THE
RICE
BIBLE

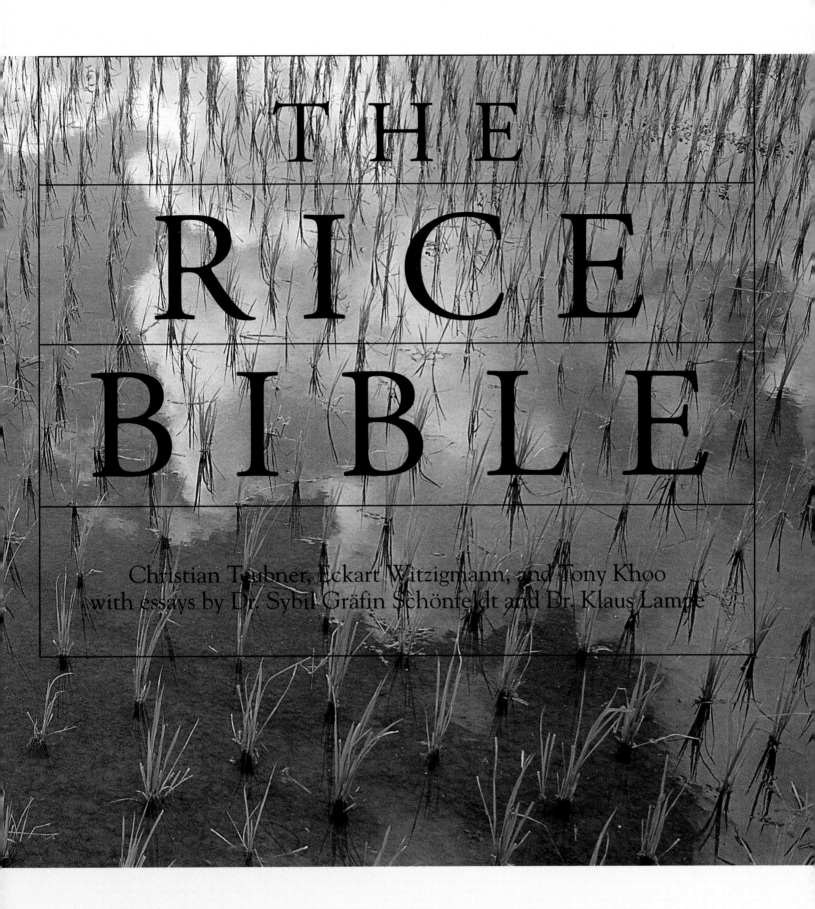

THE RICE BIBLE

Christian Teubner, Eckart Witzigmann, and Tony Khoo
with essays by Dr. Sybil Gräfin Schönfeldt and Dr. Klaus Lampe

VIKING STUDIO

VIKING STUDIO
Published by the Penguin Group
Penguin Putnam Inc., 375 Hudson Street,
New York, New York, 10014, U.S.A.

Penguin Books Ltd, 27 Wrights Lane,
London W8 5TZ, England

Penguin Books Australia Ltd,
Ringwood, Victoria, Australia

Penguin Books Canada Ltd,
10 Alcorn Avenue, Toronto, Ontario
Canada M4V 3B2

Penguin Books (N.Z.) Ltd,
182–190 Wairau Road, Auckland 10, New Zealand

Penguin Books Ltd, Registered Offices:
Harmondsworth, Middlesex, England

First published in the United States of America
by Viking Studio, a member of Penguin Putnam Inc.,
August 1999

10 9 8 7 6 5 4 3 2 1

Original edition published under the title
Das grosse Buch vom Reis, 1997
Copyright © Teubner Edition, Germany, 1997

English language text copyright © Transedition Ltd,
England, 1999
All rights reserved
Photographs other than those listed in the Picture
Credits: Christian Teubner, Odette Teubner, Andreas
Nimptsch, Julia Christl, Oliver Brachat

Translation: Debra Nicol for Translate-A-Book
Layout: Christian Teubner, Gabriele Wahl
Origination: walcher repro, Isny im Allgäu
Editorial management: Barbara Horn
Design and production: Richard Johnson

Library of Congress Catalog Card Number: 99-70425

ISBN: 0-670-88602-5
Printed and bound in England by Butler & Tanner,
Frome & London

Contents

On the trail of rice

Rice has been grown since ancient times, although we will probably never know exactly when its cultivation began. Its beginnings are shrouded in myth: Heaven loved Earth. As he bent over her, grains of rice fell out of his pockets, and as the Earth brought forth people, they found their food waiting for them. Another tale recounts how a divine virgin strode over her father's rice fields, .letting her long silk cloak drag behind her so that the rice grains would cling to it for the mortals, her friends. Rice as the gift of a benevolent goddess is a graceful image. At the beginning of the twentieth century, it was still thought that rice had not been known before 3000 BC. This assumption was based on Chinese legends, according to which the first rice had been sown personally by the Second Sovereign, Yandi, later known as Shen-nung, the Divine Farmer. In the 1920s archaeology furnished the first reliable data. At

appeared to be the most ancient agricultural settlements, dating back to about 5000 BC. The houses stood on posts at the edge of a swampy area, and the supply of rice, which had been stored in artistically worked clay pots, led to the conclusion that the people who had once harvested, threshed, and stored it were well versed in the cultivation of this grain. Was this, then, the original home of rice, or were the traces on the Huang actually older?

The question had still not been answered when the Spirit Cave was discovered in the mountains of northern Thailand. The cave contained remains of rice that was harvested between 10,000 and 7000 BC and placed in food containers, probably as ritual offerings for the spirits of the dead. This find, the most ancient yet, prompted a reassessment by the scientific community. Now rice appeared to be indigenous to an

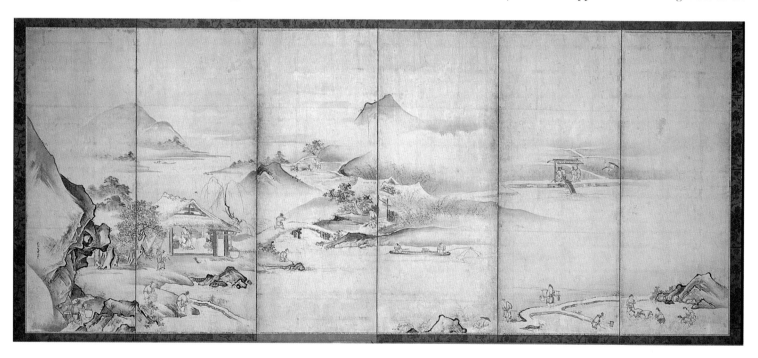

the site of a neolithic dig at Yangshao, along a tributary of the Huang, or Yellow, River, two Swedish botanists discovered a clay pot with the imprints of grains that were identified as rice. Even before that identification was confirmed, however, the next finds came from the slopes of the Himalayas, and indicated that the rice plant might have originated in India. In the 1950s and 1960s the focus was again on China, especially the Chang, or Yangtze, River delta and, in the following years, numerous other places, as more evidence emerged. In a village on the estuary of the Chang in southeastern China scientists found what

area stretching from the Himalayas across the river valleys in northern Assam, Thailand, and Burma, up to northern Vietnam and southern China. Huang-ti, the Yellow Emperor, who founded the Chinese empire, was the "Father of the grains," or *fan*. It is said that Chinese culinary culture developed from *fan* (which includes millet, wheat, and barley as well as rice): Whoever ate *fan* was considered to be Chinese; and those who did not were deemed barbarians.

In the area where it was originally cultivated, rice became the people's food. From there, it began to spread throughout the world, from the mouth of the

Yangtze to the islands to the south. Rice arrived in Indonesia and the Philippines in the third millennium BC, presumably with emigrants from the north, and quickly spread throughout the islands north and south of the Equator, where there was fertile land, jungles, sufficient moisture, an equable climate and temperature all year around — in short, paradise. In India the oldest literary sources, written in Sanskrit, refer to various species of rice around 2400 BC: dark rice was offered to Agni, the god of fire; a fast-ripening strain was dedicated to Savitar, the sun god; and a large-grained one given to Indra, both the king of gods and the god of storms in the Vedic tradition.

At this time, Japan had also finally opened its doors to trade after a long period of isolation, and rice was introduced from the area that is now Korea in the third century BC. Six hundred years later, Chinese rice growers emigrated to the south of Japan, and it was their techniques of cultivation, including the use of new tools and buffalo, that contributed to the spread of rice, which became a pillar of Japanese agriculture and

that the poor rice farmers preferred to live on millet instead. Centuries later, shortly before the First World War, Japanese settlers introduced rice-growing to Australia, which has since become a major producer.

In spite of the great importance of rice in the diets and lives of Asian peoples for many thousands of years not a single printed word about it can be found in China before the first century BC. Rice is not mentioned in the Bible, nor on the bas reliefs or papyruses of ancient Egypt. The reports of the campaigns of Alexander the Great from Greece to India in the fourth century BC contained the first written references to rice in the West. They described the rice, which by this time had been cultivated in the Euphrates valley for 2,000 years, and illustrated the layout and system of the enclosed, flooded rice fields.

However, the ancient Greeks did not think much of rice. It was considered, oddly, to be both indigestible and a nutritious food for invalids. Its continuing dissemination is attributed to the spread of Islam and the Arab campaigns of conquest toward the West and

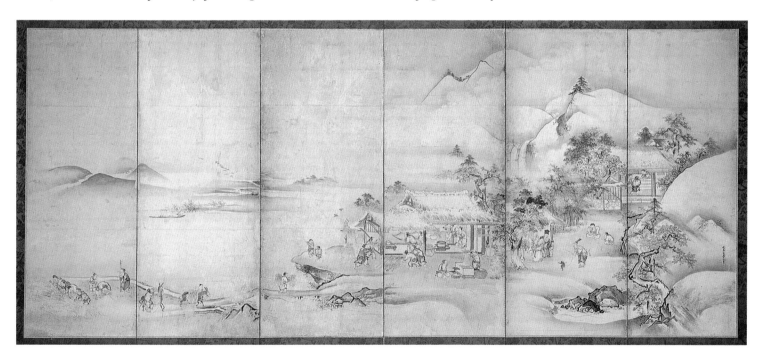

culture. Rice became not only the food of the people, but also common currency. In this feudal society, farmers paid their taxes by delivering half of their harvests to the samurai. Paradoxically, even though rice was the staple food, the Japanese did not eat the rice they harvested themselves. Japanese glutinous rice was extremely popular on the Asian continent, since it could be used in different ways, in contrast to the upland varieties in which the cooked grains remained distinct. For this reason, glutinous rice was exported to China at high prices, while inferior, cheap varieties were imported and often sold on at such high prices

the Mediterranean. The Nile delta was perfect for rice cultivation, as were the estuaries of the Guadiana and Guadalquivir, and the marshes of Valencia, where rice found its first home in Europe after the Moorish invasion of Spain in the eighth century AD. Where natural conditions were not as accommodating, the Arabs built canals and created flooded fields so that they could plant their favorite grain. If the yield was good, they would sell the surplus to their non-Arab neighbors, and thus the Asian plant flourished along with Arabic science and culture. With the Christian reconquest of Spain in the fifteenth century, the

Rice cultivation in the four seasons
Left: sowing, planting, and watering. Right: harvest, threshing, and milling; a traveling entertainer can be seen in the penultimate section. Kusumi Morikage, Japanese screens, india ink and light colors on paper, mid-17th century.

Rice cult on Bali
Offerings placed on a
small altar at the edge
of a rice field are meant
to dispose the gods
favorably so that the
next harvest will be a
good one.

Spanish took over the Arabs' rice fields and spread their methods of cultivation with their own campaigns of conquest to southern France and northern Italy.

Rice was by no means new to this part of Italy, which lay right in the center of trade between East and West. There exist bills for small quantities of rice purchased in the middle of the thirteenth century, and there is a report of the Duke of Milan sending a friend a dozen small sacks of rice that had been harvested in his own dukedom in 1475. It was the Spanish, however, who got their new subjects to tackle rice cultivation systematically. The grain was first grown where canal systems and irrigation facilities were well established, in the Po plain and in the Veneto. Rice was transported over the Alps at the end of the fifteenth century, mainly to the southern German free cities. The rice-growing areas increased in size until the Duke of Milan restricted both the export of rice and the expansion of cultivation because of disease. In China, rice-growers had put carp in the wet fields to nibble away at the roots of weeds and eat the insect larvae there. In Italy rice was planted without these guardians in the flooded fields. Mosquitoes soon flourished and malaria broke out. Since the connection between the insect and the disease was not yet known, a miasma, or bad air (from which the disease gets its name), was attributed to the rice plants, so rice fields were prohibited in the vicinity of towns, and rice cultivation was again neglected.

**Early Italian harvest
scene** In the
foreground, a farmer
takes away the cut
stalks; in the
background, the harvest
is still in full swing.

Although rice had found its way over the Alps, it had little economic or culinary importance in medieval Europe. The Arabian rice grown in Spain, as well as the Spanish rice grown in Italy, were probably sufficient only for domestic use. Although other pockets of rice cultivation did exist in the Middle Ages — for example, on the southern lowland plains of Hungary, on the fringes of the Islamic world — yields were low and the quality extremely poor. This rice was poor man's food, wholly unlike the grain that arrived from the orient. Compared with the very expensive spices, rice from the East was a relatively cheap commodity bearing in mind its weight and the long journey it had to make, but it was still costly enough to be afforded only by the rich at those times when it was available. With the shaping of the status-conscious society, imported rice became the food of the ruling class.

In the eighteenth century, when the maritime route to India around Africa's Cape of Good Hope was established, one European merchant company after the other sprang up along the coast of India. When the State power in India collapsed, the Europeans began to meddle in the politics of the huge empire and set themselves up as colonial powers. Generations of European, particularly English, children were brought up by Indian *amahs* on Indian food. Every morning they inhaled the scent of onions roasting in fat in a large pot, to which the cook would add a variety of freshly ground spices and then stir and stir until the aroma of the resulting *kari* would fill the whole house. The English anglicized the spelling of *kari* to "curry," and, like other European colonists, ate curried meat and vegetable dishes with rice throughout their lives there. Gradually, these dishes found their way onto the tables of European aristocracy, since it was considered elegant to show off one's wealth by serving food made with spices from the exotic East. Thousands of years after rice reached Indonesia, Dutch plantation owners returning home introduced the Indonesian *rijsttafel* to Amsterdam and made it, together with nasi goreng, the favorite food and national dish of the Netherlands.

In Germany, meanwhile, the ability of the poor rice grains, pulped and pushed through a sieve, to set like plaster was used primarily by court and hotel chefs to create a firm base for the table centerpieces with which they dazzled the diners with their virtuosity and stunning variety. The bourgeois successor to these rice edifices was the rice ring, which also had to be solid as a rock, and served merely to hold a filling. The last imperial courts in Russia and Austria, France and Germany showed that rice could be used as a base in a much more sensible and tasty way. The cuisine there, which was as international as the aristocracy, had to give an impression of sumptuousness while secretly being thrifty. Thus, it needed dishes in which leftovers could be turned to impressive account. The Rice Meridon was a case in point. This mold combined rice with all sorts of meat, fish, poultry, and vegetables as well as fresh fruits in season, and jam during the winter. Throughout most of Europe rice was, and remained, a special food until cheap rice began to be imported at the beginning of the twentieth century.

Rice arrived in South America with the Spanish and Portuguese who began to explore and colonize the continent in the sixteenth century. It is still a crop of major importance in the majority of countries in South America as well as in Guatemala, Belize, and Nicaragua in Central America.

The story of North American rice began on Madagascar. There, around the time the Arabs were advancing into the Mediterranean, Malays had established rice cultivation, farming it intensively in flooded fields. A Dutch brig sailing from Madagascar around Africa ran into a storm on the Atlantic, and entered Charleston harbor slightly damaged. While the ship was being repaired, the captain paid a courtesy visit to the governor, Thomas Smith, and, since the latter showed an interest, made him a gift of one sack of Madagascar rice, called "Golde Seede" because of its color. The Governor possessed a piece of swampy land like the captain had described, on which nothing was cultivated because the tides brought fresh water onto the otherwise fertile soil twice daily. Here he

A kitchen scene in ancient China In the foreground, the housewife doles out the food. Clearly visible in the background is a wok with several steaming-baskets stacked one on top of the other.

planted the rice. When the rice thrived, the swampy areas around Charleston were cleared, and the land was diked to create an irrigation system. First Native Americans, then African slaves farmed the flooded fields, and the harvests were so plentiful that rice was the earliest significant export from the colony to England and the West Indies. Charleston and, later, George Town became centers of the rice trade, and the quality of "Carolina Golde," as the variety was now called, was so high that it became the standard. By 1776 South Carolina and Georgia exported 65 percent of their rice to Europe.

After independence, American rice farmers benefited from one of the inventions that also revolutionized European agriculture. In 1787 Jonathan Lucas built the first water-driven rice mill, from which the first tide-driven mill was developed five years later. This not only saved on labor, but also kept the rice grains unharmed to a greater extent than when they were pounded. By the middle of the next century, 150 rice plantations had been established on the banks of the rivers, and their owners had become millionaires. The Civil War put an end to all that. Union troops blockaded the rice ports in 1861, and later burned the rice fields, plundered the plantations, destroyed the working quarters, and freed the slaves. The rice fields lay fallow until the end of the war, and were never restored to their former use.

However, rice soon found another home. After the Louisiana Purchase in 1803, the size of the country had doubled, and people moving into the Southwest brought rice with them. After the Civil War, discharged soldiers given land on the Gulf Coast began growing rice there. In 1884 a farmer from Iowa ventured the opinion that rice could also be grown on the prairies in southwest Louisiana and southeast Texas, and harvesting could be simplified by using a reaper-binder he employed in Iowa for his wheat. He proved to be right, and rice cultivation spread to Louisiana, Texas and Arkansas, up to California, and into the upper Mississippi delta by the the middle of the century. Rice was instantly socially acceptable in America, even being served at dinners given by some of the early presidents: there was rice soup, rice pudding (of which President Grant was particularly fond), as well as pilaf with pine kernels (Thomas Jefferson's favorite). Ever since then, rice has continued to be an important crop and a popular food in America.

Dr. Sybil Gräfin Schönfeldt

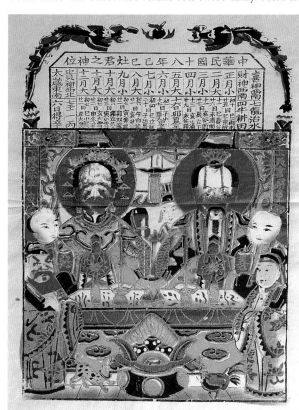

The hearth god and retinue In China, the hearth god's portrait is burned and a new one is hung at New Year.

Cultivation

Would you be able to sell a car with the name "potato field" in the United States? Surely not, even though the potato is an extremely popular food. So the fact that "Toyota," or more properly "Toyoda," actually means "rich rice field" is some indication of the central role of rice in Japan. And you won't escape from rice for long by choosing a Honda instead, since this word means "main rice field," originally the basis of survival of an entire family. Even today rice is much more than just a staple food for many people. In many of the languages of Asia, the term for "rice" is synonymous with "life," "food" pure and simple, or "agriculture" in general. Rice was, and still is, a food of major importance. Worldwide, it accounts for 23 percent of all calories consumed; in Cambodia, the figure is 80 percent; in Vietnam, 70 percent; and in Thailand the people derive almost 60 percent of their calories from this one food. At one time the emperor of Japan was believed to embody the god of the rice plant; to this day he plants rice every year in a special ceremony and is the patron of the annual harvest ceremony. Similarly, following an ancient tradition, after the rainy season the king of Thailand personally leads a festival in which the first furrow is plowed to prepare the rice field for planting. Rice is a culture that binds past and present, rich and poor, citizens and kings. Moreover, it determines, at least in part, the rhythm of life in those rice-growing regions where small-scale agricultural structures predominate and traditional village structures persist.

Ancestors

As we have seen in Chapter 1, rice originated in the Far East and made its way to the West with nomads, conquerors, and traders. Wild forms of rice, in other words possible "ancestors" of present-day varieties, can be found in Asia, Australia, Africa, and South America, although rice cultivation developed mutually independently in Asia and West Africa. (The wild forms we refer to here are distinguished from so-called wild rice, which is not actually a rice at all and which will be discussed in the next chapter.) These wild forms are often completely unlike modern cultivated varieties. The multiplicity of wild species and varieties fascinate botanists, breeders, and others who are involved in attempting to make use of this large reservoir of breeding characteristics to create new cultivars.

In spite of the many different wild species of rice that have existed on four continents over the millennia, all the modern cultivated varieties are based on only two species: *Oryza glaberrima* and *Oryza sativa.*

Oryza glaberrima

The African species *Oryza glaberrima* was originally a red rice, which developed independently of Asian rice over 3,500 years; Asian rice reached the African continent only around 500 years ago. *O. glaberrima* flourishes on very poor soil, withstands drought relatively well, and quickly covers the ground with its long, hanging leaves. In doing so it suppresses the many weeds that compete with it. However, because the panicles bear very few grains, the yields are very low and commercial fertilizers are of little help in increasing them. The most important rice-producing nations of Africa are Egypt, which grows 4.6 million metric tons a year, followed by Nigeria (3.9 million metric tons) and Madagascar (2.3 million metric tons). Rice also plays an important role in many small West African countries. For this reason, the Regional Rice Research Center (WARDA/ADRAO) in the Ivory Coast concentrates on promoting the growth and breeding of new varieties for the region. Here, West African *O. glaberrima* and Asian *O. sativa* have been crossed successfully for the first time.

Oryza sativa

The original parent of all Asian cultivars is called *Oryza sativa*. It can be broken down into three distinct subdivisions. Japonica, distinguished by its dark, straight-standing leaves, its small number of shoots, and, above all, its comparatively short, thick grains, is classified as short-grain rice. Because of its high starch content, it is usually sticky when cooked, and therefore easy to eat with chopsticks. Javanica, or tropical japonica, has straight, upright leaves and very long panicles bearing a large number of medium-length grains. Because the plant puts forth few tillers (basal side shoots), only a few, but very long, stalks grow from one seed. Indica is larger than japonica, and is classified as long-grain rice. Its light green leaves are longer and do not stand upright, but bend, together with a relatively long panicle, toward the ground, which makes the plant prone to "lying down," or falling over, in stormy weather. While indica is less tolerant of the cold than japonica, it is more resistant to drought, pests, and diseases. Owing to their high amylose content, the long, slender grains stick together far less during cooking and retain their texture to a greater extent than japonica grains.

This subdivision into three types is only the beginning. Rice's great variety is expressed in the number of cultivars produced from them. Until after the Second World War, there were far more than the 150,000 varieties in existence today, which had been handed down and developed further over many generations. Today, in the gene bank of the International Rice Research Institute (IRRI) in Los Baños in the Philippines, seeds of more than 80,000 cultivars are stored in an earthquake-proof large cold store in such a way that they remain capable of germinating for many years. Seeds of the remaining cultivars are stored in regional agricultural institutes around the world. These "banks" are truly crucial capital for the future. Without the old varieties and the wild forms of rice, over twenty of which are known nowadays, rice cultivation would be unimaginable. This gene material forms the basis for constant improvement of the resistance of rice plants to diseases, pests, and extreme climatic conditions, such as cold and drought.

Not just a marsh plant

Rice flourishes not only in lowlands below sea level, but also in uplands more than 8200 feet above sea level. A rice belt runs around the Earth from 50° latitude in the southern hemisphere up to 40° in the northern hemisphere. No other cultivated plant of similar importance can boast such a spread. Moreover, rice is not an exclusively aquatic plant, as we tend to assume. It flourishes in normal fields in rotation with many other cultivated plants, but tolerates much higher levels of rainfall than any other cultivated plant. For example, rice grows in Saudi Arabia, where rainfall does not exceed 4 inches a year, and the crop must be artificially irrigated, and it grows in Myanmar (Burma), where there may be up to 197 inches of rain during the wet season — on average, four times the annual rainfall for Jacksonville, Florida, or more than eleven times the annual rainfall for Sacramento. In northern latitudes, rice can grow in temperatures as low as 63°F, and does fine even up to 95°F in the shade. It is only above this temperature that yields fall noticeably.

Different types of rice and different methods of agriculture apply to these different locations. Upland rice is one of the most undemanding types. It grows on poor soils on mountain slopes and hilly land, and in flat valleys. It is totally dependent on the amount of rainfall during the growing season, but the fields are not leveled off and are only seldom enclosed by levees to trap the rain water. This rice is subject to slash-and-burn growing methods and is often grown as a mixed culture with other cultivated plants. Where soil conditions permit, upland rice is also part of a permanent crop-rotation system, for example with corn or other vegetables.

Worldwide, 12 percent of all land on which rice is grown is given over to upland rice. Of the total 47 million acres that are planted with upland rice, over

In West Africa, the native strains of *Oryza glaberrima* grow almost as high as an adult, so people hardly have to stoop at all during the harvest. Although the panicles bear comparatively few grains, this rice has an excellent flavor.

30 million are in Asia, about 8 million are in Latin America, and more than 7 million in Africa. However, upland rice crop yields are very low, averaging only 0.4 metric ton an acre, which is why only 4 percent of the world harvest comes from this system of cultivation. The main problem is not only that there has been insufficient research, but also that the conditions of production themselves cannot be influenced to any large extent. The soils are, for the most part, poor in nutrients and can absorb rain water only over a short period. During the growing season, between 47 and 138 inches of rain fall. This would be more than enough if distribution were not so uneven, and were not frequently interrupted by periods of drought, which severely damage the crop. For small-scale rice growers in many regions, the vigorous weed population is the most difficult problem to solve.

Rainfed lowland rice is always planted in levee-enclosed fields in which the soil remains flooded to a depth of up to 20 inches for at least part of the growing season. Worldwide, approximately 30 percent of rice plantations, or about 99 million acres, are given over to lowland rice. Yields average 0.5 metric tons an acre, owing to the somewhat better growing conditions than upland rice enjoys. The poverty of small-scale growers, who farm 7–10 acres at best, becomes clear when the harvest is seen in monetary terms: between $154 and $182 gross an acre after four to five months' work. Because of the irregular weather conditions, the high risk of disease and pests, and the so-far fairly unsuccessful breeding efforts, lowland rice farmers hardly have a chance to improve their situation. Wherever possible, families try to support themselves by finding an additional means of income.

The cultivation of lowland rice is to all intents and purposes limited to Asia. Less than 5 percent of the total cultivated area is distributed between Africa and Latin America. More research is essential in order to

Mr. Veerasak, who works for the Thai Rice Research Institute, demonstrates how the panicles of a particular species bend under their heavy load. Harvesting is often still done by hand with a narrow sawtooth sickle.

achieve the necessary increase in yields in the coming decades. In addition to greater yield potential and a better ability to absorb nutrients, the most salient feature new strains need is resistance to drought, flooding, disease, and pests.

Rice grown in irrigated fields is often considered to be rice per se, since 50 percent of rice fields are irrigated and more than 75 percent of rice crops come from this ecosystem. Average yields stand at 1.2–3.6 metric tons an acre, and, in exceptional cases, maximum yields of over 8.5 metric tons have been achieved under especially favorable conditions. Accounting for 94 percent of all rice-producing areas, irrigated rice is primarily at home in Asia. Farmers in the United States, Australia, and Europe grow irrigated rice exclusively, but this accounts for only 2.7 percent of the total rice-growing area of the world. The remainder is distributed between Africa and Latin America.

This Korean memorial commemorates the fact that rice gave a boost to national agriculture.

Irrigated rice constitutes one of the most intensive forms of agriculture. It is concentrated on the best soils with the highest water absorption and retention capacity. It took a great deal of work to create the levees that enclose all the fields, and they are maintained with special care, particularly in sloping fields, which are terrace-farmed. In some areas these levees are more than 2,000 years old, and prove that, in the case of rice, monoculture (the continuous growing of a single crop) is possible without harming local natural resources. Because of the importance of irrigated rice in the diet of non-self-sufficient populations, policies, research, and development have always focused on increasing yields. It is expected that at least 70 percent of the necessary increase in production of rice in the first quarter of the twenty-first century will come from irrigated rice. An important breakthrough has been achieved not only with new, high-yielding strains, but with earlier-ripening varieties too. There are now strains of rice that ripen in little more than 100 days, instead of the standard 160–180 days. In regions blessed with favorable climatic conditions, three, rather than one or two, harvests are thus possible. Three high-yielding crops per year, however, will in future not be achieved without negative effects on the soil, even in the case of alluvial soils. For this reason, new strains are in preparation that should enable current harvests to be doubled. Then another food plant — for example, soy or mung beans, which improve the soil by their nitrogen-fixing ability — can be grown for the third season. The aims of current research are to achieve more efficient absorption of nutrients, a longer grain, improved flavor, and higher yield after husking.

Deepwater rice, floating rice, and tidal wetland rice are types adapted to different deepwater conditions. Deepwater rice grows in what are probably the most extreme conditions for agriculture, exploiting land whose depth of flooding can be influenced by human intervention only to a very limited extent. It grows for up to three months in rainfed but not flooded low-lying lands, and then must be able to withstand complete flooding for a month or more during the rainy season. By nature, it can do this for up to about four days; new strains can remain under water for more than ten days. Tidal wetland rice is also subject to fluctuating water conditions, but on a daily basis.

Floating rice protects itself against the slowly rising flood waters in which it grows: its stalks grow up to 4 inches a day, thus keeping the canopies above the surface of the water. A root support system helps this rice, which can grow to over 20 feet long, not only to stay alive, but to produce yields that, at an average 0.6–0.8 metric tons an acre, are better than those of upland rice.

The great advantage of deepwater rice lies in its high degree of adaptability. It can survive different water depths, which often change in a short period of time, and is able to flourish in acid soils. Some varieties of rice cultivated in the large delta regions of Bangladesh, India, and Vietnam even grow in brackish water. The total area devoted to the cultivation of deepwater rice is only 25 million acres in Asia, about 3 million acres in West Africa, and about 57,000 acres in Ecuador. It is generally harvested from boats. It is hardly surprising that the 100 million people whose lives depend on this rice ecosystem are among the very poorest in the world.

Unfair comparisons

Soil quality and water supply, sunshine and day length play equally important roles and are at least as critical in determining yields as choice of variety and growing methods. China, for example, harvests on average 2.4 metric tons an acre, while rice farmers in India achieve less than half that amount with 1.1 metric tons an acre. The farmers themselves are not to blame. Whereas well over 90 percent of the very fertile rice-growing land in China can be irrigated, this is not possible, for example, for even half of the cultivated land in India. The majority of rice-growing land there is dependent upon rainfall; the soil is often not very fertile, and commercial fertilizers are not universally available. Another reason for the difference in yields between India and China is that rice breeders have developed high-yield varieties for irrigated rice, while breeding successes for other rice ecosystems are still comparatively modest. China cultivates new, modern varieties almost exclusively, but this is true for only about 75 percent of the area under cultivation in India. Finally, the harvest in India is also strongly influenced by the monsoon rains.

A lunch makes history

In the late 1950s, when the world had only just recovered from the wartime and post-war famines, a study by the United Nations indicated that the next food crisis was looming. Asia was declared the potential focus of a major food shortage, and many people thought that the Indian subcontinent would suffer the same fate. However, the crisis was averted — because of decisions made at a lunch. The agricultural directors of the Ford and the Rockefeller foundations received the United Nations' report while lunching together, and resolved to take joint action. It was the starting gun for perhaps the most important and, above all, the most sustained world nutritional program of the post-war era. A small planning group traveled around Asia analyzing the problems of rice as the most important cultivated plant. A couple of years later, in 1960, the IRRI was founded as a joint project by the two foundations.

The venture was rewarded with success. Just five years after it was created, the IRRI succeeded in developing a new strain of rice, called simply IR-8, which was to make history. This rather uninventive name became a watchword for the doubling of potential yield, for a key to preventing starvation. The breeders in Los Baños had crossed a japonica variety with a domestic variety from Indonesia. The result was the first high-yielding, low-growing strain for the tropics and subtropics. It stood firm even when rainfall was fairly heavy and grew equally well in different latitudes, regardless of the length of day. It was capable of absorbing commercial fertilizers and converting them into increased grain yield, and also ripened more quickly than other varieties.

IR-8 was not a miracle rice, as IRRI researchers knew from the start. However, because of political pressure and the specter of famine on the doorstep, the new variety spread more quickly than many scientists would have wished. The high-yielding strain required

not only additional applications of fertilizer, but also, above all, protection from diseases and pests. The old domestic varieties, with yields of 0.4–0.6 metric tons an acre, had been adapted to local conditions for centuries. They had developed a high degree of resistance to diseases and pests, which the new strain still lacked. Yields of 1.6–3.2 metric tons an acre, however, meant that the voices of the skeptics were ignored. Heavy insect infestation was combated with more and more pesticides. Where the means of production or the money to buy chemicals was not available, there were setbacks. The wrong policy decisions, for example in the case of credit terms for agriculture, combined with harvest losses caused by storms have cast shadows on a development that, wrongly described as a "green revolution," has protected several hundred million people from hunger and starvation. Without the modern strains of rice and wheat, India would have to be twice as large as it is in order to provide its population (which increased by more than 90 percent between 1961 and 1991 alone) with staple foods. In this respect, plant breeding and modern cultivation methods changed the world in a way that few people were aware of because the great crisis was successfully averted.

Since the IRRI was established, a large number of national rice research institutes have been set up, linked to one another and to the IRRI via networks and cooperation programs.

These farmers in Samoeng, Thailand are growing onions in their rice fields as an in-between crop. Other kinds of vegetables are also grown in alternation with rice where soil and water conditions permit.

The continuing work of the IRRI

A few thousand books and articles in scientific journals represents only a small, and by no means the most important, part of the work of the IRRI following the launch of IR-8. Nearly every second rice strain worldwide nowadays is related to a variety cultivated by the IRRI, and they all have pedigrees that would put the best thoroughbred to shame. Resistance to diseases, pests, and stress situations such as cold, drought, and flooding, to name but a few examples, are permanent components of a breeding program, for high yields alone are of little use to small-scale growers, who live on their harvests and cannot afford

In regions with irrigated rice fields, here, for example, in Sri Lanka, the water is brought to the fields using a time-honored system of carefully maintained channels and gutters.

to buy new seed every year. A long-term secure yield with low production costs must be the goal.

IR-8, a rice for irrigated fields only, failed to impress gourmets. It was a highly welcome seed rice, but it was hardly a delight to the palate. High yields, early ripening, and strength of aroma and flavor are characteristics that cannot always be encompassed in a single variety — at least not until the present. Rice yields are determined not only by the strain, but also to a considerable extent by environmental factors and cultivation methods. Therefore a large proportion of domestic and international research work focuses on improving production technology. There are socioeconomic reasons too. The work in rice fields is among the hardest agricultural labor there is. The levees and terraces for wetland rice cultivation must constantly be cared for, and plowing, harrowing, planting, applying fertilizer, and weeding all require intensive manual labor. Whoever can, therefore, tries to trade in the role of small-scale farmer for that of a worker in the city. Mass migration from the countryside to the cities is in full swing in many rice-growing areas, and will have serious consequences. If agrarian production fails to develop attractive, labor-saving production methods, it will stagnate. At the same time, an annual 3 percent increase in yield is necessary to keep pace with population trends and to adequately nourish the 1 billion people who even now suffer from hunger. Let us not forget that while rice is merely a delicious side dish for many people, it is an essential, irreplaceable staple food for almost 2 billion people, most of them very poor.

Unfortunately, the willingness to continue financing rice research has decreased drastically.

Unlike wheat and corn, rice is of little interest to the big international seed-growing companies. Therefore, governments, public and private foundations, and development banks will have to take over the financing. In the twenty-first century there will be almost 5 billion people for whom rice is the basis of their diet. In order to feed them, an annual increase in production of 2.5–3 percent is needed. In the history of farming to date it has never been possible to achieve this over a relatively long period. For this reason, in 1988 a group of scientists from the IRRI set themselves new strategic targets reaching far into the next century: to break through the currently insurmountable yield barriers, and at the same time develop production methods which would be socially, ecologically, and economically tenable for future generations. From among the large number of research programs, we present here just a couple of particularly interesting projects.

From the drawing board

Rice 2000 will be the first "drawing board rice" in the history of the cultivation of the grain, since it really evolved on paper. Breeders, growers, and economists combined forces to produce a sketch of their ideal plant. They came up with a short rice plant with especially strong stalks, and thick, broad, long, dark-green leaves that would stand erect like solar panels and absorb a great deal of light. The panicles had to be long, bearing over 300 grains instead of the usual 120

Scientists from more than twenty nations at the International Rice Research Institute (IRRI) develop rice strains for the future on around 250 1-hectare (2.5-acre) fields, using both conventional breeding methods and biotechnology.

to 150. Naturally, the plant would be resistant to diseases and pests, and produce high-quality grain in spite of early ripening, and this with a yield of 6 metric tons an acre instead of the maximum limit of 4 metric tons an acre, which seemed unbeatable.

Many people thought this project was unrealistic, but today, we are most of the way to achieving this target. New breeding methods, such as embryo cultivation in which resistant wild strains are crossed with high-yielding varieties, were a key factor. Yields of more than 5.2 metric tons an acre were already being achieved in 1998, well on the way to the target. By crossing two high-yielding inbred lines, yields can be increased by around 15 percent without additional applications of fertilizer. By 2008 a hybrid Rice 2000 could be available to Asian farmers.

High-tech hybrids

Although the hybrid vigor of rice was discovered in 1926, research into rice hybrids for the temperate zones was begun only in 1964, and the first ones released for use in 1974. Similarly, the first systematic program for developing rice hybrids for the tropics began at the IRRI in 1979, and the first cultivars were released only in 1995. These crosses have one great drawback, however: for each culture, the seed must be bought afresh, because the hybrid effect comes to fruition only in the first generation. Small-scale farmers often cannot afford to buy the seed each season, and the prerequisites for hybrid seed generation and marketing simply do not exist in many poor countries. Scientists are therefore looking for a solution: apomixis. Apomixis means the ability of plants to reproduce asexually, that is, without pollination. Many grasses possessing this ability have already been identified, but, to date, all efforts to discover an apomictic strain of rice have met with failure. If scientists do not succeed in finding an apomictic rice, there are still other avenues open to them. Modern biotechnological methods enable the genes responsible for asexual reproduction to be pinpointed. They also allow an individual gene to be isolated and transferred to a rice plant. Creating an apomictic rice by genetic engineering will benefit even the small-scale farmer.

Genetic engineering

In the last 100 years people have changed the world. We have long since taken electricity, automobiles, airplanes, television, computers, robots, and space travel in our stride. Now, however, a new technology has arrived that many of us find sinister: biotechnology. Here, we must distinguish between "old" and "new," "red" and "green." Yeast for beer and bread, and rennet for cheese are areas of application of classical biotechnology, some of which have been used since prehistoric times by people of many different cultures without knowing or understanding the correlations. Modern biotechnology makes use of the findings of biochemistry and microbiology, and attempts to influence directly what is going on in the cell. Although rice researchers, particularly in the United States and Japan, were quick to recognize the potential usefulness, other economically more attractive plants underwent genetic engineering much sooner. Biotechnology arrived in medicine even earlier. Medicines produced by genetic engineering are already widespread, and the United States is the largest consumer worldwide. Skepticism of this "red" genetic engineering has long since been overcome.

The misgivings triggered by genetically engineered foods are to a large extent based on inadequate knowledge of the facts. Reticence and resistance are the consequences. We insist that our food should be good value, if not actually cheap, as well as tasty, healthy, and fresh. Gourmet cuisine, to name but one example, links a maximum amount of "naturalness" to these requirements. Is genetically engineered rice less natural than the old upland rice from a high-lying valley in Laos? The answer is no, but because most of us are not familiar with what genetic engineering means, reservations are common. In exactly the same way that many people once regarded the usefulness of computers with skepticism, one might wonder: Do we really need genetically engineered rice? What risks does it entail? And what benefits, if any, does it bring?

Of course, a rice connoisseur does not need to be a rice geneticist. However, in order to be able to form our own judgments based on an understanding of the

Rice, rice and more rice The most successful strains from every country in the world find their way into a trial-and-exchange program through an unprecedented network of international voluntary cooperation. This accelerates the breeding of new varieties.

subject, a brief look into the genetic kitchen is necessary. First of all, we need to know that all life on Earth, from rice to seals, from Brussels sprouts to human beings, is composed of the same DNA building blocks. Over millions of years of differentiation, species and forms have arisen whose individual evolution we

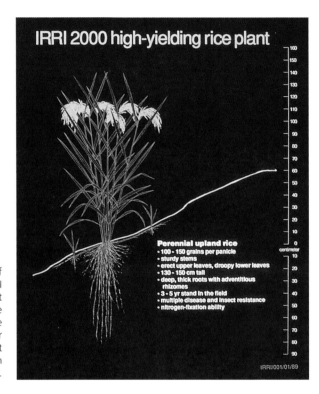

IRRI 2000 high-yielding rice plant

Perennial upland rice
- 100 - 150 grains per panicle
- sturdy stems
- erect upper leaves, droopy lower leaves
- 130 - 150 cm tall
- deep, thick roots with adventitious rhizomes
- 3 - 5 yr stand in the field
- multiple disease and insect resistance
- nitrogen-fixation ability

IRRI/001/01/89

Perennial rice is one of the targets the IRRI breeders have set themselves. The advantage of such a rice is that it would crop for several years without having to be resown after each harvest.

cannot yet explain. The interrelatedness of different species, however, remains undisputed. The more distant these "family connections" are, the more difficult it becomes to cross a highly selected strain with a distant wild relative. Either no offspring at all result, or they are infertile, like, for example, a mule or hinny, the product of a cross between a donkey and a horse. Genetic engineers have found a solution for this problem with regard to plant breeding. The program is called embryo rescue, and works in the following way. After pollination, an embryo develops from the egg cell, just as for human beings. In order to prevent it from dying, the embryo is detached prematurely from the mother plant and kept in a nutrient solution in a test tube. There it grows into a rice plant. If the breeder is lucky, the new genetic combination will encompass the desired characteristics of both parents. In an arduous process of back-crossing, all undesired characteristics must be eliminated, without losing those needed to achieve the previously determined breeding goal.

Modern breeders are forced to fall back on the characteristics of wild forms or other species when these hereditary factors are not present in the strains used today. This is particularly true for pest and disease resistance, and special tolerance for poor, acid, or

excessively salty soils. The embryo rescue method has two major drawbacks, however: It does not allow for the purposeful selection of the desired hereditary factors, and it works only where the degree of relatedness is at least close enough to permit fertilization. It is thus not possible to transfer a wheat gene to a rice plant using this method. However, a genetic engineer has succeeded in pinpointing a large number of hereditary factors on the twelve rice chromosomes. It will probably not be very long before we have the "gene map" for rice. The next step will be a matter of isolating specific genes or gene combinations. When this has been accomplished, purposeful gene transfer will be possible, even surmounting natural barriers to crossing.

More than a dozen food plants have already been provided with new characteristics through biotechnological processes, including soy, potatoes, corn, wheat, beets, sugar cane, tomatoes, pumpkin, cabbage, and melons. Today genetically modified plants have characteristics that for the most part hardly touch the consumer directly. A good example of this is the soil bacterium *Bacillus thurengensis*. It is found in the wild in the soil, and produces a very specific poison, which kills the corn earworm caterpillar as well as the rice-stem borer. Eating a carrot or radish freshly pulled from the ground, human beings take in countless bacteria of this sort. They are not harmed by it, as this poison has no effect on warm-blooded creatures. That is why the specific gene for the poison was isolated and transferred to the rice genome. Now, when the rice-stem borer attempts to bore into the stalk, it does not get very far. The rice plant has produced its own pesticide. It is not contained in the rice grain that we eat — although the hereditary factor for its production is — but in the plant stalk. A research team at the Eidgenössische Technische Hochschule (ETH) in Zurich, which was deeply involved in this development, is also in the process of increasing the provitamin A and iron

Wild forms, native, and high-yielding strains from around the world are guarded like treasure at the rice seed bank at the IRRI in Los Baños, where over 80,000 varieties of rice are currently stored.

content of rice in the same way, through the transfer of foreign genes. This will contribute to a future in which children in rice-growing countries no longer go blind due to vitamin A deficiency. It could also help alleviate the anemia from which almost half of all women in developing countries suffer. Here, "green" and "red" genetic engineering form a particularly advantageous alliance. In the first two decades of the twenty-first century plant breeders will use genetic engineering to help solve many, but by no means all, problems that they face.

Do we really need our rice to be genetically engineered? Those of us who live in the Western industrialized countries certainly do not; our annual consumption averages less than 22 pounds a head. For China, India, Nigeria, Indonesia, and Bangladesh, however, to name but five countries with a total of 2.6 billion inhabitants, biotechnology is indispensable. There the annual per capita consumption of rice is between 155 and 365 pounds. By about 2045, around 4.3 billion people will live in these countries. Without research making use of the most modern technologies, it will not be possible for them to feed their populations. The question "Genetically engineered rice — yes or no?" has therefore long since been answered in the affirmative, and been succeeded by the question "When?" We in the West owe it to those who sit before empty bowls to use our knowledge, abilities, and all scientific discoveries at our disposal to help conquer hunger. We need to remain immune to polemical hysteria. In a few years genetically modified foods, including genetically engineered rice, may be as much a part of everyday life as the computer, the airplane, and the railroad.

Burning the forest, or wading in the mud?

Rice farmers in Asia and Africa may have a lot of work to do to prepare their land for sowing. If they do not have enough water and are dependent on upland rice, their work often begins with the clearing of land. Trees are felled, the timber piled up and burned. "Slash-and-burn" is the name given to this ancient method, which dates back to semi-nomadic times; and was much better for the land than its reputation now reflects. Originally, between productive periods of two to four years there was a long fallow period of up to fifty years in which the forest and soil were allowed to regenerate and recover. The sharp increase in population threw this system out of kilter and forced farmers to reduce the fallow period to just a few years.

The price paid for this was high: loss of soil fertility. Thus, out of pure need, people began to live at the expense of future generations.

If the forest and the land are cleared, the land is prepared by hoeing between tree stumps, timber remains, and, not infrequently, large rock formations, and then immediately sown. With irrigated rice cultivation also, the preparation of the soil on smallholdings has hardly changed until recently. For thousands of years, a yoke of buffalo, driven by a farmer wading deep in the mud, would go round and round, first with a wooden plow, then with a rake-like harrow, and finally with the leveling board. The compacting of the plowed soil that thus took place over time ensured that the water would not trickle down into the lower soil layers so quickly, and would therefore remain available for the plants. Modern technology is slowly reaching small farmers, thanks largely to the IRRI and many national institutions. In addition to other technical aids, the IRRI has developed a simple two-wheel tractor, which can be manufactured, to a large extent, by a semi-skilled village blacksmith. These "iron buffaloes," as they are called, are not much to look at, but they are cheap, easy to repair, do the work of two buffaloes, and make the work easier. Almost every bit as important, however, is a side effect that many people overlook. It is not often that you will still find young people who of their own free will are prepared to walk behind a yoke of buffalo in the water. In order to ready 2.5 acres of land for planting rice, they must wade in water for 43 miles. With the "iron buffalo," this task is not only accomplished much more quickly, but because the job involves an engine and its care and maintenance, it is also considerably more appealing to the younger generation.

With large-scale farming, for example in the United States, Malaysia, and Australia, soil preparation methods do not differ substantially from those of other cultures. The soil is plowed and harrowed as for other types of grain. Only the leveling-off process and the ultimately finer topsoil distinguish a rice field that is "flooded," to a depth of 2–6 inches, either before or after the seed begins to grow. Originally, wet rice was grown in many places to turn to good account marshlands that were otherwise unproductive. Later, irrigation systems were set up to make better use of soil and water reserves, and to enable the cultivation of rice during the dry season as well. This preparation of the soil for wet rice cultivation swallows up almost half of the quantity of water needed for growing rice. At one time, there was no reason to dwell on the waste of water this entailed. This will have to change, however, for it is forecast that water will become scarce almost everywhere in the years to come.

IRRI employees at work. Scientists and technicians from around the world work in state-of-the-art laboratories to produce better crops and search for the "super rice" of the future.

The table and the map show the major rice producing areas of the world. Only 4 percent of world production is sold on the international market. Although the United States is not the largest rice producer, it is the single largest exporter, contributing 32 percent of its total production to export markets. It consumes 33 percent of its own production and keeps the rest in reserve.

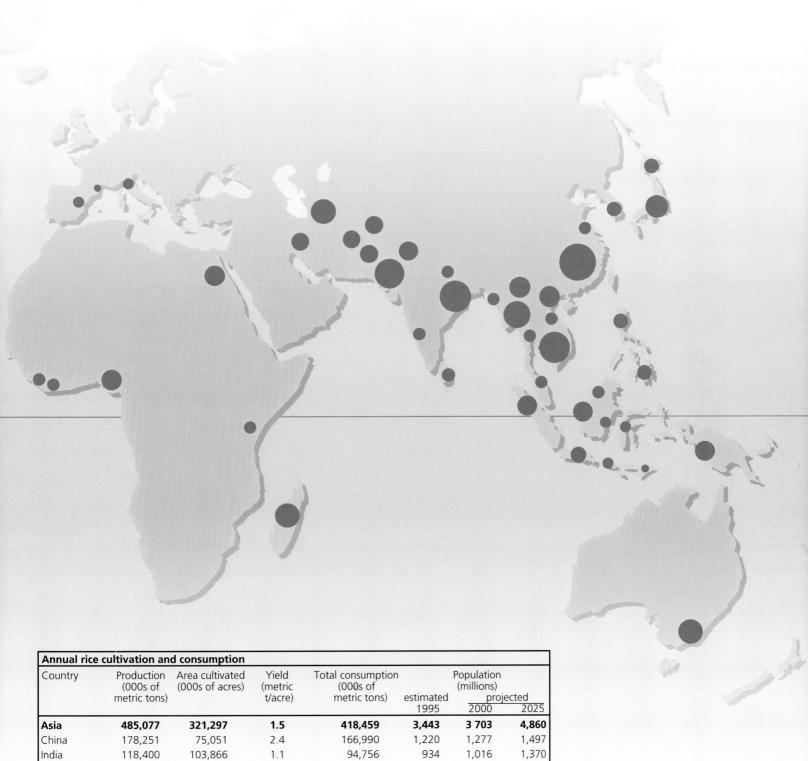

Annual rice cultivation and consumption						
Country	Production (000s of metric tons)	Area cultivated (000s of acres)	Yield (metric t/acre)	Total consumption (000s of metric tons)	Population (millions) estimated 1995	projected 2000	2025
Asia	**485,077**	**321,297**	**1.5**	**418,459**	**3,443**	**3 703**	**4,860**
China	178,251	75,051	2.4	166,990	1,220	1,277	1,497
India	118,400	103,866	1.1	94,756	934	1,016	1,370
Indonesia	46,245	26,306	1.7	39,994	193	206	265
Japan	14,976	5,466	2.8	11,505	125	127	124
Thailand	18,447	20,959	0.9	11,216	60	65	81
Latin America	**20,036**	**16,788**	**1.8**	**17,188**	**475**	**512**	**686**
Brazil	10,582	10,986	1.0	9,419	161	172	224
Africa	**15,855**	**17,878**	**0.9**	**15,741**	**719**	**821**	**1,431**
Egypt	4,582	1,430	3.2	2,514	58	63	86
Nigeria	3,857	4,171	0.9	3,353	111	128	217
United States	**8,972**	**3,301**	**2.7**	**2,704**	**263**	**276**	**323**
Europe	**2,113**	**934**	**2.3**	**2,550**	**731**	**739**	**744**
Australia	**1,017**	**301**	**3.4**	**215**	**18**	**19**	**23**
Others	**1,631**	**1384**	**1.2**	**636**	**43**	**43**	**55**
Worldwide	**534,701**	**361,883**	**1.9**	**457,493**	**5,692**	**6,113**	**8,122**

Source: IRRI Rice Facts, January 1997

Water buffaloes could not till the very hard, heavy soil without water, but now this work can be done with a two-wheeled tractor. This saving on water will change rice culture in other ways. In Egypt, for example, water is scarce, but high yields are especially crucial on account of the low arable land area and the sharply increasing population. For this reason, the farmers have accepted a new method, which does not sacrifice yields. In many cases, rice no longer stands in water; the soil is simply kept moist. Irrigated rice, after all, is not drought-resistant, and if there were no water at all over a fairly long period, the crop would fail. For the majority of small-scale farmers in the developing world who live for, with and from rice, their very existence depends directly on each harvest. For them, rice is synonymous with life.

farmers in developing countries preparation begins with the previous harvest. The purchase of new seed does not take place on a regular basis, as it does in the United States, Europe, and Australia, but only occasionally. For this reason, the farmers' own seed production is particularly important, and it is carried out with great care, from harvest to storage to sowing. For example, in the north of the Philippines, experienced women go through the fields before the main harvest and cut down the biggest and healthiest panicles individually. Tied together in bundles and protected from mice and rats, the panicles are hung from the roofs of dwellings or storage sheds until the next sowing. In the new sowing season they are threshed and sorted. Before sowing, the seed is left to

Just how little some aspects of rice-growing have changed down the centuries can be seen on the following pages, which juxtapose ancient Chinese etchings (on the left-hand pages) from the *Gengzhitu* — the book of plowing and weaving, known in China since the eleventh century and subsequently often copied — and the photos depicting rice cultivation today (on the right-hand pages). Shown here: rice farmers soaking the seed, which must swell and germinate before it is sown.

Sowing or planting?

Only upland rice, which does not grow on fields that are enclosed by levees or that are flat, is sown exclusively, as is the case with other cereals. Before this stage, though, the seed, regardless of the type of rice, must be prepared. For many small-scale rice

soak and swell in water for twenty-four hours. It is then washed and pregerminated for a further two days. Now, perhaps after disinfection to prevent diseases, the rice is ready to be sown. Nature, however, does not make things that easy. There is a dormancy period for almost all seeds, so that they do not germinate immediately after they are ripe for harvesting. Otherwise, during damp weather in particular, the

Rice terraces in Banaue, Luzon In the north of the Philippines, the Ifugao people cultivate their rice by hand on the slopes of the Cordillera Central. In the foreground, the bright green of young plants; behind, flooded rice fields.

grains would sprout on the stalk during the harvest period. The dormancy period for rice lasts about four weeks. The very first cultivated rice was presumably grown on dry fields, without any artificial water supply. Usually spaced out by hand with a great deal of skill, so that the seeds are evenly distributed and germinate at the same time, sowing is generally regarded as men's work. The grains are then worked into the soil with the harrow, and left to themselves and the next rain. This age-old method of cultivation is also found in modern irrigation rice for quite different reasons: the increasing lack of labor for planting, and rising production costs. In America, even machine-sowing has become too expensive. Airplanes have taken over this job, and the irrigated fields are sown from the air

sown in the flooded field. This can be accomplished with simple little machines that sow in rows. In this way, the necessary weed-control can also be made easier.

As a result of selective breeding over many generations, irrigation rice in Asia has also been adapted for transplantation. But if rice can be sown in all ecosystems, why does the (usually female) farmer torture herself with arduous planting? There are good reasons. A watered field can be rid of weeds mechanically, with a harrow, before planting. The approximately three-week-old plants, which have been raised in a special nursery bed, are then transplanted into the prepared field. This is backbreaking work, as was impressively shown in the

Plowing. Brandishing a stick, the rice farmer drives on the water buffalo yoked to his wooden plow, furrow by furrow. But plowing is only part of the job. It is followed by harrowing, then fine-harrowing, or leveling of the soil, which should be as even and compact as possible before sowing.

after the weeds have been eliminated with herbicides.

Not every rice germinates and grows in the very oxygen-deficient conditions of water. It must be an innate characteristic, or one that is bred into it, or the cultivation methods must be appropriately adapted. Irrigation rice, for example, can be dry sown or wet sown. With the former method, the rice is allowed to germinate and begin growing in a dry field, which is flooded later. In the case of wet sowing, the grains are

1948 Italian movie classic *Bitter Rice*. Although this transplanting subjects the rice to a shock, it not only recovers swiftly, but seems to grow better as a result. During the period of shock its root system is wholly transformed, and it becomes an aquatic plant. This gives the irrigation-rice farmers a head start of three weeks. Where water and climate also make a positive contribution and modern early-ripening strains are used, three crops a year can be achieved in this way.

Before sowing In these irrigated rice terraces on Bali the water is more than ankle-deep, and the bottom of the basin is absolutely even, so that the water depth is the same everywhere. The rice needs a lot of oxygen to germinate. For this reason, it is pregerminated in the case of wet-sowing.

In large parts of Asia, depending on the geography, not much has changed in the preparation of the soil. Water buffalo are still used today for plowing, harrowing, and, as shown here, leveling the field. However, machines specially developed for small farmers are increasingly being employed.

The tractor makes lighter work of soil preparation. Italy's rice fields are plowed and harrowed when dry, since only then can the tractor drive over the ground. The rice fields are then flooded just before sowing.

A rice that needs be sown only once

Many grasses are perennial, but although many strains of rice have the ability to send out new shoots, yields decrease sharply after the second and third crop. A few wild strains of rice form runners from their roots, like couch grass, an extremely stubborn wild grass. If this ability could be successfully transferred to cultivated varieties, many problems would be solved simultaneously. This is particularly true for upland rice, which is grown on dry slopes. Here, not only is soil preparation especially difficult, but the risk of erosion is high, since heavy rains — especially at the beginning

annual plants, from the legume family, for example, have this nitrogen-fixation ability, and therefore are not dependent on nitrogen fertilizers. Some species of trees also have their own system for absorbing nitrogen. Such achievements by the plant's own chemical factory do not come free of charge, however. The energy expended on the absorption of nitrogen from the air is very high, so nitrogen-absorbing plants cannot be expected to give maximum yields. Upland rice, however, whose yields will not be greater than 1.6–2 metric tons an acre, even with new strains, could cover part of its nitrogen requirement by itself if this ability were made possible through the transfer of the appropriate genes. Researchers still have some way to go before they crack this problem.

Sowing The seed sits in a basket on the rice farmer's arm, waiting to be sown in special nursery beds that are already flooded.

of the growing season, when the rice plants do not yet cover the ground — can easily wash away the topsoil. A perennial rice, with its deep, solid network of rhizomes, could relieve the farmers of the chores of soil preparation and sowing, and serve as an edible erosion-protection plant, safeguarding the topsoil. Such a plant would make the lives of the poorest rice farmers considerably easier, especially if it could be endowed with the ability to gather nitrogen from the air. Many

Fighting weeds, diseases, and pests

Farmers in the tropics and subtropics, particularly those who are dedicated rice-growers, hardly get a moment's rest. Ask rice farmers how much land they plant with rice, and you will often receive the reply,

The flooded rice fields of the Italian Rice Institute near Mortara are prepared for sowing (wet rice cultivation). The subsoil must be reinforced before sowing, in order to keep nutrient and water losses from seepage to a minimum. Separated according to variety and subdivided into plots, the grains are then planted in the soil.

Seed to be sown directly into water must pregerminate. The soaked rice grains are then sown either in special seed beds or broadcast. For 1 acre of planted-out rice, 35–45 pounds of seed are needed, depending on the variety.

Sowing by hand is widespread in Italy to this day. The rice grains are strewn as evenly as possible over the flooded rice field.

In the United States, by contrast, rice is sown in flooded fields from an airplane, since labor is scarce and expensive. Other methods are not economical in the case of huge cultivated areas.

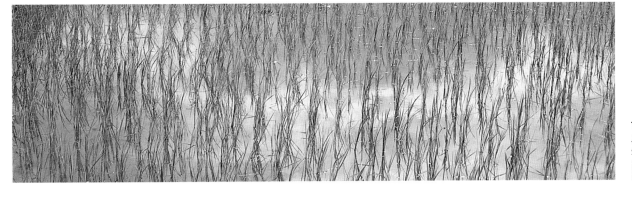

The first green. Just 20–40 days after sowing, the young rice plants are 6–8 inches high.

"As much as we can keep free from weeds." Weed control is not only one of the most arduous, but also one of the most time-consuming activities. Sunlight, high humidity, and water provide good growing conditions for the rice, but also for its competitors.

In Bangladesh a farmer needs around forty days to keep just 2.5 acres of land free from weeds. This is accomplished mostly by hand-weeding; the plants pulled up often serve as animal fodder, so at least they serve a purpose. The weeding is almost always done by women, who are responsible for half of all the work involved in rice-growing. Where wet rice has been sown or planted in rows, weeds can be flattened with a roller hoe. With dry rice, however, a hand hoe must be used. Alternatively, chemical agents can be used, but

being, refuse to employ this technology. If they were to dispense completely with weed control, however, they would easily forfeit half of their crop.

Unfortunately, weed control is only part of the story. Rice has no more enemies than other cultivated plants, but there are insects, for example cicadas, that not only live off the rice plant, but also transmit dangerous viral diseases. For a long time, people believed that they could bring this plague under control, even in the tropics, through the use of insecticides alone. Today, the solution for this, too, is integrated plant protection. Spraying is used only where necessary, as the last means of choice. The fact is that while rice not only has enemies, a rice field plays host to around 500 useful species, some of which

Planting out the stalks After about three weeks, when the rice shoots are growing close together, the small, light-green plants are pulled up from the ground and brought to their new destination in large baskets.

they often have a number of drawbacks: they cost money, work only very selectively, take a long time to break down in the soil, and in some cases are even hazardous. By contrast, so-called total herbicides, which work against all green plants, are harmless, but they can be used only in conjunction with biotechnologically produced seed that is resistant to the active substance in question, or before sowing. Farmers who cannot afford new seed will, for the time

eat rice pests. Insecticides do not usually work selectively, but also kill the useful insects, although not the eggs of the rapidly reproducing cicadas. When the next generation of cicadas hatches, it is met with only a small number of natural enemies, and hence reproduces in greater numbers. Many years of observation of and investigation into the life cycles of the ecosystem were required to recognize these relationships, but they have paid off. The result: lower

The age-old rice terraces in the north of the Philippines, some of which were laid out 2,000 years ago, are steep and narrow. In some places proper supporting walls have been erected to make use of every last bit of the valuable land. Rice is grown here according to the classic cultivation method: first sown in seed beds — clearly visible here on the top plot — and later thinned out, as has already taken place on the lower terraces.

use of pesticides, less environmental pollution, and lower costs for the same yields. The next generation of the green revolution will thrive because of the successes of the breeding of resistant strains, modern growing methods, and the deliberate promotion of useful insects.

A rice that protects itself from weeds?

The rice plant is already a highly complicated chemical factory, capable of producing protein, fat, and carbohydrates from water, nutrients, and sunlight,

with a catalytic converter." It may take ten or fifteen years to develop such a plant, but we know that it is possible. Even before that, there will be a rice that produces its own weedkiller. The roots of the rice plant not only absorb water and nutrients from the soil, they also exude chemical compounds. In this way, the plant protects itself against competitors such as specific aquatic weeds. If scientists succeed in reinforcing this ability — and initial trials, particularly in the United States, are promising — it will be possible to dispense with at least a large part of industrially manufactured herbicides. The potential financial benefits of this research are considerable, as about $1 billion are spent worldwide each year on herbicides for rice cultivation.

Planting Many hands are needed to plant the young rice plants, correctly spaced out, in the beds, which are flooded to above-ankle depth. They are then temporarily left to their fate.

under a number of very different environmental conditions. The special aspect of irrigation rice is that it can stand in water without further air supply because the pipe system in its stems and roots makes it self-ventilating. It does, however, also give off methane into the atmosphere through its stems and leaves, thus having an unfortunately negative impact on the ozone layer. Breeding can influence this characteristic. We might call the breeding aim "Rice

Fertilizers have become essential

Before commercial fertilizers changed the face of agriculture, hundreds of generations of farmers around the world had been successful; they survived. If we were all prepared to become small-scale farmers

Young plant production is finished when the rice shoots are 6–8 inches high. Here, usually three, but sometimes five, young plants are planted in one place at intervals of 4–6 inches.

Endless rows of rice plants are planted in the soil — here, in a Japanese rice field. The gap between rows is usually 6–8 inches. Planting out is arduous work, but has the advantage that the rice shoots do not have to compete immediately with the weeds.

Transplantation of the young rice plants by hand, eighteen to forty-five days after sowing, is a very labor-intensive job. With bent backs and in the full glare of the sun, the planters often stand ankle-deep in water for hours at a time, as here in Italy, protected only by their broad-brimmed hats.

Several rows at a time are planted by this Japanese planting machine. Only a Japanese weekend worker whose main income is drawn as a non-agricultural worker or employee can afford such a machine.

again, if we would take on the onus of laboring twelve hours a day, six days a week, we could produce enough food to live on, without commercial fertilizers, just as our great-grandparents did. However, to be part of a subsistence-farming family is not a desirable goal even for all those people who must live on this basis.

Increased harvests depend only in part on the breeding of correspondingly higher-yielding varieties, which absorb commercial fertilizers via their root systems. According to the rule of thumb, variety, nutrient availability, and water supply each bear a third of the responsibility for the size of the yield. Of course, this rough division applies only if all other factors, such as light, temperature, and plant

Nitrogen fertilizing, which is still used nowadays, is actually very uneconomic. Only about half of the fertilizer that is applied is directly absorbed by the plant. The rest vanishes into the air, contributing to environmental pollution, or is deposited in the soil. A considerable proportion winds up in the groundwater. These environmental burdens are particularly high in the case of heavy applications of fertilizer (more than 134 pounds an acre) and insufficient spreading over the growing period. Applying excessive amounts of fertilizer not only harms the environment and is costly for farmers, but also damages the rice itself. Even modern strains fall over when too much fertilizer is applied, because the stems are not strong enough to stand up to the wind. Farmyard fertilizers — that is,

Weeding The young rice plants cannot survive untended for very long, as the weeds sprouting up amidst them threaten to choke them. In addition to regular watering, therefore, farmers must remember to weed in good time. The unwanted plants are pulled up by hand as many as three times.

protection, provide favorable growth conditions for the rice plant. For example, the rice plant grows best at a temperature of 77–95°F. If it gets hotter, the chances for a good harvest sink quickly. Nitrogen, phosphoric acid, and potash are the most important nutrients, with nitrogen playing a central role (not because the other nutrients are less important, but because they are present to a larger extent in the soil and are available to the plant).

animal manure and green manure (from green plants) — which would be a good alternative to commercial ones, are seldom available to rice farmers, who have few animals and little land. Today, however, there are many methods of using commercial fertilizers more judiciously. For example, little nitrogen balls placed in the soil give off only very small quantities of fertilizer over a relatively long period, thus reducing losses to a minimum. The cost of manufacturing the balls and

Javanese rice farmers weeding After applying fertilizer and ensuring that the plants are watered, weed control is the most important measure in rice cultivation. There are several ways of doing this: pulling out the weeds by hand; using a hoe, as above; or using small machines. Chemical weedkillers or herbicides are also employed, except in organic rice cultivation.

Rice cultivation in terraces — still widespread today in South and Southeast Asia — is an impressive example of the fact that long-term food production is possible without harming nature. In fact, wet rice is the only cultivated plant that has been grown as a monoculture for millennia without any negative consequences.

inserting them in the flooded soils, however, is still high, so this method is not common yet. Simpler and more widespread is the multiple application of small quantities of fertilizer, according to the stage of development of the plant. With the aid of a small device that works like a light meter, it is possible to measure the nitrogen requirement of a rice plant. The fertilizer is then applied only when the plant shows signs of nutrient hunger.

Harvest

Rice is ready for harvesting about four months after planting. If the rain does not thwart plans, as is all too

areas of Indonesia, for example, rice is not cut off with its stalks. Women with baskets tied to their backs move through the field of standing stalks, using a hidden knife, the *ani-ani*, to cut off just the panicles, which they throw over their shoulder into the basket. This is so the spirits in the stalks will not be disturbed.

The sickle, the common harvesting implement, varies little from one part of Asia to another. Although much narrower and sharper than a garden sickle in the West, it usually has a serrated cutting edge to make cutting off the often-tough stalks easier. Depending on the season and region, the sheaves, bound together with straw, are heaped high on the field, or taken to a private or communal threshing place, on the backs of people, animals, or any other

The harvest Two to three weeks before the grain is ripe, the water is drained out of the rice fields (as can easily be seen here — the farmers are no longer wading in the water) and the harvest can begin. Using slender, narrow sickles or special harvesting knives, they cut down the stalks , bundle them into sheaves and take them away.

frequently the case, these days become the high point of the season. Helping one's neighbors is a way of life. Working as a group, farmers harvest one field after the other with sickles, and bind the rice into sheaves. During the history of 10,000 years of a plant of such central importance a great deal of country wisdom and many stories have developed. In fact, no other plant is linked to so many myths, rituals, and superstitions, and this is especially true for the harvest. In many

available means of transportation, to be dealt with later. However, threshing in the fields right after harvesting is becoming increasingly popular. When one thinks of modern combine harvesters with their air-conditioned cabins, it is hard to imagine people in America using flails, threshing machines, and hand-operated grain cleaners until after the Second World War. But in many parts of the world and in most of the rice-growing regions of Asia, it is only very recently

Stalk by stalk, the rice farmers harvest their crop when the panicles have turned yellow — in Italy (left) as in Thailand (right). At harvest, some of the leaves and stems are still green. In the case of hand-harvesting, which is much the same everywhere, the grains have a moisture content of around 20 percent.

Rice harvest in Japan using a small combine harvester. In the background, the sheaves are hung up to dry. Since the invention of a special small threshing machine — and Japan is one of the leading inventors of machines for small farmers — it is increasingly used in the harvest.

In the Ebro delta, in Spain, the rice harvest is fully mechanized. Heavy-duty combine harvesters harvest the grain from the fields. The threshed rice is brought by the tankload by tractor to the edge of the field, and transferred onto the waiting truck by means of a blower.

After the harvest the rice straw is often burned, as it is here in the Camargue, to make subsequent soil preparation easier, and to save on labor costs.

that some, if not many, technological changes have been implemented. Threshing by driving animals in a circle around a stake to trample the grain is still as common as beating out the rice sheaves over a grid. Even threshing with one's bare feet is still to be found in remote regions. The flail, however, has had its day in almost all parts of the world.

Rice breeders must look for many compromises between what are often mutually exclusive characteristics. This also holds true for threshing. Wild strains of rice and simple native varieties lose their grains easily in the late stage of ripening: they fall out, as nature intends, in order to encourage spread and the growth of new plants. Modern cultivated strains, by contrast, possess the ability to keep the seeds firmly in

turning wheel, the loops knock the rice grains from the panicles. But who wants to tread the pedals when it is well above 90°F in the shade, and extremely humid as well? At this level of mechanization, threshing remains an arduous activity. The next step, therefore, was to replace the pedal with a motor, and make the loop roller a proper pin thresher. Here too, the IRRI was substantially involved in development up to the ready-for-production stage. In most developing countries, however, there is no agricultural machinery industry that can take on production, sales, and servicing. The manufacture of such devices therefore is dependent on small and very small businesses, often coupled with a vehicle repair service. To enable these manufacturers to build the apparatus,

Threshing Once the harvest is in, the individual grains must be freed from the panicles. The rice plants are laid out on bamboo mats and beaten with a flail.

the panicle. This is advantageous only if the threshing method can beat out all the grains, thus avoiding harvest losses. With very simple methods such as hand-threshing, this can be achieved only by a great deal of effort, if at all. The first step in modernization was the invention of the pedal thresher. It is driven by a foot pedal, which activates a roller with wire loops, a concept copied from the treadle sewing machine. When the little sheaves are held up to the rapidly

there have to be models to copy or drawings that can be read by self-taught manual workers.

With modernization continuing apace, especially in Asia, the degree of mechanization is rising more quickly than was originally expected, even in rural areas. In countries such as China, India, Indonesia, Pakistan, and Thailand, progress is particularly apparent. In Malaysia rice is produced mainly on big farms, and is already mechanized. Just how small

With manually harvested rice there is usually a several-day-long drying phase between harvesting and threshing. In Bali, the panicles, either loose (top left) or tied into sheaves (center left), are spread out in the sun. Next comes the threshing, in which the grains are beaten out of the panicles. On Lombok, Bali's neighboring island, threshing is done by beating the sheaves over wooden frames (left). In Thailand (top right), they are threshed on the ground. The rice farmer uses big fans, like here in Thailand (center right), to separate the chaff from the heavy rice grains, still in their husks.

farmers can make use of modern technologies is a question that often remains unanswered. The size of their fields, the size of their farms, the lack of capital and the lack of credit are among many other factors that leave them little leeway for experimentation and investment. In addition, these farmers face increasing labor shortages, especially at peak periods such as harvest time. Paid labor is therefore becoming more and more common, even in regions where small farms are the rule. Payment is made either in cash or, even more frequently, in rice, which served as a form of currency long before coins and paper money. Threshing is almost always carried out right in the field, using fairly small motor-driven threshing machines operated by a small team. Even so, the

The mechanization of rice cultivation or opting out, wherever this is possible, are the answers for many rice-growers today. In Japan small combine harvesters were developed some time ago. It is not just the technical requirements for a high degree of mechanization that are present there, however. Rice farmers in Japan are often weekend farmers only. Their cultural ties to the land have so far kept them from giving up farming, or at least labor-intensive rice cultivation. Instead, they have diverted a substantial part of their income from their industrial or white-collar jobs into mechanizing rice cultivation — and the State foots a large part of the bill. Nowhere in the world does rice farming receive such strong State support as in Japan, and nowhere in the world is rice

Winnowing To separate the chaff from the grain, a separate step, winnowing, has always been necessary. This is done by tossing the threshed grain into the air, allowing the lighter stalk and leaf residue to be carried away by the wind, while the heavy rice grains fall to the ground.

harvest work itself is hard. There will have to be more improvements, since agricultural labor costs are rising, even in Asia's rice-growing regions. This is not because there are other employment opportunities in the village, but because more and more of the workforce are moving away to urban centers in search of a better job and an income above the minimum survival level, often in vain.

as expensive as it is there. In Australia, the United States, France, and Italy, rice is only combine-harvested with large machines, often operating in convoy with several threshing units. A large combine can harvest up to 25 acres a day. For the many small-scale farmers of Asia, whose terraced fields often are accessible only with difficulty via small paths, these are, unfortunately, not solutions.

In the traditional manner women from Lombok winnow (left) by tossing the threshed grain into the air. The photo top right shows the rice being dried on Bali. Rice generally needs another subsequent drying, since paddy suitable for storage may not contain more than 14 percent moisture, or it will spoil. For lack of a suitable drying place, the rice is simply spread out on the street to dry in the sun, turned occasionally with a rake.

Until further processing in modern rice mills or in the traditional fashion, the rice is stored temporarily — here, for example, in an Italian warehouse. Great care is taken to keep its moisture at a constant 14 percent.

Rice mills in the United States are huge factories. In these gray concrete "temples" with their huge, round silo towers, the rice passes through various fully mechanised processing stations. After the grains are cleaned and husked and the bran is removed, convoys of trucks stand ready to transport the rice to its destination.

Paddy, or raw, rice is not yet ready to eat, as the inedible husks must first be removed.

Helping small farmers

The technology of the most modern pickup loader can be exploited and scaled down in such a way that it can be operated with a two-wheeled tractor. As with the first pedal thresher, a roller strips the grains into a basket, leaving the straw standing in the field. Once such harvest technology is fully mature, labor will be reduced to three working days an acre for a single person, as opposed to sixteen with the old sickle.

Even once the threshing is finished, however, the rice crop is still not in, and must first be freed from impurities and straw- and panicle residue. This is accomplished by winnowing: tossing the threshed rice

without technical assistance. Normally, the threshed rice is spread out thinly over every available surface and raked until it is dry enough to be stored without going moldy. Since the 1970s many scientists have tried to build a simple, cheap, efficient drying plant for small farms. At last they found a solution that is now used for drying special crops. Technically it is very simple, except for the solar cell that supplies the power for a small ventilator, even in cloudy weather.

Ready for the pot?

Self-sufficient rice farmers who harvest their crop every four to five months and do not need to store the

Husking The final stage involves removing the rice grains from the inedible husk that surrounds them. This is done either with a mortar and pestle (seen in the foreground of the picture) or with a treadle apparatus (shown in the background).

with a pitchfork or flat, woven shawls. In the wind, the chaff separates from the rice. Hand-operated grain cleaners or similar devices have so far hardly found acceptance in traditional rice cultivation. The biggest problem, especially when the harvest falls in the rainy season, is drying the grain. Rice is harvested with a moisture content of 20–25 percent. This must be reduced to 13–14 percent for storage. Where atmospheric humidity is high, this is almost impossible

rice for longer, are often satisfied with the husked rice. Health-conscious consumers in the West also swear by untreated whole-grain rice. The small grain acquires its white appearance only after milling, removal of the bran, and polishing. The grain itself constitutes a complicated little world of its own, of which every cook and gourmet should know the basics. For this reason, the next chapter is devoted to it.

Dr. Klaus Lampe

Rice processing for the Ifugao In Banga-an, a small village in the north Philippines, among other places, the rice grains are still husked almost as they used to be in ancient China. The only difference is that here the grains are stripped by hand from the panicle. Next, they are worked with poles in a huge mortar to loosen the husks. When they are tossed into the air, the heavy grains fall back into the sieve, and the husks and bran are used for animal fodder. The rice is not yet white, though, so it is pounded and sieved again. Three to four processing stages are required to produce the white grains in this sieve.

The rice grain

awn

Bran layers:
pericarp and testa (seed coat),
protein-rich aleurone layer

lemma

endosperm
(containing starch granules)

germ (embryo)

rudimentary husk

start of stem

Varieties and uses

The genus *Oryza* is a member of the family of cereal grasses (Gramineae) and, within this, of the subfamily Oryzoideae. Its flower cluster, or panicle, which reaches a length of 12 inches, and up to 20 inches in a number of varieties, develops at the top of the stalk. The upright panicle then usually flowers within a week, from the bottom upward. The flower cluster consists of single-flowered spikelets situated on twisted lateral branches. The unimposing flowers — in traditional varieties, up to 150 per panicle, in new strains, twice as many — are hermaphroditic, and therefore self-pollinating. Unlike the flowers of most other grasses, rice flowers have six, rather than three, anthers. The ovary bears two stigmas. On each spikelet there is a lancet-shaped upper bract, or palea, and a boat-shaped lower bract, or lemma, which grow together with the ripening grains (caryopses). The grains are protected by the hard husks, most of which are also topped with slender bristles called awns. After flowering, it generally takes another thirty to forty days for the grains to ripen. During this period the grain develops its most important nutrients, the majority of which are to be found in the various layers of the bran, which consists of pericarp and testa (seed coat), and the protein-rich aleurone layer. In addition, the bran layers gives the rice grain its reddish-brown or greenish-yellow hue. Important nutrients also lie in the germ, or embryo, which is located under the endosperm and is composed mainly of starch.

The grains and the inedible husks grow together, so husking is necessary before the rice can be used as food. The traditional method, which is sometimes still used, involves pounding the rice. The drawback here is the high proportion of broken rice that results, as well as the considerable time taken. Today's modern rice mills, by contrast, can achieve substantially higher yields and quality, since a more gentle processing means that far fewer grains are broken. The raw rice, or paddy, is separated into brown rice and husks

Wholegrain rice, husked rice with the bran intact, also called brown rice, is the result of an initial processing of raw rice in the rice mill. Generally speaking, the rice is usually husked in the country where it is grown.

Broken rice is a by-product of milling. Three grades are distinguished, according to size. Small broken rice is used as animal fodder, in processed foods, and in beer-brewing.

Rice hulls, which accrue during the hulling process (accounting for about 20 percent of dry paddy weight), are used chiefly to generate energy.

From paddy to white rice
Short-grain rice, left, as paddy, and, right, in five different milling grades. If the rice is not pretreated (parboiled), the rule is: the whiter the grain, the lower the nutrient content.

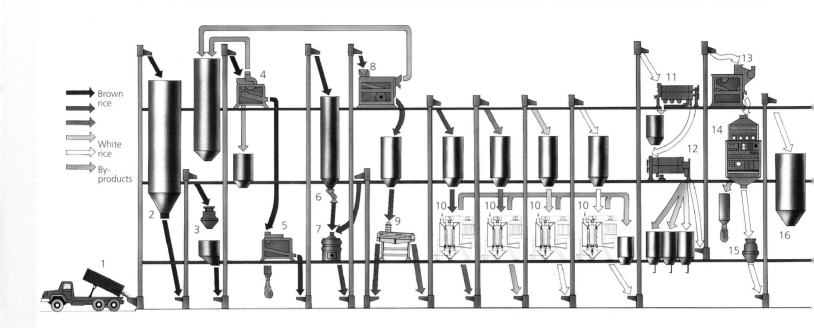

Brown rice

White rice

By-products

between two rubber rollers running at different speeds. The husks are used in the manufacture of fuel, and packaging and insulating material. Husked rice is the usual format for shipping abroad, and is therefore also known as "cargo rice." Loaded into the hulls of big ships, it is transported to the rice mills, where it undergoes further processing. First, magnets and sieves are used to remove foreign bodies as well as larger

impurities from the rice before it is sorted according to grain length. During the sorting small foreign particles and broken rice are removed. Next comes the stripping off of the bran layers and embryo. There are two ways this can be done. The first is to rub the rice grains against stone. This produces fewer broken grains, but gives the rice grains a rough surface. The second option is to rub the rice grains against rice grains. This gives the grains a smoother surface, but there are more broken grains because of the necessarily higher pressure. The rice is then often polished: the dust still clinging to the grains from the stripping process is removed. The final milled product — white rice — is very popular, particularly in many Asian countries. It would be healthier, however, to skip the milling process and leave both the bran layers and the germ on the grain, since these contain the lion's share of minerals, trace elements, and vitamins, particularly B-complex vitamins (B_1, B_2, niacin, pantothenic acid, and B_6) as well as vitamin E. About 10 ounces of brown rice provides 18 percent of the daily protein requirement, and it contains a much higher percentage of fiber. Whether milled or unmilled, however, rice is healthy — low in sodium, but high in potassium, which regulates the body's water balance.

Processing in the rice mill:
1 Delivery of raw rice (paddy)
2 Temporary storage in large silos
3 Weighing the rice
4 Removing large foreign bodies
5 Removing small foreign bodies
6 Magnet removes iron particles
7 Hulling the paddy with rubber rollers
8 Suctioning off the husks
9 Elimination of unhulled grains
10 Removing the bran
11 Removing too-small grains
12 Sorting into whole grains and three sizes of broken grains
13 Final polishing: cleaning of dust from grains
14 Visual sorting; elimination of black or discolored grains
15 Weighing the rice
16 Collection silo, where the grain is stored before packing

Nutritional content of rice, corn, and wheat				
	Rice		Corn	Wheat
	unpolished	polished		
Moisture	13.1	12.9	12.5	13.2
Carbohydrates	73.4	77.8	64.7	61.0
Protein	7.2	6.8	8.6	11.7
Fat	2.2	0.6	3.8	2.0
Fiber	2.9	1.4	9.2	10.3
Magnesium (mg)	157.0	64.0	120.0	147.0
Calcium (mg)	23.0	6.0	15.0	43.7
Phosphorus (mg)	325.0	120.0	256.0	344.4
Iron (mg)	2.6	0.6	–	3.3
Potassium (mg)	150.0	103.0	330.0	502.5
Thiamin B_1 (mg)	0.41	0.06	0.36	0.48
Riboflavin B_2 (mg)	0.09	0.32	0.20	0.14
Energy kJ	1,454	1,461	1,389	1,310
Energy kcal	342	344	327	309
Average values in g/per 100 g edible part of grain				

From short-grain to long-grain

It seems only a short time ago that we could just about manage to distinguish between long- and short-grain rice. Since then the rice section in supermarkets has expanded, and the selection in natural food stores and Asian groceries has also increased. Compared with the over 100,000 varieties of rice in existence worldwide, however, this is still small beer. Some of the varieties presented in the following section might still be difficult to track down, since the exporting of rice is limited to relatively few countries and varieties. Ninety percent of the world's rice is produced in Asia, but the Asian share of the export market is comparatively small. Of the 535 million metric tons of rice produced in total, only a fraction reaches the international market because rice, a staple food in Asia, is consumed mainly in the rice-growing countries themselves. Of the approximately 16 million

metric tons that are exported worldwide, around one quarter comes from Europe, the United States, and Australia. Of the Asian countries, Thailand, Vietnam, China, Pakistan, and India are significant exporters, with Thailand being by far the biggest. Taken as a whole, however, the world market for rice is of subordinate importance to the market for other cereals, such as wheat and corn.

In principle, the trade distinguishes between short-grain, medium-grain, and long-grain rice. Generally speaking, short-grain rice is between 5.0 and 5.2 mm long, medium-grain rice is between 5.2 and 6.0 mm, and long-grain rice is over 6.0 mm long. The slender indica rice grains usually have a length-to-breadth ratio of greater than 3:1. In a number of countries, further distinctions are made. Thus, for example, the subdivision of Italian short- and medium-grain varieties into *commune* or *originario*, into *semifino*, *fino*, and *superfino*, does not refer to the "fineness" of the grains, but to grain size: *commune* or *originario* means shorter than 5.2 mm, *semifino* can be between 5.2 and 6.4 mm long, and *fino* means longer than 6.4 mm; *superfino*, of the same length, is of particularly high quality. Rice is also divided into non-glutinous and glutinous (sticky) varieties. The latter are found mainly among the japonica varieties, but there are also some among the indica.

Rice is sold according to the following classification: top-quality rice, which may contain a maximum of 5 percent broken rice grains; standard rice, with a maximum of 15 percent broken rice; household rice with a maximum of 25 percent broken rice grains; household rice with a maximum of 40 percent broken grains; and broken rice, with a minimum of 40 percent broken grains. Because of its low moisture content, rice has a long shelf life. When stored in a cool, dark, dry place, milled rice keeps for several years. Brown rice, with its higher fat content, can be kept for up to one year without going rancid. The following pages illustrate a selection of the most important varieties, shown both raw and cooked. In addition to the usual trade name and origin, the cooking time is given for each variety as a guide, and refers to the absorption method unless indicated otherwise.

Rice on sale in Bangkok
An amazing variety of rice types are offered for sale in Asian markets. Not all rice is the same: price differences of up to 100 percent are not at all uncommon.

Tio João, long-grain rice, Brazil.
Cook for about 20 minutes.

Patna rice, long-grain rice, USA.
Cook for about 20 minutes.

Long grain, USA.
Cook for 15–18 minutes.

Carolina rice, long-grain rice, USA.
Cook for about 20 minutes.

Brown long-grain, integrated cultivation, USA.
Soak, then cook for about 40 minutes.

Texmati, long-grain rice, USA.
Cook for 12–15 minutes.

Brown short-grain, integrated cultivation, USA.
Soak, then cook for about 30 minutes.

Medium-grain rice, USA.
Cook for 15–18 minutes.

Brown short grain, organically grown, USA.
Soak, then cook for about 25 minutes.

Sushi rice, Japanese medium-grain rice, USA.
Cook for 12–15 minutes.

Shinode, Japanese medium-grain rice, USA.
Cook for 12–15 minutes.

Nishiki, Japanese short-grain rice, USA.
Cook for 12–15 minutes.

Shiragiku, Japanese short-grain rice, USA.
Cook for 12–15 minutes.

Brown sweet rice, organically grown, USA.
Soak, then cook for about 30 minutes.

Sweet rice, Japanese short-grain rice, USA.
Cook for 10–12 minutes.

Hitomebore, short-grain rice, Japan.
Cook for 12–15 minutes.

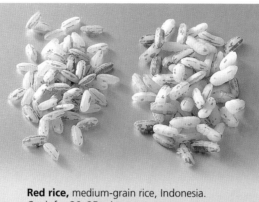

Koshihikari, short-grain rice, Japan.
Cook for about 15 minutes.

Akitakomachi, short-grain rice, Japan.
Cook for 12–15 minutes.

Short-grain rice, Bali.
Cook for 15–20 minutes.

Red rice, medium-grain rice, Indonesia.
Cook for 20–25 minutes.

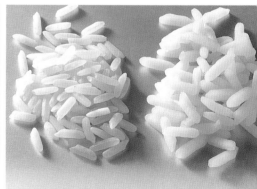

Black rice, Indonesia.
Cook for 25–30 minutes.

Aplati, uncolored green rice, Thailand.
Sauté in a little oil for 2–3 minutes.

Long-grain glutinous rice, Thailand.
Cook for 12–15 minutes.

Neow san pha tong, long-grain glutinous
rice, Thailand. Cook for 10–12 minutes.

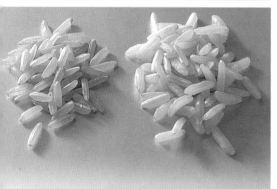

Jasmine rice, unmilled, Thailand.
Soak, then cook for 20–25 minutes.

Thai organic fragrant rice, Thailand.
Cook for about 30 minutes.

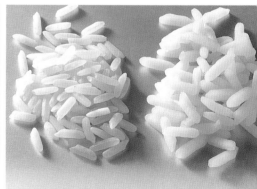

Kaew, long-grain rice, Thailand.
Cook for 10–12 minutes.

Khao dowk mali, long-grain rice, Thailand.
Cook for about 10 minutes.

Five-star basmati, long-grain rice, India.
Cook for about 15 minutes.

Supreme basmati, long-grain rice, India.
Cook for about 15 minutes.

Sweet mochi rice, short-grain rice, Japan.
Cook for 30–35 minutes.

Long-grain rice, China.
Cook for 15–18 minutes.

Short-grain rice, Philippines.
Cook for 10–12 minutes.

Fragrant rice, long-grain rice, Indonesia.
Cook for 12–15 minutes.

Aplati, colored green rice, Vietnam.
Steam in a little water for about 2 minutes.

Short-grain glutinous rice, Vietnam.
Cook for 12–15 minutes.

Patna rice, long-grain rice, Thailand.
Cook for 15–20 minutes.

Kao luang, long-grain rice, Thailand.
Cook for 15–18 minutes.

Jasmine rice, long-grain rice, Thailand.
Cook for 12–15 minutes.

Red rice, medium-grain rice, Thailand.
Cook for about 20 minutes.

Red rice, long-grain rice, Thailand.
Cook for 20–25 minutes.

Black rice, long-grain rice, Thailand.
Cook for 30–35 minutes.

Brown basmati rice, India.
Soak, then cook for about 25 minutes.

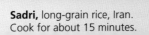

Sadri, long-grain rice, Iran.
Cook for about 15 minutes.

Dom Siah, long-grain rice, Iran.
Cook for 10–12 minutes.

Long-grain rice (Oryza sativa), Africa.
Cook for 10–12 minutes.

Short-grain rice, unpolished, Spain.
Soak, then cook for 30–35 minutes.

Bomba, short-grain rice, Spain.
Cook for 15–20 minutes.

Bahía, short-grain rice, Spain.
Cook for 12–15 minutes.

Thai bonnet, long-grain rice, Spain.
Cook for 10–12 minutes.

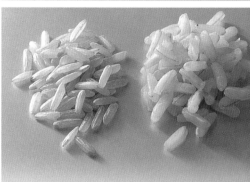

Thai bonnet, long-grain brown rice, Spain.
Soak, then cook for about 30 minutes.

Short-grain brown rice, France.
Soak and cook for about 40 minutes.

Arborio, short-grain rice, Italy.
Cook for 15–18 minutes.

Carnaroli, short-grain rice, Italy.
Cook for 18–20 minutes.

Vialone nano, short-grain rice, Italy.
Cook for 15–18 minutes.

Vialone nano semifino, short-grain brown rice, Italy.
Cook for 30–35 minutes.

San Andrea, short-grain rice, Italy.
Cook for 18-20 minutes.

Roma, short-grain rice, Italy.
Cook for 15–18 minutes.

Ribe, short-grain rice, Italy.
Cook for 15–18 minutes

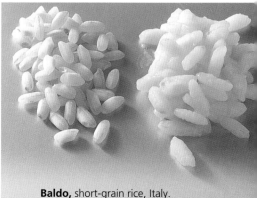

Baldo, short-grain rice, Italy.
Cook for about 18 minutes.

Thainato, short-grain rice, Spain. Cook for 15–18 minutes.

Red rice, Camargue, France. Soak, then cook for 20–25 minutes.

Loto, short-grain rice, Italy. Cook for 17–20 minutes.

Padano, short-grain rice, Italy. Cook for 15–18 minutes.

Originario, short-grain rice, Italy. Cook for 12–15 minutes.

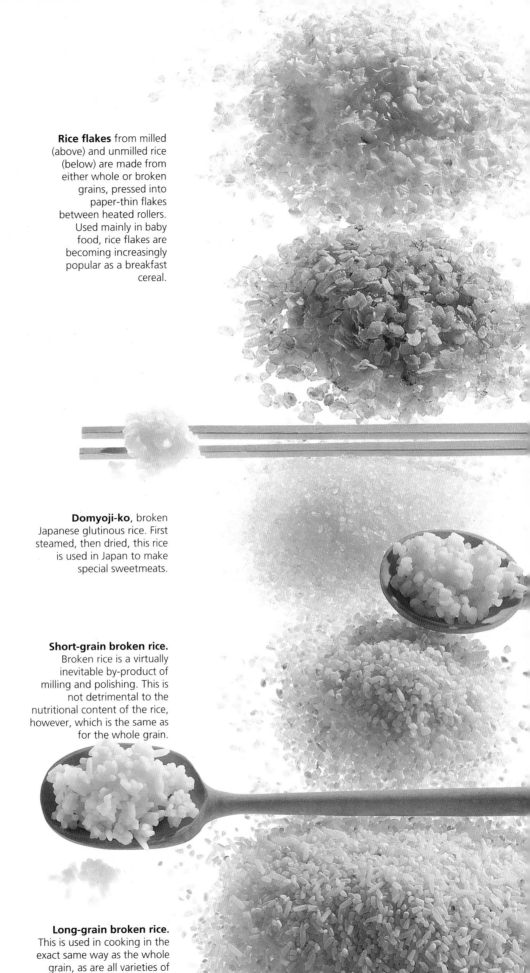

Rice flakes from milled (above) and unmilled rice (below) are made from either whole or broken grains, pressed into paper-thin flakes between heated rollers. Used mainly in baby food, rice flakes are becoming increasingly popular as a breakfast cereal.

Domyoji-ko, broken Japanese glutinous rice. First steamed, then dried, this rice is used in Japan to make special sweetmeats.

Short-grain broken rice. Broken rice is a virtually inevitable by-product of milling and polishing. This is not detrimental to the nutritional content of the rice, however, which is the same as for the whole grain.

Long-grain broken rice. This is used in cooking in the exact same way as the whole grain, as are all varieties of broken rice. Nevertheless, broken rice is substantially cheaper than the whole grain.

Parboiled rice
Almost as nutritious as brown rice, thanks to a special treatment

Whereas "white" rice has lost most of its valuable nutrients after milling, parboiled rice still contains a majority of the vitamins and minerals present in brown rice — up to 80 percent, in fact, even after the bran and germ are removed. This is a good thing, even if a bit of the rice's flavor is sacrificed. Around one fifth of the world's rice crop is processed into parboiled rice, generally in situ, in the rice-growing countries themselves. The process is not new. Traditionally, it is carried out by steaming the raw rice and then drying it in the sun. The modern parboiling process using steam and pressure was developed in America in the 1940s, and has been employed increasingly since the Second World War. In parboiling, the nutrients in the outer layers are transferred to the inner portion of the grain by means of a special hydrothermic treatment. If the rice is treated according to this method (illustrated schematically below) —that is, using pressure and a vacuum — it is also called "converted" rice. After being subjected to this procedure, parboiled rice is processed further in rice mills in exactly the same manner as other raw rice. A further advantage of the parboiling procedure is that it reduces losses resulting from broken grains. Finally, parboiled rice is photoelectronically sorted in order to eliminate brown and black grains, which have been overheated. Milled parboiled rice is translucent and yellowish in color. We do not yet have a full scientific explanation for this change in color, but the heat applied during the parboiling process is partly responsible for it — the higher the temperature, the darker the grain becomes. In addition, pigments from the testa are drawn into the endosperm with the steam. Rice connoisseurs can tell the degree of processing and the nutritional content of the grain merely from its color.

Parboiled rice and untreated rice of the same variety have different cooking properties. The former cooks more quickly, and the final steam treatment hardens the surface starch that seals the grain. For this reason, the grains of parboiled rice remain fluffy and separate rather than sticking together, and the vitamins and minerals are retained.

A wooden spoon makes light work of fishing this boil-in-the-bag rice out of its cooking water. Almost all of the bags are equipped with an extra tab designed for this purpose.

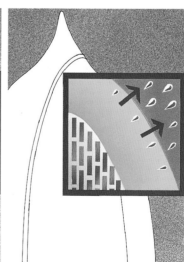

Cook-in-the-bag rice is widely available in stores from the United States to Thailand. Its advantages are that it doesn't stick to the pan, burn, or become sticky. The perforations in the bag enable the rice to absorb the necessary quantity of liquid during cooking.

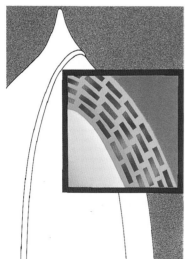

The parboiling process: The enlarged cutout diagramatically illustrates the vitamins and minerals contained in the bran. The modern parboiling process works as follows:

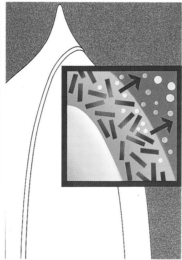

All the air is drawn out of the raw rice in vacuum containers by means of low pressure. The rice is then steeped in lukewarm water, which detaches the nutrients from the bran and germ.

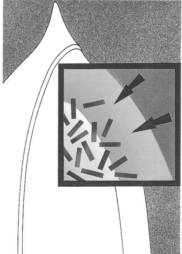

Next, the grains are treated with steam and high pressure, which forces the water-soluble vitamins and minerals back into the center of the rice grain.

The rice grains are again subjected to hot steam, which hardens the surface starch. This seal keeps the nutrients in the grain. Lastly, the rice is dried.

US white rice, long-grain rice, parboiled.
Cook for 18–20 minutes.

Pai João, long-grain rice, parboiled, Brazil.
Cook for 20–25 minutes.

Long-grain rice, parboiled, USA.
Cook for 15–20 minutes.

Short-grain rice, part-milled, parboiled, India.
Cook for about 20 minutes.

Long-grain brown rice, parboiled, USA.
Cook for about 25 minutes.

Long-grain rice, parboiled, Spain.
Cook for 18–20 minutes.

Ribe, short-grain rice, parboiled, Italy.
Cook for 18–20 minutes.

Ribe integro, short-grain brown rice,
parboiled. Cook for 20–25 minutes.

Avorio, short-grain rice, parboiled, Italy.
Cook for 20–22 minutes.

Vialone, medium-grain rice, parboiled, Italy.
Cook for about 20 minutes.

A very wide range of rice comes in perforated polyethylene bags in practical portions. Cook-in-the-bag rice is extremely popular because it is so easy to prepare. Before you cook it, it pays to read the instructions on the package. Bring the given amount of water to a boil in a pot and lay the bag down flat. It should be completely covered by the water. Cooking times vary according to variety. Generally, parboiled long-grain rice cooks in 12–15 minutes, untreated long-grain rice in around 15 minutes; parboiled long-grain brown rice has a cooking time of 20–25 minutes, and untreated long-grain brown rice of 25–35 minutes. These times are just guidelines, however, and may vary by several minutes according to the variety. In addition, there are different types of quick-cooking rice on the market, for example the moist, sterile-packed minute rice, which only needs to be heated to the desired eating temperature. Also available is dry instant rice, over which a given quantity of boiling water is poured to rehydrate before eating. Lastly, there is the dried, precooked, and then redried quick-cook rice, which cooks in 5–10 minutes, depending on variety.

Crunchy snacks and convenience foods
From puffed rice and crackers to risotto mixes

Rice-producing countries such as the United States, Japan, Korea, and China are naturally trailblazers in the matter of rice snacks. Puffed rice is eaten as a breakfast cereal, plain or flavored, for example with a chocolate or sugar glaze. Puffed rice is made from rice grains that are heated to a very high temperature and subjected to high pressure. When the pressure is reduced suddenly, they expand to many times their original volume. The same process is used to produce rice cakes. These are usually made from brown rice, which is sometimes mixed with wild rice, corn, or sesame seeds. In spite of such combinations, however, or the addition of flavorings, these puffed rice products do not exactly deliver an intense taste experience. Even their nutritional value is relatively low, but they are quite useful within the context of a reduced-calorie or gluten-free diet.

Asian rice snacks are available in an amazing variety of shapes and flavors. Until recently, they tended to be sold for the most part in health food stores, but have gained entry into many grocery stores due to their growing popularity. The most widely available are Japanese rice crackers, which can be made both from glutinous and non-glutinous rice varieties. The different structure of the two types

makes them easy to tell apart: whereas crackers made from glutinous rice are relatively open-textured and melt quickly on the tongue, those made from nonglutinous rice are harder to the bite, with a rougher surface. Although many recipes are jealously guarded company secrets, the manufacturing process for both sorts has certain elements in common: the rice is dried, glazed with a mixture of soy sauce and sugar or other seasonings, and then oven-baked, after which the crackers are sometimes also wrapped in nori leaves, which have a strong sea tang. In addition, deep-fried rice crackers, often spicy-hot with chile and closer to Western snacks in taste, are now on the market. In Japan one can also buy individually shrinkwrapped rice cakes that can be seasoned and fried or broiled according to taste.

People who don't have the time to prepare, say, their own tomato, saffron, or spinach risotto from scratch can buy specialties of this sort in a package, ready-seasoned, to make in any quantity they wish. The basis of this almost instant meal is parboiled rice, the individual grains of which are coated in their own sauce according to a patented process. Red, yellow, or black, these quick risottos need to cook in boiling water for a mere 12 minutes until the grains have swollen.

Also available in some places are rice flakes of various colors and flavors, including chocolate, that can be stirred into milk, other dairy products, or fruit juices straight from the package, and, like the quick risottos, can also be made into near-instant sweet soups, hot cereal, or puddings.

These are some of the products made from and with rice, from cereal to cookies and other snack foods.

Rice flour is made by grinding whole grains or broken rice. However, a mixture of pearling-cone meal, left over from the polishing of the rice grains, and fine broken rice, is also referred to as rice flour. Whereas the former forms the basis for rice noodles and thin rice paper, the latter is used chiefly as animal fodder. There are two sorts of rice flour for human consumption, which are distinguished by their grain structure. The first type is made from glassy, hard grains; the second, from glutinous or waxy rice flour. Because of its great ability to swell, the latter lends a slightly rubbery texture to doughs, and is suitable for thickening white sauces and for using in desserts. In China, glutinous-rice flour is used primarily to make sumptuous dim sum dumplings. Products made from glutinous-rice flour are well suited to freezing because, unlike most other foods, they do not absorb water when thawing.

Rice flour
Snow-white and powdery-fine: the basis for blancmanges, rice noodles, and snacks.

Like wheat or rye, polished or brown rice can easily be ground into flour after hulling. The technical process for milling rice does not differ substantially from that used for other cereals, and storage is the same. Rice flour is primarily made from polished broken rice, and is therefore usually whiter than wheat or rye flour, and is generally ground more finely. There is, however, a major difference between it and other flours: rice flour cannot be used in baking. The reason for this has to do with its chemical composition. Although rice flour contains a great deal of starch, it is very low in gluten, which has an unfavorable effect on the structure of the crumb. The protein contained in rice has a different composition than wheat protein. Whereas in wheat flour, the gluten, a specially structured protein composed of gliadin and glutenin, runs through the dough in fine strands, thus enabling it to rise, the protein contained in rice flour cannot build this netlike framework. Baked goods made from rice flour therefore do not rise, and produce very little poring of the crumb. On the other hand, rice flour, which is easily digested by people with celiac disease (a protein allergy), is used in special diets, as well as in baby food. The very fine-grained rice starch, obtained

The preparation of jaggery nests, a sweet rice-flour-based snack popular in India, looks simple. The rice-flour-and-water dough is pressed through a machine or form with a perforated insert. The noodle nests are left to dry slightly on the open weave of the basket before being gently steamed. The rice nests, which are sold at street stands everywhere, are simply eaten out of one's hand, sprinkled with freshly shredded coconut and "jaggery," the dark palm sugar.

mainly from broken rice by wet-milling, is also employed in special diets, and has been used as a cosmetic powder since antiquity.

Rice-paper and rice-noodle leaves are the ideal wrappings for fillings of all sorts. Egg rolls, for example, are often wrapped in rice paper. Rice leaves, which are fairly small in diameter, can be made into little filled pouches without too much effort — perhaps held together decoratively with a chive blade. The advantage of dry rice leaves is that they can be stored almost indefinitely, and therefore are always available for use. They taste equally delicious steamed or deep-fried, filled with crunchy vegetables or tender meat. The only tricky thing is achieving the right degree of pliability when softening the delicate, patterned leaves in water. Too dry, and the brittle rice paper breaks rather than bends; soaked for too long, it loses its suppleness and tears. Rice leaves are easiest to use when softened in cold water for a few minutes, then spread out on damp dish towels.

Tissue-paper thin and fragile, these round rice-paper "leaves" may be found in various diameters between 6 and 12 inches in Asian food stores.

Crackling variety
Fresh or dried, rice noodles come in a wide variety of guises

Dried rice noodles have a glassy, almost transparent appearance, and a fragile, brittle texture. Dry and raw, they are a great deal more transparent than when cooked, and could almost be mistaken for oriental glass noodles, which, however, are made not from rice flour, but from ground mung beans. Whereas glass noodles remain transparent after cooking, rice noodles do not. Once cooked, the thin ribbon or thread noodles made of rice flour and water have the color of their initial product, namely, milky-white polished rice. In Thailand, Singapore, China, and other Asian countries rice noodles are best bought fresh, already steamed, and packed, still moist, in plastic bags. Fresh rice noodles are ready for immediate use, straight out of the bag, as a soup garnish or in stir-fries.

Elsewhere, by contrast, rice noodles are seldom available in any form but dried. Even dried noodles, though, are simplicity itself to prepare by any one of three methods: Cook the noodles for a couple of minutes in fast-boiling water; scald them with boiling water and leave them to soak for about 10 minutes before draining; or soften them in warm water for just 6–8 minutes, then blanch them.

The cooking or blanching time depends on the width and thickness of the noodles. Without presoaking, wide rice tagliatelle should cook at a rolling boil for 4–5 minutes, semi-wide and thin

Rice noodles are available in many shapes and sizes, ranging from ⅓-inch-wide ribbon noodles of chopstick length to hair-fine soup noodles. The different varieties, from left to right, are wide rice noodles (chantaboon rice sticks), semi-wide and thin rice noodles (rice sticks), and fine rice noodles (rice vermicelli).

noodles for 2–3 minutes, and the almost hair-thin rice vermicelli is done in 1–2 minutes. In all cases, the noodles should be rinsed well after blanching to remove the starch sticking to them, and drained thoroughly in a colander, after which they are ready. Thus, in almost no time at all, dried rice noodles can be turned into an easy soup garnish or the ideal ingredient for a stir-fry.

Thin, dried rice noodles, just as they come out of the packet, are extremely crunchy and decorative when deep-fried in hot oil for about 3 minutes. Rice noodles are eaten for preference in the southern provinces of China, where rice is grown. In the north, by contrast, the noodles are mostly of wheat flour. It is not only in China, though, but also in other Asian countries that rice noodles are a common ingredient, especially as a soup garnish. Most rice noodles are manufactured semi-professionally, except for those produced at home for the family's own use. Numerous small businesses are engaged in noodle production each day, with the majority limiting themselves to a single type of dough — wheat, mung-bean, or rice. To make rice noodles the dough, made from rice flour combined with water, is worked by large kneading machines, rolled out by machine and cut, and then steamed in the steamer. All other jobs — from packing the fresh noodles to drying them — are still, for the most part, done by hand.

At this small Chinese business in Singapore the fresh rice noodles are hung over rails and then dried in large ovens.

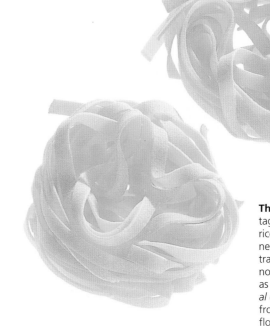

These *bretelline*, a tagliatelle-type Italian rice noodle wound into nests, look like traditional wheat noodles and are treated as such, i.e. cooked until *al dente*. They are made from a mixture of rice flour, durum semolina, and eggs.

Different varieties of rice vinegar from left to right: dark rice vinegar; mild Japanese rice vinegar for sushi; lemon-flavored vinegar-based sauces for seasoning cooked meat and fish (light) and for marinades (dark), and black Chinese rice vinegar.

then flavored with millet extracts, salt, and sugar. The slightly transparent Chinese red vinegar — especially popular for dips — is sweet and spicy, and goes well with seafood. Mild, clear Chinese rice vinegar, fermented from rice wine distillate and thinned down with water, is used in both sweet and savory dishes, as well as for pickled vegetables. The Japanese rice vinegar pictured at the front on the left (Su mitsukan) is also manufactured from rice wine distillate, thinned down with water and flavored with various extracts (wheat, rice, corn, and sake pulp). Light yellow and mild-tasting, it is just the thing for sushi. Also indispensable in Japanese cooking is miso, a protein-rich, fermented paste made from soybeans or a mixture of soybeans and grains (barley or rice), with rice miso (*komé miso*) currently the bestseller in Japan.

Sake, which, together with green tea, is the preferred drink to accompany a meal and is also popular as an aperitif or a digestive— one could hardly picture life in Japan without it — is made from fermented rice mash. Sometimes the strong, dry rice wine (usually around 16 percent by volume of alcohol)

Sweet or sour, mild or potent
Vinegar and alcoholic beverages

There is a wide range of liquid rice products, from beer to spirits, and from wine to vinegar. While fermenting rice into wine and distilling it into spirit is quite usual in the Far East, in the West the only alcoholic drink in which rice forms the basis is beer, if we ignore a rice liqueur made in Italy. And just as wine, cider, or must is fermented into vinegar in many places in the West, fermented rice (*kuji*) or rice wine forms the basis of the different kinds of vinegar in Asian countries. However, since rice vinegar is generally milder than cider or wine vinegar — it has an acidity of 3–5 percent — it cannot be kept for as long as the latter. However, there are also some very sour Asian vinegars with up to 25 percent acidity.

In oriental kitchens, rice wine is used as a seasoning, a preservative, and even as a dip, and the spectrum of flavors ranges from mildly spicy to sweet and hot. Dark or black rice vinegars have an inky consistency and a strong, malty taste; the one pictured on this page, which is suitable for marinating both meat and vegetables or for seasoning dark sauces, is distilled from brown rice, fermented into vinegar and

Beer made from rice? It may sound unusual, but it looks very much the same and is more common than you might think.

Various alcoholic drinks brewed from rice: above, Chinese Shaoxing rice wine, the best-known and most popular of its kind in China; right, the different sorts of mirin are a delicate yellow in color; far right, on the outside, arrack, a spirit made from rice and palm juice.

is heated in a porcelain carafe placed in a water bath, and served at a temperature of about 104°F; sometimes, though, it is drunk at room temperature, and on hot days it is even served cold — sake on the rocks. With an alcohol content of about 14 percent by volume, mirin, which is also made from rice, is sweeter and somewhat lighter than sake, and intended not so much for drinking as for cooking. It lends many Japanese dishes their characteristic taste.

Rice wines are to be found throughout Asia, wherever rice is the number one food. On Bali, for example, people drink the rosé-colored Brem, while the Chinese prefer the powerful, amber-colored Shaoxing, from the province of Zhejiang, to accompany a meal and for cooking. Shaoxing (15–20 percent alcohol by volume) is manufactured from glutinous white rice, yeast, and spring water. If you can't get hold of it, dry sherry can be substituted in a pinch. Bottles that have been opened are best stored, tightly corked, at room temperature. The widely available clear or slightly yellow rice brandies (20–30 percent alcohol by volume) are triple-distilled. In Japan alone there are different varieties, from sake sui shin to samshu. The best-known rice spirit, however, must be arrack (40 percent alcohol by volume) from Southeast Asia. Also very popular, because of its low alcohol content, is beer brewed from rice. Unlike other alcoholic drinks distilled from rice, however, rice beer is by no means limited to Asia, but is also manufactured in Europe. Somewhat thinner than the malted-barley brew, it keeps longer than the latter.

Sake, the Japanese national drink Usually served slightly warmed in a small carafe, sake is drunk from small porcelain cups.

Wild rice
The grain of the Native Americans

Once a culinary dark horse, and correspondingly difficult to get hold of and expensive, nowadays wild rice — also known as Tuscarora rice — is a common item in most supermarkets. *Zizania palustris* and *Zizania aquatica* are the botanical terms for the most important varieties of wild rice, which are native chiefly to the big lakeland districts of the border area between Canada and the United States, but also throughout the whole eastern half of the North American continent down to Florida. Wild rice, which is only indirectly related to *Oryza*, leads a similarly amphibious life to its more widespread namesake: while the roots of *Zizania* are anchored in lake or marsh beds, a large portion of the green plant, which grows to an average height of 3–10 feet, and can reach up to 16 feet in individual cases, raises itself above the water level, and with it, first the flowers, and later also the grain-bearing panicles. In late summer the grains are ripe and ready for harvesting. Here, too, the eccentric wild grain differs in an important point from rice and all other types of cereals: the grains do not all ripen at the same time. This means that when the grain is harvested, the stalks must not be cut off completely; rather, the harvest team must "beat down" the entire field several times in search of ripe grains. The traditional harvest method, which is still used by the Ojibwa or Chippewa tribe and yields wild rice of particularly high quality, has an old-fashioned, romantic quality to it: two-man canoes are slowly paddled or poled through the wild-rice growth at harvest time. The person responsible for harvesting is equipped with two long sticks, one of which he uses to bend the long, flexible stems over the edge of the canoe, while he carefully beats the panicles with the other stick, dislodging the ripe grains so that they tumble into the craft. When the bent stems spring back again, some grains fall into the water — serving as seed for the following year. In Canada, around 2,000 metric tons of wild rice are harvested annually in this manner; wild rice of the best quality, to be sure, but far too little to meet the huge increase in world demand. Therefore, in the United States, since 1985 — in addition to this traditional method of providing for the next year's growth, which is pursued, mainly by Indians in Canada and Minnesota — attempts have been made to grow wild rice, especially in California, Florida, and Wisconsin. Higher-yielding cultivars, with the same ripening time for all the grains, are the breeding goals, and with the use of fertilizers and pesticides — which are naturally completely taboo for genuine wild rice — it should be possible to increase yields in artificially planted wild-rice fields from 75 to 890 pounds an acre.

In terms of quality, however, this cultivated grain cannot compare to the natural wild rice of the big lakes; moreover, the grains of the cultivated types remain smaller on average.

Larger quantities, whether the truly "wild" type or artificially planted in ponds, are often no longer harvested manually, but with the aid of propeller boats or hovercraft, which either carefully comb through the vegetation several times, or, according to the combine harvester principle, cut off the panicles completely and bring in the entire harvest all at once. At first glance, the grains obtained in this fashion do not yet bear much of a

Before the stalks with their panicles rise clear above the water, the leaves of the young wild rice plants grow on the water's surface.

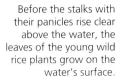

Wild rice harvest on Lac du Bois, one of the biggest natural wild rice fields in Canada. Even though the aquatic grass still grows wild in the crystal-clear lake, without fertilizers and pesticides, growers have no objection to using motorboats for the harvest. Trough-shaped basins at the bow of the boats catch the ripe wild rice grains, which fall from the panicles upon contact.

resemblance to the normally dark-brown to shiny black grain found in stores and on our tables, as they are greenish-brown in color and still contain a great deal of moisture. In order to remove the moisture, the crop is traditionally first spread out in the sun for a few days, then parched over wood fires. During this time the grains develop their characteristic color, and the parching also causes the formation of flavorings that are responsible for the typical nutty taste. After this procedure, and the moisture loss brought about by it, the grains have shrunk to such an extent that they can be husked with great ease. The traditional method of doing this is to trample the wild rice underfoot in mortar-like containers, then winnow it. Nowadays, of course, this labor-intensive procedure can be carried out by machine: on great conveyors, the grain is briefly treated with steam, dried, and husked. In this way, what took several days by the traditional method, is accomplished in almost no time at all. Traditionally grown and harvested wild rice, also called eco wild rice or mahnomen wild rice, is now sold by Indian producer cooperatives.

Golden-yellow wild rice, not yet husked. At this stage, it still differs very little in terms of color from other types of cereals.

Processing wild rice the traditional way is a job for both hands and feet: relayering the grain so that none of it burns while being parched over a wood fire, husking the grains by treading on them, and winnowing with a birchbark pan.

"Good grain"
Bursting with vital nutrients and exceedingly tasty

The black grain, which the Indians call "manomin" or "mahnomen," meaning "good grain," is often extolled for its fantastic nutritional content. There are many stories about explorers or trappers who, for lack of other food, at times had to content themselves with a diet of wild rice, which supposedly did no harm to their health. In the mid 1970s, under medical supervision, a biology teacher in the United States tested the possible truthfulness of these legends, using himself as a guinea pig. While on a wild-rice diet his blood pressure went down to normal, and his iron, cholesterol, and uric acid levels apparently improved noticeably. Of course this is not intended as a plea for people to follow his example, or to switch to a diet based on wild rice. What is indisputable, however, is that wild rice has a considerably lower fat content and an even higher proportion of protein than unpolished rice, not to mention the polished sort. In addition, the black grain contains several important B-group vitamins as well as phosphorus and copper in higher concentrations than normal rice. Admittedly, the

Cultivated wild rice, "extra fancy." Cook for about 40 minutes.

Mahnomen wild rice from Minnesota. Cook for 15–20 minutes.

Eco wild rice from Canada. Cook for 35–50 minutes.

Wild rice, harvested unripe. Cook for about 15 minutes.

proportion of these substances can vary considerably from one variety of wild rice to another — this is especially true for the different hybrid varieties from wild-rice cultures. Wild rice also differs from most varieties of rice in terms of its starch composition: the aquatic grain contains a relatively high amount of amylopectin, but not much amylose. This accounts for the ability of the grains to absorb such an amazing amount of water. During the cooking process they can swell to double their original weight, which is why they burst open toward the end of cooking. As anyone who has prepared wild rice will know, this takes quite a long while to happen, the black grains simmering away, depending on size or the processing method used, for up to an hour before they are edible. As a rule of thumb, wild rice is done when around half of the grains have burst open; you can simply sample the grains repeatedly toward the end of the cooking process to see whether they are soft enough for your personal taste. Soaking wild rice overnight can cut down its cooking time to about 30 minutes. A number of wild-rice producers have sought to eliminate the disadvantage of this long cooking time by means of "scarification." In this process, the outer skin of the grains is scratched slightly to enable them to absorb the cooking water more quickly. A number of manufacturers also offer quick-cooking wild rice, which, like the scarified version, is precooked and then dried again. Part of the starch is broken down by these processes in such a way that soaking becomes superfluous and cooking time is reduced to around 20 minutes. Admittedly, the rice is altered substantially during these procedures: the precooked grains shimmer in matte reddish-brown tones, lose their shape, and become somewhat milder-tasting. And while the original black grain can easily keep for at least five years because of its low fat content, quick-cooking wild rice can be stored for only around three years. You might find mixtures of wild rice and white long-grain rice, or even basmati rice, or wild rice and unpolished brown rice more commonly available than wild rice on its own. The advantage of these is that the rice and wild-rice varieties are combined in such a way that they are done in the same amount of time, usually within 20 minutes. Mixtures of this sort are often served primarily as an accompaniment to fish, the classic combination being with salmon. Considerably cheaper than pure natural wild rice, they nevertheless boast a (slightly less intense) fine, nutty flavor, as well as providing an attractive color contrast on the plate.

Nutritional content and energy values of Canadian wild rice (per 100 g)	
Carbohydrate	69.5–75.3 g
Protein	12.4–15.0 g
Fat	0.5–1.05 g
Fiber	1.1–3.3 g
Minerals	1.2–1.42 mg
Energy kJ	1,430–1,625
Energy kcal	339–355

Source: *Ernährung-Umschau* [Nutritional survey] 43 (1996)

Quick-cooking wild rice.
Cook for about 15 minutes.

Brown rice/wild rice mixture.
Cook for about 20 minutes.

Basmati/wild rice mixture.
Cook for about 20 minutes.

Parboiled rice/wild rice mixture.
Cook for about 20 minutes.

Cooking methods

Cooked rice is much more than a plain side dish. A simple bowl of steaming rice also carries symbolic force: according to the Chinese boiled rice is daily nourishment for the living, but also food for the dead, who, thanks to the sacrificial offering of rice at the family altar, will not be condemned to restless wandering as "hungry souls."

In Asian cuisines in particular, boiled rice is always the focal point of a meal. Whether as the Indonesian *nasi* or the Chinese *mi fan*, it plays the main role. In fact, in many Asian languages, the terms "meal" and "to eat well" are synonymous with "to eat rice." A meal without rice is hardly a meal at all, which is expressed in the Japanese word *gohan*, which means both "meal" and "to eat boiled rice." The multiplicity of ways in which rice can be prepared and used in the kitchen, as illustrated in the following pages, may surprise many who have only been familiar with it up until now as an accompaniment. So, *Mòi ong xoi com*, as the Vietnamese say, meaning "enjoy your meal," or, more literally, "Tuck into the rice!"

Dry risottos are eaten with a fork, moister ones with a spoon, if only so that one can enjoy this delicate *primo piatto* down to the last grain.

A matter of technique
For some eating habits, you need a little "manual" skill — and the right sort of rice

Everywhere in the world rice is eaten with the same implements that are used for other everyday food, whether that is a fork, spoon, chopsticks, or hands. In those regions of the world where people literally live from hand to mouth, boiled rice must be conveyed between the lips in a more or less elegant manner. For this simplest way of ingesting food, some peoples have developed special eating techniques that require a certain amount of dexterity. This is clear to any Westerners having to eat with their hands for the first time since infancy, who usually present a more or less ridiculous picture even to themselves, and often end up with at least part of the meal on their clothes. In Asia, for example, rice is often eaten from one's hand as a between-meal snack. This is not only usual for simple glutinous rice balls, but also is proper etiquette for such highly sophisticated snacks as Japanese sushi. In the case of many a pilaf or pilau, particularly in the Arab world and in India, people dig into their food enthusiastically with their fingers. A spoon is the natural utensil for eating a broth with a rice garnish; a rice pudding of a more or less liquid consistency, served as a dessert; a creamy-smooth risotto; or congee, the Chinese rice gruel that is served for breakfast or later in the day as a snack. When the rice is boiled or steamed until dry, people in the West reach for a fork as naturally as those in the Far East pick up their chopsticks. While rice itself may not determine the form and shape of eating implements, those implements influence the choice of rice varieties. Parboiled rice, whose grains do not stick together after cooking is wholly unsuitable for eating with chopsticks precisely for this reason — it would have to be consumed grain by grain. For chopstick users, the rice grains must stick together at least enough to allow a satisfactory portion to be conveyed to the mouth without the risk of some or all of it falling off the chopsticks. The same is true for eating rice by hand. All non-parboiled long and short grain varieties of rice are thus far better suited for eating habits of this kind, the ideal type in such cases being Asian glutinous, or sticky, rice, whose grains, thanks to their above-average amylopectin content, do honor to their name.

Lunch in the rice field: Rice growers in Myanmar eat their breaktime snack, consisting of, among other things, steamed glutinous rice, which they skillfully and quickly form into compact bite-size balls with their fingers.

As eating tools, the spoon and fork are actually outsiders: worldwide, a far greater amount of rice is consumed with chopsticks.

In the picture on the left, Gabriele Ferron carefully stirs a risotto to a creamy consistency. The long-grain rice in the photo below, cooked the previous day by the absorption method and of a very different consistency, is used in a stir-fry.

Cooking rice by the absorption method, like the Burmese woman in the photo on the left, does not require many utensils. By contrast, Yap Wing Sang, chef at the Ritz-Carlton in Singapore, needs a greater range of special equipment to steam glutinous rice expertly, as he demonstrates in the picture below.

Matching the rice with the method
And tips for storing cooked rice

The starch composition of a given variety of rice exerts a considerable influence on its cooking qualities. In principle, we distinguish between two different kinds of starch: amylopectin and amylose. Amylose is the water-soluble part of the endosperm, while the non-water-soluble amylopectin is responsible for the swelling and for the tendency of the rice grains to stick together. Thus, it is hardly surprising that the starch in glutinous or sticky rice grains consists almost entirely of amylopectin, and that glutinous rice is cooked preferably in steam rather than boiling water. The different properties of the rice starches are also a consideration with other cooking methods, for example when making risotto. If the cooking liquid is not meant to thicken — say, in the case of pilafs, the rice should be washed before cooking under cold running water until the water runs clear, that is until the powder-fine remains of the milling process still clinging to the outside of the grains have been rinsed away. Green rice requires special treatment when it is cooked. For its "manufacture," rice grains are pressed, still unripe, from the panicles, so that they have a somewhat crushed and irregular appearance. They are cooked in a flash, requiring no more than brief shallow-frying in fat or steaming; under no circumstances should they be boiled in water. If you should have any leftover plain cooked rice, you can store in a tightly sealed container in the refrigerator for around three to four days, or in the freezer for up to six months. It can be reheated on the stove over a low heat, or in the oven, with two tablespoons of liquid per cup of rice, and is also ideal for preparing stir-fry dishes.

Examples of cooking methods for common rice varieties, per ½ cup raw rice

Variety	Thai fragrant rice	Basmati	Parboiled rice
Cooking method	absorption	absorption	absorption
Quantity of liquid	1½ cups	1½ cups	1¼ cups
Cooking time	12–15 min.	12–15 min.	about 20 min.

Variety	Long-grain brown rice	Italian short-grain rice	Glutinous rice
Cooking method	absorption	risotto-style	steaming
Quantity of liquid	1¾ cups	1¼ cups	as needed
Cooking time	12–15 min. (presoak for 2 hrs)	12–15 min.	about 20 min. (presoak for 2 hrs)

One of the simplest methods of cooking rice: The grains are added to rapidly boiling salted water, and stirred occasionally. When the rice is done, the water is poured off and the rice is allowed to steam dry for a while longer, spread out on a baking sheet and dotted with butter, in the oven at 210°F.

With the absorption method, rice is put in a pot with the proper amount of cold water and brought to a boil. The rice is then simmered gently until it has absorbed sufficient water. The swelling need not take place on the stove: an oven or a "hay box" can also be used.

Rice for pilafs can be prepared in two ways: either it is first fried until transparent, like risotto rice, then the liquid is added and the rice is cooked by the absorption method; or the rice is poured into the boiling liquid, the heat is reduced, and the grains are allowed to swell slowly until they are done.

Steaming is a relatively time-consuming cooking method for rice used mainly in Asia, particularly for glutinous rice. The rice is cooked in a steamer — either the classic lidded bamboo basket or the more common insert with a perforated base — over the boiling water.

To make risotto, short-grain rice is first sweated in fat — usually butter — until transparent while being stirred constantly. The hot cooking liquid is then added in stages, always a little more than the rice absorbs. The amylose released from the grains provides the necessary binding agent.

In principle, rice pudding is cooked according to a mixture of two methods: first, it is added to the boiling liquid, then the heat is reduced and the rice is allowed to swell until done.

Women in northern Thailand cook long-grain rice by the absorption method. First the grains are washed until the water runs clear; then the rice is placed in the cooking pot with the appropriate quantity of water.

On top of the little "stove," the rice simmers away comfortably in an uncovered pot. Part of the cooking water is absorbed, while the rest usually evaporates. And if you are not cooking by the clock, you've got to test the rice from time to time to see if it is really done.

When the rice is done, any excess cooking water is drained off. The rice is then transferred back to the pot on the stove and steamed, uncovered, until the grains are quite dry and separate.

The absorption method
It sounds so technical, but is quite simple

The principle of the absorption method is that the rice cooks by swelling slowly in hot liquid. The preparation itself actually has surprisingly little "method" to it. The rice is put in a pot with only as much liquid as it can absorb while it cooks. Both the necessary quantity of liquid and the cooking times are dependent on many factors: whether or not the rice has been soaked, and for how long; whether or not the pot is covered during cooking; what variety of rice is used; how long the rice has been stored and consequently how much moisture it contains; and lastly, of course, personal taste — some people like rice firm to the bite, others prefer it more tender. It would therefore be impossible

Cooking parboiled rice by the absorption method:

Pour the rice into a sufficiently large pot, together with the appropriate quantity of water.

Allow the rice and water to boil, then reduce the heat and simmer the rice.

When the rice is done, drain off any remaining liquid, or simply allow the rice to steam dry. Fluff with a fork.

Although this Burmese woman has prepared her rice with the simplest utensils, it has turned out perfect and tastes wonderfully aromatic.

to give a single basic recipe that would apply to all rice for all people. However, the photo sequence on this page illustrates the principle, using parboiled rice as an example. The table on page 68 offers a few guidelines for cooking times and quantities of liquid.

An overwhelming proportion of the rice that is prepared worldwide is cooked by the absorption method. This becomes more obvious when you bear in mind that not only is plain white rice as an accompaniment to main dishes prepared according to this method, but so, basically, are risotto, pilaf, paella, and even rice pudding: in all these dishes, the rice cooks by swelling in hot liquid, even if it has perhaps also been sweated in hot fat first. Even rice that is prepared in a larger quantity of rapidly boiling water, in the last analysis, cooks by absorbing hot liquid.

You can prepare rice by the absorption method in a particularly energy-saving fashion, since the rice does not necessarily need to spend the whole time on top of the stove to cook thoroughly — it merely needs to be kept hot for as long as possible. For this reason, just a few generations back, in order to save fuel, people would bring the rice, or other grain, to a boil and then put the pot in a wooden hay box lined with cloth or blankets, or wrap it in thick cloth and stow under the quilt until the rice had finished cooking. Nowadays there are special pots that can be placed in a suitable Styrofoam box to cook rice according to the same principle.

Rice by the absorption method for the advanced cook
Special gadgets for connoisseurs

If you enjoy rice and eat a lot of it, you may find it worth your while to purchase an electric rice cooker. Not only does it allow you to prepare fairly large quantities of rice effortlessly, as shown in the photo sequence below on the left, but the device also switches itself off automatically at the exact moment when the grains are perfectly cooked. Only water should be used as the cooking liquid in this device, however, since the heat-conducting metal compartment could be tainted with the flavor of other liquids. Therefore, if you wish to make your absorption-method rice with stock, for example, you should plump for the traditional cooking method in a pot. The advantages of the electric cooker are that it guarantees perfectly cooked rice that steams dry beautifully, and can even be kept warm in the cooker for several hours without any loss of quality. It also contains a special steamer insert in which cold rice can be reheated effortlessly.

To cook rice in an electric cooker:

Wash the rice until the water runs clear. Drain and transfer to the pot insert of the cooker.

Pour the cooking liquid over the rice. In the electric cooker, this should always be water — never stock, broth, or milk.

Add water to reach the mark corresponding to the appropriate quantity of rice.

Place the pot in the cooker, turning it back and forth until the bowl is firmly in place.

Cover the cooker and allow the rice to soak for 30 minutes, then switch on the device.

Allow the cooked rice to steam dry for another 15 minutes in the covered cooker, then lift out the pot insert and serve the rice.

To cook rice in the aluminum cylinder:

Fill the cylinder no more than half full with soaked and drained rice.

Pour enough water into a roomy pot to allow the cylinder to float freely.

Place the cylinder in the rapidly boiling water and cook the rice for 12–15 minutes.

Remove the cylinder, drain, allow to cool somewhat, then open and push out the rice.

By contrast, a bit more attention is required when cooking rice in the aluminum cylinder demonstrated in the second photo sequence. These cylinders are popular in Southeast Asia for cooking glutinous or long-grain rice. Small wonder, since the result —rice that can simply be cut into rounds to serve — makes for an especially decorative presentation. With the model shown here, the rice must be soaked for about two hours before cooking, otherwise the grains escape through the holes in the sides, top, and bottom of the cylinder while the rice cooks. Rice in the cylinder is also best cooked in water, and the gadget should be filled no more than half full, as the grains require plenty of room to swell. To push out the cooked rice roll, you will need a ladle or gravy spoon of the same diameter as the cylinder, and a bit of strength. Unfortunately, these cylinders may be difficult to find locally; you must either take advantage of the chance to buy them if you visit the Far East, or commission a globetrotting friend to bring one back for you.

If you wish to prepare brown rice by the absorption method, you will have no such difficulty in obtaining the necessary equipment. Brown rice does, however, take a bit longer to cook than white rice: The bran, which has not been removed, not only contains nutrients and fat, but also protects the endosperm from penetration by the cooking water for quite some time. Even when it has been soaked, brown rice must cook for 15–20 minutes longer than white rice. It is a good idea to use a bit more liquid too, because quite a lot evaporates over the longer cooking time. The cooking liquid can be seasoned more strongly than for white rice, as the bran also impedes the penetration of flavorings. Brown rice is best cooked in chicken or vegetable stock. Both contribute a great deal of flavor, which the brown rice will ultimately absorb.

Preparing brown rice by the absorption method:

Pour the brown rice into a strainer and wash thoroughly several times under running cold water.

Place the rice in a bowl with cold water to cover and soak for at least 1 hour, but preferably overnight.

Melt 4 teaspoons butter in a roomy pot, and sweat ¾ cup finely chopped onion until translucent.

Drain the soaked rice thoroughly and pour into the pot, stirring constantly.

Sweat the rice, stirring constantly, until the grains are evenly coated in the butter.

Add 3½ cups cooking liquid and season with salt. Chicken or vegetable stock are particularly suitable.

Bring to a boil, reduce the heat to as low as possible, and cook for about 25 minutes, until the rice has swelled and absorbed the cooking liquid.

The shape of the rice grains, which look like little bones, is an unmistakable sign that this patna rice was overcooked or reheated in soup for too long.

A Thai farmer steaming glutinous rice. As soon as the rice is cooked, it will be packed in portions and sold as a snack. While the water in the steaming pot is brought to a boil, the soaked rice is left to drain thoroughly.

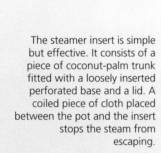

The steamer insert is simple but effective. It consists of a piece of coconut-palm trunk fitted with a loosely inserted perforated base and a lid. A coiled piece of cloth placed between the pot and the insert stops the steam from escaping.

When the rice is done, it is emptied into a big bowl — the base of the steamer insert falls out on top — and allowed to steam dry for a short time before being divided up by hand into portions, which are placed in woven baskets with lids.

Steaming rice
A very gentle method of preparation, particularly ideal for cooking glutinous rice

Delicate or especially nutritious foods such as fish, vegetables, and potatoes are often cooked in hot steam instead of water. Steaming is a particularly gentle cooking method, since the food that is being cooked does not come into direct contact with the hot liquid, which, when boiling, leaches out a considerable proportion of the water-soluble vitamins and nutrients. The fact that rice, too, can be cooked to perfection in steam is common knowledge in Asia. This cooking method is usual both for non-glutinous and glutinous rice varieties. Non-glutinous rice turns out distinctly drier when steamed in a bamboo basket

Towards the end of the cooking time, a check is made to see whether the rice is ready. The Thai farmer in this photo seems to be highly insensitive to the heat, taking a sample with his bare hands.

than when cooked by the absorption method, but in some cases takes more than twice as long to cook. With glutinous or sticky rice, however, the cooking method depends on the intended use. If the rice is to be eaten with chopsticks or with the hand, it must be steamed; because of its extremely high amylopectin content, this rice, when boiled, sometimes sticks together so firmly that it can be cut into slices. Boiled glutinous rice is used chiefly in sweet dishes; these look especially unusual and attractive when prepared from black rice, or from a mixture of black and white glutinous rice.

In Thailand, which produces some of the most delicious varieties of long-grain rice, steamed glutinous rice is popular in the northern regions, as it is in neighboring Myanmar. In both countries, it is eaten warm, and is also a popular snack for the midday break, packed cold in small woven baskets.

Rolled by hand into little balls, it is eaten plain or dipped in spicy sauces. More sophisticated culinary demands can also be satisfied with steamed glutinous rice: little rolls, for example, are prepared from seasoned sticky rice mixed with strips of roast chicken, mushrooms, vegetables, or coconut milk. Wrapped in banana leaves, or other large leaves, these rolls are then steamed again. Chinese "lotus dumplings" are also prepared in this way. Besides being food for people, cakes made of steamed glutinous rice are prepared as offerings to the gods and venerated ancestors, and, in Vietnam, for example, are traditionally placed on the house altar as offerings for the New Year celebrations. In China, too, since time immemorial, steamed glutinous rice cakes, either savory or sweetened with sugar and sometimes also with dried fruit, have been served at the New Year.

Rice that is to be steamed is always washed first in order to remove the starch clinging to the grains.

Authentically Asian
In the East, it's full steam ahead with rice — in a bamboo basket, or in a pot

Asian cooks have developed the most varied methods of cooking rice in steam. A steam bath alone, though, does not suffice. The grains need prior treatment, and are either soaked in cold water or boiled briefly before steaming. The method shown below, which for brevity's sake alone we will call "Vietnamese," is classic: This is how breakfast glutinous rice is prepared in Vietnam. While the rice is being steamed, there should always be enough boiling water in the wok to come up about ⅜ inch high on the outside of the basket. Be sure to replenish the hot water before it all evaporates! During the steaming process, check the rice in the bamboo basket frequently. If it threatens to

The "Vietnamese" method:
Serves 4

Line a steaming basket made of bamboo and raffia with half of a moistened steaming cloth that has been wrung out.

Soak 1½ cups glutinous rice in cold water for at least 2 hours or overnight. Drain the rice and spoon into the cloth.

Place the other half of the cloth over the rice and the steaming basket, and cover the basket with the lid.

Pull the eight corners of the cloth into the center of the lid and place the steaming basket in boiling water in a wok.

After about 30 minutes' cooking time, remove the lid and the top half of the cloth. Lift out the rice and serve.

become too dry, sprinkle it with a little water. Special steaming cloths can be purchased in Japan.

The Japanese and Iranian methods are hybrids of the absorption and steam-cooking methods: In both, the rice is first boiled briefly, and then continues to cook in steam. The steam rises from the cooking water, and must not be allowed to escape. For this reason, keep the pot sealed while the steam is circulating. Place a cloth between the pot and the lid to stop condensation on the inside of the lid dripping onto the rice. The Japanese and Iranian steaming methods differ on one point: In the latter, the "butter base" causes a crust, called *tahdig*, to form, which no one willingly foregoes once they have tasted it. If you cannot get hold of the marvelously aromatic Iranian long-grain rice — and it is virtually unavailable outside its country of origin — use basmati.

The Japanese method:
Serves 4

Place 2 cups nishiki rice in a bowl with cold water to cover. Carefully knead the rice with the ball of the hand.

Pour off the cloudy water, then cover the rice with fresh water, stir through vigorously and knead again.

Repeat the process until the water stays clear. Pour the rice into a strainer and drain for 30–60 minutes.

Put 3 ¾ cups water into a pot and tip in the drained rice. Cover the pot and bring the rice to a boil.

Turn down the heat. Place a dish towel between the pot and the lid, and steam the rice for 12 minutes over a low heat.

Take the rice off the heat, and leave undisturbed for about 15 minutes. It should now be dry, but still slightly sticky — ideal for eating with chopsticks.

The Iranian method:
Serves 4

Wash 2 cups Iranian long-grain rice. Boil in plenty of salted water, stirring, for 5–10 minutes, then drain.

Meanwhile, place ¼ cup butter in a large, heavy-bottomed pot and melt over a low heat.

Add the drained rice to the pot a heaping tablespoonful at a time, trying to keep it away from the sides.

Use the handle of a wooden spoon or a chopstick to make holes in the rice structure to help the steam circulate better.

Wrap the lid of the pot in a cloth and cover the pot. Steam the rice for 20 minutes over a moderate heat.

Continue to steam for an additional 30 minutes over the lowest possible heat. Plunge the pot with the cooked rice in a bowl of ice water.

Hold the pot in the ice water until the contents are loosened, then unmold the rice with the golden-brown crust into a bowl and serve.

Shaping up nicely
Few accompaniments can be served as

In Thailand these split bamboo sticks serve simultaneously as molds and travel containers for the sweet, black glutinous rice that was cooked in them.

Quenelles molded with tablespoons and rice turned out of cups, as shown on these pages, are examples of how rice can be served decoratively with the simplest tools. Of course, timbale, savarin, ring, and oval molds can be used to mold rice into attractive shapes; just remember to oil them well, so that the rice turns out effortlessly. Alternatively, place a pastry cutter on a board that has been moistened or spread with parchment paper, spoon the rice into the cutter, smooth flat, and lift off the cutter. While with these methods, the rice is first cooked and then molded into shape, in Asia the rice is often cooked in the mold. The photo sequence below shows how glutinous rice is steamed into a roll inside a banana leaf.

Seasoned and colored rice and rice salads make eye-catching accompaniments pressed into small molds and turned out before serving.

Steamed rice rolls:
Serves 4

Soak 1½ cups glutinous rice overnight. Drain, and mix with ½ cup coconut milk and ½ teaspoon salt. Spoon into 4 rolled-up banana leaves.

Tie each roll at both ends with strong kitchen twine. (They should not be filled too tightly, as the filling will expand further during cooking.)

Place the filled banana-leaf rolls in an Asian bamboo-and-raffia steaming basket, and steam in the wok for 1 hour.

Take the banana-leaf rolls out of the steamer, cut into slices, remove the leaves, and serve the glutinous rice.

Rice quenelles:
Serves 4

Cook 1½ cups long-grain rice with 1 cup cubed tomatoes, and season with thyme. Fold in another cup cubed tomatoes. Scoop out "dumplings" with a tablespoon.

Use a second tablespoon to round off the top of each quenelle, then remove the rice from the first spoon with the second one.

Slide the finished tomato-rice quenelles from the spoon, placing two side by side on each plate.

The contrast between the yellowish rice and the red tomato flesh is especially attractive.

Rice molds:

Brush the inside of the molds — cups, timbale, or ring molds — with oil.

Spoon the rice mixture into the greased molds, pressing down firmly.

Turn out the individual molds onto plates and serve as soon as possible, before the hot rice cools down.

Seasonings and colorings

Who says that rice always has to be white? After all, apart from the necessary water, the grains can absorb a wide range of colorings and flavorings during the

cooking process. Spiced and colored rice, which for the most part can be prepared without much effort, can be used to impart some very special culinary accents. When it is cooked with spices, herbs, fruit, vegetables, mushrooms, spicy sauces, coconut milk, or stock, the sky's the limit to creativity when it comes to enhancing the appearance or flavor of rice. Where rice is the main food everyday, additional ingredients of this sort are designed to make a complete and tasty meal from a simple grain. Therefore it is hardly surprising that Asian cuisines in particular boast an amazing variety of recipes for spiced and colored rice, as well as taking particular pains with decorative presentation

and garnishing. The celebratory Indonesian rijstafel offers perhaps the most impressive example of this culinary tradition. Elsewhere, on the other hand, spiced, colored rice is used more as a classic accompaniment or hors d'oeuvre. For a particularly attractive presentation, it is used to fill small molds and then turned out as individual portions on each plate.

Southern Asia is the home of turmeric *(Curcuma longa)*, the rhizome of which is first scalded, then dried to obtain the spice of the same name. Curcumin, which is responsible for the yellow coloring, decomposes rapidly when exposed to light. Therefore, to preserve the intensity of its color, store ground turmeric away from the light, for example in an opaque container or in a cupboard.

The name of the most expensive spice in the world, "saffron," comes from the Arabic *za'fran*, meaning "yellow." And the coloring crocin really does produce a bright yellow hue, even when heavily diluted with water. Only the stigmas of the *Crocus sativus* flower, hand-stripped from the crocus calyx, are used for the highest-quality saffron. The highly esteemed saffron flavor, develops only during the drying process.

Yellow, orange, and aromatic
By using spices containing coloring, rice dishes are transformed in a flash into a delight for both the eyes and palate

Four hues of yellow rice: rice with turmeric (see recipe on page 98), saffron (see recipe on page 134), annatto (see recipe on page 98), and dandelion flowers (see recipe on page 130) show the various dyeing strengths of these spices. Their taste also varies: while turmeric provides burning heat, saffron furnishes a subtle, delicately bitter taste. The longer the dandelion flowers cook with the rice, the more marked the bitter flavor they impart to it. Annatto oil, used in the recipe for annatto rice, also tastes more or less bitter depending on how long the seeds are roasted. The oil is easily made: Heat ½ cup vegetable oil over a moderate heat, stir in 3 heaped tablespoons annatto seeds, and fry for 1 minute. Allow to cool, then strain.

Annatto seeds impart yellow-to-reddish-orange hues. They are supplied by the tropical tree *Bixa orellana*, which originated in the Amazon region but is now cultivated throughout most of South America, as well as in Jamaica, East Africa, and India. The actual dye, bixin, is obtained from the arils surrounding the seeds in the pods, and is usually sold as a dried paste. Annatto is used mainly in the manufacture of cheeses; many varieties of cheddar owe their attractive color to bixin.

As well as the tender leaves of the dandelion, the yellow petals are edible, and not only in a salad — the flavonoids contained in them impart a delicate yellow hue to, for example, a risotto. Although they do not dye foods very dark, the petals leave stubborn stains on the skin, so wear rubber gloves when stripping them from the flower heads. Apart from the color, the petals provide an unusual flavor, which becomes stronger the longer they are cooked.

Chiles, mushrooms, and olives

Aromatic rice accompaniments, seasoned in the classic Italian style

BROWN RICE WITH CHILES

Unmilled rice requires a considerably longer cooking time than the milled product. This apparent disadvantage can be offset by soaking brown rice for a relatively long time before use. In addition, brown rice can take far greater amounts of seasoning than one could reasonably expect of white rice.

Serves 4
1⅔ cups brown rice
4 green chiles (about 3 oz in total)
4–5 scallions
2 tablespoons olive oil
3 garlic cloves, finely chopped
2¼–2¾ cups vegetable stock
10 oz tomatoes
salt, freshly ground pepper
1 tablespoon chopped herbs (basil, thyme, oregano)

Soak the brown rice overnight in cold water. Tip into a strainer and drain thoroughly. Halve the chiles, remove the seeds, and cut the flesh into thin strips. Trim the scallions and cut into thin rings. Heat the oil in a pot and sweat the garlic and scallions. Add the chile strips and sauté for 2 minutes. Stir in the rice and sauté for 2–3 minutes. Add half of the vegetable stock, bring to a boil, and season with salt and pepper. Reduce the heat and simmer the rice for about 30 minutes, topping up with the remaining stock as and when needed. Meanwhile, blanch, skin, and seed the tomatoes, and dice their flesh. Ten minutes before the end of cooking time, mix the tomatoes into the rice. Season the finished rice to taste and fold in the chopped herbs.

RICE WITH MUSHROOMS

This rice dish is in season from late summer to late fall, when fresh wild mushrooms are to be found. The yellowish-to-gray-hued chanterelles and horns of plenty suggested here might seem somewhat unprepossessing, but lend a distinctive flavor to mixed-mushroom dishes and sauces.

Serves 4
1½ cups long-grain rice
¼ cup dried cèpes

10–11 oz mixed fresh mushrooms
½ cup finely chopped white onion
3 tablespoons butter
salt, freshly ground white pepper
1 tablespoon chopped parsley

Bring some salted water to a boil in a large pot. Reduce the heat, stir in the rice, and simmer for 15 minutes. Tip into a strainer and drain well. Meanwhile, pour some lukewarm water over the dried cèpes and allow to rehydrate for 10 minutes. Drain, squeeze out all excess water, and chop finely. Thoroughly clean, trim, and prepare the mixed mushrooms, for example cèpes, chanterelles, and horns of plenty: slice the cèpes, and leave the chanterelles and horns of plenty whole or halve, depending on size. Melt the butter in a pan and sweat the onion until translucent. Add the mushrooms and sauté for 3–4 minutes. Mix the cooked rice into the mushrooms, season with salt and pepper, and sprinkle in the parsley. Sauté for 2–3 minutes more, then serve on warmed plates.

RISOTTO TUTT'OLIVE

Describing this dish as a risotto is slightly misleading. Strictly speaking, it is not a classic risotto, but a rice dish seasoned with olives and chiles. Unlike a risotto, the rice is not first sautéed in fat, then cooked in liquid while being stirred, but is simply boiled in salted water. That's why this "risotto" lacks the typical, creamy consistency — more than made up for by its strong olive flavor!

Serves 4
1½ cups short-grain rice
½ cup black olives
½ cup green olives
1 small green chile
3 tablespoons olive oil
2 garlic cloves, finely chopped
salt, freshly ground white pepper

Bring some salted water to a boil in a large pot. Add the rice and boil for 10 minutes, then drain. Pit half of the black and green olives. Halve, seed, and core the chiles. Finely chop the pitted olives and the chiles. Heat the olive oil in a pan, add the chopped olives, chiles, and garlic, and sweat for 2–3 minutes. Add the rice, mix well, season with salt and pepper, and cook until everything is hot. Either serve the rice with the remaining olives on warmed plates, or use to fill oiled timbale molds, turn out onto plates, and garnish with the olives.

With bell peppers and chiles
Mild and hot peppers: the classic addition to rice

ARROZ VERDE

Countless variations of this "green rice" dish exist in all Spanish-speaking countries. The basic ingredients, however, are always rice, green peppers, and chiles of the same color. When cooked, *arroz verde* should be creamy in consistency, comparable to a risotto. The following recipe gives the ingredients for *arroz verde* as an accompaniment. If it is to be served as a main dish, double the given quantities and sprinkle the *arroz verde* with grated Manchego cheese. Black olives also go very well with this dish.

Serves 4
1 cup long-grain rice
2 green chile poblano peppers, 1 green bell pepper
3 garlic cloves, finely chopped
2 tablespoons chopped cilantro
3 tablespoons chopped flat-leaf parsley
4 tablespoons vegetable oil
3½ cups finely chopped onions,
1¾ cups chicken stock, salt
You will also need:
cilantro to garnish

Thoroughly wash the rice under running cold water and drain well. Halve the chile poblano and bell peppers, remove the stem, seeds, and ribs, and finely dice the flesh. Pound or process the diced pepper and chiles, garlic, cilantro, and parsley to a smooth paste in a mortar or a blender. Heat the oil in a pot, add the onions, and sweat them without letting them color. Add the rice and continue to sweat for 2 minutes, stirring constantly. Mix in the chile-and-bell-pepper spice paste and cook for a further 2 minutes. Add the chicken stock and salt to taste. Bring to a boil, reduce the heat, and simmer the rice for 18–20 minutes, stirring from time to time. Remove from the heat and leave, covered and undisturbed, for 5 minutes. Fluff the rice with a fork, garnish with the cilantro, and serve. If the dish is intended as an accompaniment, pack the hot rice into oiled timbale molds and turn out onto plates.

SPICED RICE WITH BROILED VEGETABLES

The hot-sweet combination of cayenne pepper and turmeric on the one hand, and cinnamon and dried apricots on the other, lends this rice dish an unusual note, inspired by oriental seasoning traditions. In this recipe, however, the bell peppers are not cooked with the rice, but, just like the eggplant slices, they are broiled in typically Mediterranean fashion and served separately alongside the rice.

Serves 4

For the rice:

1⅔ cups long-grain brown rice
1 small onion
1 tablespoon olive oil
2 garlic cloves, finely chopped
½ teaspoon cayenne pepper
¼ teaspoon ground turmeric
1 teaspoon ground cinnamon
3½ cups vegetable stock
⅓ cup dried apricots, finely diced

For the vegetables:

2 red peppers
1 small eggplant
salt, freshly ground black pepper
3 tablespoons olive oil

You will also need:

⅓ cup pine kernels
1 tablespoon chopped mint

Thoroughly wash the rice under cold running water. Place in a bowl with cold water to cover and leave to soak overnight. The next day, drain the rice well. Slice the onions into thin rings. Heat the oil in a pot, then add the garlic and onions, and sweat until lightly colored. Sprinkle in the spices and sauté briefly. Add the rice and stir vigorously. Pour in the lightly salted vegetable stock and bring to a boil. Stir in the apricots and simmer the rice for 20–25 minutes. In the meantime, quarter the red peppers, remove their stems, core, and seeds, and cut the flesh into 1¼-inch-wide strips. Remove the stalks from the eggplants and cut the flesh lengthwise into slices about ½ inch thick. Season the red-pepper strips and eggplant with salt and pepper, and brush with the olive oil. Cook the vegetables under a fairly hot broiler for 4–5 minutes on each side. Alternatively, the vegetables may be cooked in the oven. Preheat the oven to 425°F. Prepare the red peppers and eggplants as described above, place on a baking sheet lined with silicone paper, and bake for 15 minutes; halfway through the cooking time, turn the vegetables. Dry-roast the pine kernels in a heavy-based frying pan, mix into the finished rice, and adjust the seasoning. Divide the broiled vegetables among the plates, spoon the rice on top, sprinkle with chopped mint, and serve.

Colorfully spiced rice
At home the world over

HERBED RICE

Serves 4
1 tablespoon olive oil, ½ cup finely chopped white onion
1 garlic clove, finely chopped
1¼ cups long-grain rice, 2¼ cups vegetable stock
2 tablespoons chopped parsley, 2 tablespoons chopped chives
1 tablespoon chopped chervil, 1 tablespoon chopped tarragon, 1 tablespoon sliced basil leaves
salt, freshly ground pepper

Heat the oil in a pot, and sweat the onion and garlic until lightly colored. Add the rice, and sweat for 2–3 minutes. Pour in the stock, season with salt, bring to a boil, then reduce the heat, cover, and simmer for 15 minutes. Add the herbs, adjust the seasoning, and simmer for 5 minutes.

Cranberries dye this tart, fruity rice accompaniment from Sweden nearly purple. The cardamom, cinnamon, and allspice in *gesmoorde rys* hint at the Indian influence on South African cooking, while the combination of honey-sweet and chile-hot reveal the Arabian origins of pistachio rice.

PISTACHIO RICE

Serves 4
1¼ cups long-grain rice, 2¼ cups water, salt
1 red chile pepper, ¼ cup seedless golden raisins
¾ cup chopped pistachios
freshly ground black pepper
¼ teaspoon ground cinnamon, 4½ teaspoons butter
You will also need:
1 tablespoon honey

Sprinkle the rice into the boiling water, add salt, reduce the heat, cover, and simmer for 10 minutes. Remove the stem and seeds from the chile pepper, and cut the flesh into thin rings. Mix the chile, raisins, pistachios, pepper, and cinnamon with the rice, and cook, stirring, for a further 10 minutes until done. Stir in the butter. Press the rice into oiled semicircular molds, turn out on plates, and drizzle with the honey.

GESMOORDE RYS

Serves 4
3 tablespoons vegetable oil, 2 garlic cloves, halved
¾ cup finely chopped onion
1 teaspoon cumin, 2 cardamom pods
2 inches cassia bark or cinnamon stick, 4 allspice berries
2 cups long-grain rice, salt, 1 quart water
4½ teaspoons butter
You will also need:
cilantro to garnish

Heat the oil in a pot, add the garlic and onion, and sweat for 4–5 minutes until golden yellow. Add the spices and sweat for a further 2 minutes. Season with salt, pour in the water, and bring to a boil. Simmer the rice for 20 minutes. Remove from the heat and stir in the butter. Serve sprinkled with cilantro.

CRANBERRY RICE

Serves 4
2¼ cups chicken stock, 1¼ cups long-grain rice
1¼ cups cranberries, ½ cup orange juice
grated zest of ½ orange
1 teaspoon hot mustard, a pinch of ground cloves
salt
You will also need:
strips of orange zest and cranberries to garnish

Bring the chicken stock to a boil in a pot, sprinkle in the rice, season with salt, reduce the heat, cover, and simmer for 20 minutes, until the rice has absorbed all the liquid. Wash and sort through the cranberries. Bring the orange juice, orange zest, mustard, and ground cloves to a boil in a saucepan. Add the cranberries and simmer for 3 minutes, then mix into the nearly cooked rice and simmer gently for a further 3 minutes. Spoon the rice into well-oiled timbale molds, press down firmly, turn out onto warmed plates, and garnish with strips of orange zest and cranberries.

The art of seasoning, Southeast Asian style

Rice with cinnamon and cloves, lemon, dill, ginger, and curry powder

FRIED RICE

Serves 4
1½ cups Thai long-grain rice
3 tablespoons vegetable oil
½ onion, sliced into thin rings
1-inch-long cinnamon stick
1 bay leaf, 3 cloves, ½ mace
1 heaping tablespoon brown sugar, salt, 2¼ cups water

Thoroughly wash the rice under cold running water. Transfer to a bowl, cover with cold water, and soak for 20 minutes, then drain well. Heat the oil in a pot, then add the onion rings and sauté until golden brown. Add the spices and sauté for a further 3 minutes. Sprinkle the sugar on top and caramelize, stirring constantly. Add the rice and stir for a further 3 minutes; season with salt. Add the water, bring to a boil, reduce the heat, and cook for 10–15 minutes, until done.

LEMON RICE

Serves 4
1 cup basmati rice, ¼ cup cashew nuts
1⅓ cups water, ½ teaspoon turmeric
1 green chile pepper, 2 tablespoons vegetable oil
¼ teaspoon mustard seed, 8 fresh curry leaves
juice of ½ lemon, salt,

Thoroughly wash the rice under cold running water. Transfer to a bowl, cover with cold water, and soak for 30 minutes, then drain. Soak the cashew nuts in cold water. Bring the water to a boil in a pot with some salt. Add the rice and turmeric, and simmer for 10 minutes, during which time the rice should absorb all the liquid (take care that it does not get too soft). Transfer the rice to a bowl and leave to cool. Meanwhile, remove the stem from the chile and cut the flesh into rings, removing the seeds at the same time. Heat the oil in a wok and briefly stir-fry the chile rings. Mix in the mustard seed, the well-drained cashew nuts, and the curry leaves, and stir-fry for 30 seconds. Stir in the lemon juice. Heat the rice briefly in the spiced oil and serve.

DILL RICE

Serves 4
1 cup Thai long-grain rice

1 green chile pepper, 2 tablespoons vegetable oil

2 green cardamom pods, 4 tablespoons chopped fresh dill

salt, 1½ cups water

You will also need:

dill fronds for garnishing

Wash the rice under cold running water till the water runs clear. Transfer to a bowl, cover with cold water, and soak for 15 minutes. Drain well. Halve the chile pepper lengthwise, remove the seeds, and finely dice the flesh. Heat the oil in a pot, fry the cardamom pods for 1 minute, then add the diced chile, and fry briefly. Stir in the dill and salt, and sauté over a low heat for a further 2–3 minutes. Sprinkle in the rice and sauté for 2 minutes. Add the water, bring to a boil, and simmer the rice for 10–12 minutes. Season to taste. Serve in individual bowls, garnished with dill fronds.

GINGER RICE

Serves 4

1½ cups Thai long-grain rice

1½-inch piece fresh ginger root

1 stalk lemon grass

2–3 scallions, 1 red chile pepper

2 tablespoons vegetable oil, a pinch of brown sugar, salt

juice of ½ kaffir lime, 2¾ cups water

You will also need:

4 scallions for garnishing

Thoroughly wash the rice under cold running water. Peel the ginger and cut into paper-thin slices. Slice the lemon grass and the trimmed scallions into rings. Halve the chile pepper lengthwise, remove the seeds, and finely chop the flesh. Heat the oil in a pot. Add the ginger, lemon grass, scallions, and chile pepper, and sweat for 2–3 minutes. Add the rice and continue to sweat with the other ingredients. Season with sugar,

salt, and lime juice. Pour in the water, bring to a boil, reduce the heat, and simmer the rice for 15 minutes. Meanwhile, prepare the scallions for the garnish: trim off most of the green part to leave scallions about 2½ inches long. Make repeated lengthwise incisions in the scallions from the top down to ¾ inch short of the root, and place briefly in ice water so that the strips roll up decoratively. Serve the rice in small bowls, garnished with the scallions.

CURRIED RICE

Serves 4

1½ cups basmati rice, 2 tablespoons vegetable oil

½ cup finely chopped white onion

1 teaspoon curry powder

2¾ cups vegetable stock, salt

¼ cup golden raisins, 2 teaspoons mango chutney

You will also need:

peppermint leaves to garnish

Thoroughly wash the rice under running water. Transfer to a bowl, cover with cold water, and soak for 15 minutes. Drain well. Heat the oil in a pot, add the onion, and sweat without allowing to color. Add the rice and continue to sweat for a further 2 minutes. Sprinkle in the curry powder and cook, stirring for a further minute. Add the vegetable stock and season with salt. Bring to a boil, then reduce the heat and simmer the rice for 15–20 minutes, stirring several times during this period. Wash and drain the golden raisins. Mix into the rice with the mango chutney 5 minutes before the end of cooking time. Divide the curried rice among individual bowls, garnish with the peppermint leaves, and s

Remove all visible fat and reserve. Lightly salt the chicken inside and out.

Stuff the cavity of the chicken with the garlic, half the ginger, and 1 screw pine leaf.

Bring 7 cups salted water to a boil with the remaining ginger, the other screw pine leaf, and the chicken.

Pour the broth through a fine-mesh strainer into a bowl or pot and reserve for later use.

Heat the oil and chicken fat, then sweat the garlic; pour in the rice and salt lightly.

Hainan chicken rice

Flavored rice with tender chicken, spiced in three different ways

Serves 4–6
For the chicken:
2 screw pine leaves or 1–2 drops pandan essence
3½ lb chicken, 2 garlic cloves, halved
4-inch piece fresh ginger root, peeled and sliced, salt
For the chicken-rice sauce:
4 tablespoons dark soy sauce, 6 tablespoons oyster sauce
2 tablespoons sesame oil
½ cup chicken broth
For the chicken-rice chile:
3–4 fresh red chile peppers
¼ cup chicken broth, salt, juice of 1 lime

For the chicken-rice-ginger paste:

⅔ cup coarsely chopped fresh ginger root, salt

4 teaspoons sugar, ¼ cup chicken broth

For the rice:

3 cups Asian long-grain rice, 3 tablespoons oil

3 garlic cloves, thinly sliced

salt, 1 screw pine leaf, 4½ cups hot chicken broth

You will also need:

cilantro and red chile rings to garnish

Wash the screw pine leaves and tie them into little packets. Wash the chicken, pat dry, and proceed as shown in the first three photos on page 92. Reduce the heat and simmer the chicken for 25–30 minutes. Plunge the chicken into ice water in order to stop the cooking process; remove and set aside. Strain the broth as shown in the fourth photo in the sequence. To make the chicken-rice sauce, stir all of the ingredients together. To make the chile, halve the chile peppers lengthwise, and remove the seeds. Bring the chicken broth to a boil, add the chiles, and simmer for 10 minutes. Season with salt and lime juice, and purée to a fine paste in the blender. To make the ginger paste, purée the ginger in the blender with salt, sugar, and chicken broth. To make rice, wash the rice until the water runs clear. Finely chop the reserved chicken fat and proceed as shown in the last photo in the sequence. Knot the screw pine leaf and add to the pot, and sauté all the ingredients for several minutes, stirring. Add the chicken broth, bring to a boil, reduce the heat, and simmer until the rice is only just covered with liquid. Meanwhile, preheat the oven to 300°F. Remove the rice from the heat and place it in the oven for 20 minutes. Meanwhile, bone and skin the chicken, cut into bite-sized pieces, and briefly reheat in the remaining chicken broth 5 minutes before the rice is finished cooking.

▲ Hainan, the big island in the South China Sea, is famous for its culinary artistry. This dish confirms its reputation. Serve the rice with the sliced chicken, the sauce, and chile paste, and garnish with cilantro and chile-pepper rings.

With coconut milk and shrimp
Culinary excursions to the Caribbean and Asia

Coconut milk determines the flavor of the rice dishes in the first two recipes on this page. Although you can buy coconut milk in cans, the unique taste of the sweet-tart coconut water combined with the nutty flesh is stronger when freshly prepared. Make it as follows. First, hammer a nail into two of the three "eyes" of the coconut and pour the coconut water into a bowl. Use a sharp saw to saw halfway through the coconut, then break open with a hammer. Break off the hard husk piece by piece, with the hammer if necessary. With a knife or peeler, remove the brown skin from the white flesh, rinsing the latter briefly. Next, finely grate the flesh into the bowl with the coconut water, or cube the flesh and process it in the blender with the coconut water (see also page 227).

COCONUT RICE

This very mild rice goes superbly with fish dishes. Served as an accompaniment to spicy meat curries, it tones down the heat slightly. The liquid contained inside really fresh coconut should "glug" quite audibly when the fruit is shaken.

Serves 4
1 fresh coconut (about 1–1¼ lb), 1¾ cups hot water
2 tablespoons coconut oil
½ cup finely chopped white onion
1¼ cups long-grain rice, 1¼ cups cold water, salt

First open the coconut as described above. Cut about one-third of the flesh into pieces and purée in the blender with the reserved coconut water. Add the hot water gradually and blend thoroughly. Strain the coconut milk. Heat the oil in a pot, add the onion, and sweat until lightly colored. Tip in the rice and continue to sweat for 5 minutes, stirring constantly. Pour in the cold water and bring to a boil, stirring. Add the coconut milk, season with salt, and allow to boil. Immediately reduce the heat to the lowest possible setting. Cover the pot with aluminum foil, crimping tightly around the edges. Replace the lid and simmer the rice until it is soft and has absorbed all the liquid, about 20–25 minutes. Meanwhile, preheat the oven to 400°F. Shave the remaining coconut flesh into thin strips, toast on a baking sheet in the oven, and use to garnish the rice.

JAMAICAN COAT OF ARMS

Just where this Jamaican dish gets its name is a mystery. One possible explanation is that "rice and peas," as the recipe is also called, could be described as a culinary emblem of the island, the combination being one of the most popular dishes there. In Jamaica, Coat of Arms is prepared with gungo peas, a whitish-brown speckled native legume, referred to as a pea because it is round, but botanically a variety of bean. The legume is not normally exported, and is accordingly difficult to track down; however, you can use the somewhat larger borlotti or pinto beans, which are also speckled, as a substitute.

Serves 4
1 fresh coconut, water as needed
¼ cup finely chopped shallots, 2 cups gungo peas
2 cups long-grain rice, salt, 3 thyme sprigs

First, open the coconut as described above. Place the flesh and water from the coconut in a blender and purée very finely. Add hot water a little at a time to make 4½ cups liquid, and strain this coconut milk. Bring the coconut milk to a boil in a large pot. Sprinkle in the shallots and gungo peas, remove the pot from the heat, and allow the legumes to steep for 20 minutes. Stir in the rice, season with salt, and add the thyme sprigs. Cover the pot and simmer over a low heat for 30 minutes. Stir in a little more coconut milk or water if necessary.

SHRIMP RICE

Dried shrimp are used in quite a few Asian cuisines, first and foremost as an intensely flavored condiment. Together with the fish sauce, they lend a maritime note to this rice dish from Myanmar, known in its native country as *Htamin*. The fresh flavors of lemon grass and lime harmonize brilliantly with the fishy taste.

Serves 4
For the spice paste:
5 tablespoons dried shrimp
2 red chile peppers
1 cup finely chopped onion
2 garlic cloves, finely chopped
5 tablespoons peanut oil
4 tablespoons fish sauce, 1 tablespoon lime juice
salt
For the rice:
1¾ cups Thai long-grain rice
1 stalk lemon grass
1 quart water
You will also need:
3 shallots
3 tablespoons peanut oil
4 red chile peppers to garnish

To make the spice paste, first soak the shrimp in cold water for about 10 minutes, then drain well. Halve the chiles, remove the seeds, and chop the flesh. Place the shrimp, onion, garlic, and chiles in a blender and process to a smooth paste. Heat the oil in a pan, add the paste, and sweat, stirring, for 3–4 minutes. Season with fish sauce, lime juice, and salt. Pour the rice into a large pot. Cut off the top third of the lemon-grass stalk, halve the lower part lengthwise, and crush slightly with a large kitchen knife. Place the lemon grass on top of the rice and add the water. Bring to a boil, reduce the heat, and simmer the rice, covered, for 15–20 minutes, stirring occasionally. Five minutes before the end of cooking time, fish out the lemon grass and stir the spice paste into the rice. Remove the pot from the heat and let the rice rest for 5 minutes.

Peel the shallots and slice into rings. Heat the peanut oil in a pan and fry the shallots until they are golden brown and crispy. To make the garnish, halve the chile peppers from the tip upwards to about ¼ inch below the stalk. With a small, pointed knife, remove the seeds and slice the flesh into fine strips in such a manner that the strips are held together by the stalk. Soak the "palm trees" briefly in ice water until the strips bend decoratively outward, then remove them and drain well. Serve the rice in bowls, garnished with the crispy shallot rings and the chile palm trees.

Fragrant rice
Exotically scented and spicy

The recipes on these two pages are fragrant rice recipes in two senses: they are prepared from Thai fragrant rice — one variety of which has such a fine, enticing aroma and flavor that it is called, quite poetically, "jasmine rice" — and the well-balanced spice mixtures and kaffir limes contribute additional nuances of fragrance. Incidentally, almost every part of the kaffir lime — juice, leaves, and zest — can be used as a flavoring.

BROWN FRAGRANT RICE

Unmilled Thai fragrant rice needs to cook for a little longer than milled rice to develop its full flavor.

Serves 4

1½ stalks celery, 4 scallions

2 red chile peppers

2 tablespoons peanut oil

2 garlic cloves, finely chopped

⅜ cup diced carrot

1 tablespoon finely chopped fresh ginger root

1⅔ cups unmilled Thai fragrant rice

4½–5½ cups chicken stock

1 kaffir lime leaf, 1 tablespoon lime juice

salt, freshly ground pepper

You will also need:

lime slices to garnish

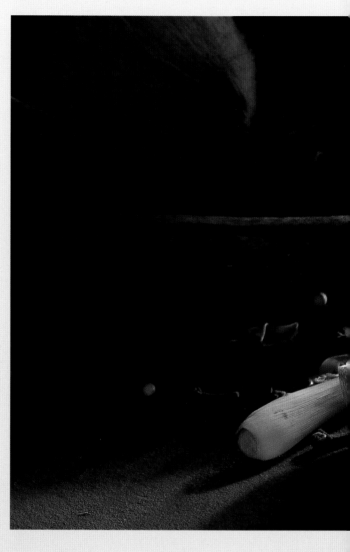

In Southeast Asia baskets are used not only to display fruit and vegetables in the markets but also to serve ready-made dishes like the brown fragrant rice here. Baskets are often lined decoratively with lettuce or banana leaves before the rice is served.

Trim the celery and scallions. Slice the celery and cut the scallions into rings. Halve the chile peppers lengthwise, remove the seeds, and finely chop the flesh. Heat the oil in a large pot and sweat the scallions and garlic without allowing them to color. Add the chiles, ginger, celery, and carrots, and sweat for a further 2 minutes. Tip in the fragrant rice, stirring vigorously. Add half the chicken stock. Stir in the kaffir lime leaf and the lime juice, and season with salt and pepper. Bring to a boil, reduce the heat, and simmer for 45–50 minutes, adding the remaining chicken stock a little at a time. Serve garnished with lime slices.

FRAGRANT RICE

For this highly aromatic rice, fresh curry leaves are a must. The dried leaves cannot be sautéed in hot oil, and it is only by this procedure that the curry leaves can contribute their flavor and aroma, along with that of the kaffir lime and mace, to the fragrance of this dish.

Serves 4–6

1 stalk lemon grass
2 tablespoons peanut oil
10 fresh curry leaves
zest of ½ kaffir lime
2 mace blades
6 cloves
2½ cups jasmine rice
1¾ cups water
salt, freshly ground pepper
1¼ cups coconut milk (see page 227)

Preheat the oven to 300°F. Cut the lemon grass into thin rings. Heat the peanut oil in a large pot and sauté the curry leaves until their aroma wafts up. Add the lemon grass, lime zest, mace, and cloves, and sweat for a further 2–3 minutes. Pour in the rice, stirring vigorously. Add the water and bring to a boil. Reduce the heat, season with salt and pepper, and pour in the coconut milk, mixing it in thoroughly. Cover the pot and place the rice in the oven for 20–30 minutes, until all the liquid has been absorbed.

With turmeric and annatto
Four yellow rice dishes, from simple to sophisticated

NASI KUNYIT

Serves 4
scant 1 teaspoon turmeric, 2 tablespoons vegetable oil
1 cup Thai fragrant rice
7/8 cup water, 1¼ cups coconut milk (see page 227), salt

Preheat the oven to 400°F. Proceed as illustrated in the photo sequence opposite.

TURMERIC RICE

Serves 4
2 scallions, 2 tablespoons peanut oil
2 teapoons turmeric, 1¼ cups Thai fragrant rice
2¼ cups chicken stock, salt

Trim the scallions and slice into thin rounds. Heat the oil, add the scallions, and sweat until lightly colored. Add the turmeric and rice, and sweat briefly. Pour in the chicken stock, season with salt, and bring to a boil. Reduce the heat and simmer for 15 minutes, stirring several times. (See picture on page 82.)

ANNATTO RICE

Serves 4
2 tablespoons annatto oil (see page 82)
1 garlic clove, finely chopped
¼ cup finely chopped onion, 1¼ cups long-grain rice
1 heaped teaspoon annatto seeds, ground
3 cups vegetables stock, salt

Heat the annatto oil in a pot and sweat the onion and garlic. Add the rice and sweat briefly, stirring. Stir in the annatto seeds, pour in the stock, season with salt,

Mild nasi kunyit, which is cooked in coconut milk, is superb as an accompaniment for fish and poultry dishes.

Heat the oil in a flameproof pot, add the turmeric, and cook for 1–2 minutes.

Tip in the rice and sweat briefly, stirring. Pour in the water and bring to a boil.

Reduce the heat, stir in the coconut milk, and season the rice with salt if necessary. Cover the pot, transfer to the oven, and cook for 20–25 munutes, until done.

and bring to a boil. Reduce the heat and cook the rice for 20–25 minutes. (See picture on page 83.)

NASI KUNCI

Serves 4
2½ cups Thai long-grain rice
2¼ cups coconut milk, 1¾ cups chicken stock
1 stalk lemon grass, finely chopped
1 tablespoon finely chopped galangal
1¾ teaspoons turmeric
1 screw pine leaf, 1 kaffir lime leaf, salt
For the vegetables:
10 oz broccoli florets (5 cups), 3 oz snow peas
1 carrot, 4 scallions, 3 oz shiitake mushrooms
¾-inch piece fresh ginger root
⅓ cup chicken stock, 4–5 tablespoons light soy sauce
¼ teaspoon cornstarch, 2 tablespoons vegetable oil
1 garlic clove, thinly sliced; salt, freshly ground pepper
For the shrimp:
1 red chile pepper, 2 tablespoons vegetable oil
⅜ cup finely chopped onion, 1 garlic clove, finely chopped
12 raw shrimp, shelled; 2 tablespoons fish sauce
You will also need:
a cone made of strong, transparent film (2-quart capacity)
1 banana leaf, 1 tablespoon vegetable oil
cilantro to garnish

Wash the rice thoroughly and drain. Slowly bring the coconut milk and the stock to a boil in a pot. Stir in the lemon grass, galangal, turmeric, salt, and rice. Add the screw pine and lime leaves, reduce the heat, and simmer for 20 minutes; keep warm. To prepare the vegetables, blanch the broccoli florets and drain well. Cut the snow peas into ½-inch-long diamond shapes. Peel the carrot and cut into rounds. Trim the scallions, slice the green parts into pieces about 1½ inches long, and halve the white parts. Remove the mushroom stems. Peel the ginger and cut into thin batons. Mix together the stock, soy sauce, and cornstarch. Cover this sauce and set aside. Make the rice cone as shown in the first three photos below. Heat the oil in a wok. Add the garlic and ginger, and stir-fry briefly. Add the vegetables and mushrooms, and stir-fry for 8 minutes. Stir in the sauce, bring to a boil, and season. Remove from the wok and keep hot. To prepare the shrimp, remove the stems and seeds from the chile pepper, and cut the flesh into rings. Clean the wok, then heat the oil. Add the onion, garlic, and chile rings, and stir-fry briefly. Add the shrimp and stir-fry for 2–3 minutes. Add the fish sauce and mix well. Serve the rice as shown, garnished with cilantro.

Arrange the banana leaf in the tip of the film so that it fills about ⅓ of the cone. Brush the remaining ⅔ with oil.

Remove the lime and screw pine leaves from the cooked rice. Spoon the rice into the prepared cone.

Press the cooked rice firmly into the cone with a potato masher, flattening and smoothing the surface.

Turn the rice out onto a plate and remove the film. Arrange the vegetables and shrimp all around.

Claypot rice
Rice gently cooked in a covered clay pot: a specialty of *nonya* cooking

"Nonyas" was the name originally given to the descendants of the Chinese traders who settled on the Strait of Malacca, so it is hardly surprising that *nonya* cooking succeeds in combining Chinese and Malay ingredients and preparation methods in a most harmonious fashion. Indonesia and Thailand contributed their impetus, which undoubtedly helped to make *nonya* cooking one of the most creative cuisines in Singapore. Delicacies prepared in the *nonya* style are found in the popular food stalls on the streets of the metropolis.

SINGAPORE CLAYPOT RICE

Serves 4
1 cup Thai long-grain rice
1 oz salted dried fish

2 oz air-dried Chinese sausage
⅔ cup cubed chicken meat from the thigh
3 tablespoons vegetable oil
3 garlic cloves, diced
1½ oz dried shiitake mushrooms
2 tablespoons oyster sauce
1½ tablespoons dark soy sauce
1¾ cups chicken stock
2 tablespoons sesame oil
salt, freshly ground white pepper
You will also need:
2 shallots
2 tablespoons vegetable oil
flat-leaf parsley
cilantro

Rinse the rice under cold running water until the water runs clear. Drain well. Soak the shiitake mushrooms in warm water for 30 minutes; remove the hard stalks, and squeeze the mushrooms dry. Slice the salted fish and the Chinese sausage. Preheat the oven to 300 °F. Heat the oil in a purpose-made clay pot or in an earthenware

Add the Chinese sausage, chicken, and mushrooms, stir-frying with the other ingredients.

Add the well-drained rice and stir-fry everything for a few more minutes.

Stir in the sauces, moisten with chicken stock, and bring to a boil.

Evenly distribute the shallots and the oil over the rice, meat, and mushroom mixture.

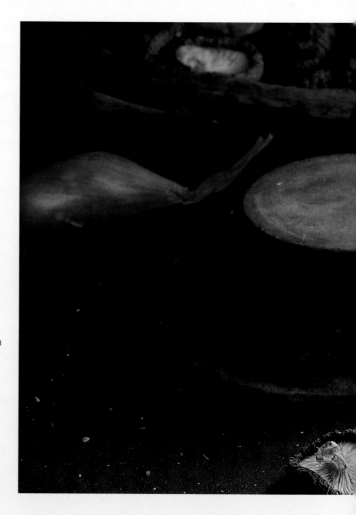

pot with a lid. Add the garlic and the fish, and stir-fry briefly. Proceed as shown in the first three photos in the sequence below. Cover the pot and place it in the oven for 20–25 minutes. In the meantime, slice the shallots into rings and fry in the vegetable oil until golden brown. Take the clay pot out of the oven and remove the lid. Proceed as shown in the final photo. Season with salt and pepper. Garnish with parsley and cilantro, and serve in the pot.

CLAYPOT RICE WITH VEGETABLES

Serves 4
1 cup Thai long-grain rice
1½ oz dried cloud ear mushrooms
8 baby corn cobs, salt, 3½ oz choy sum
3 oz small round eggplants
3 tablespoons vegetable oil, 2 garlic cloves, chopped
1 teaspoon shrimp paste
2 tablespoons vegetarian oyster sauce
1½ tablespoons dark soy sauce
freshly ground white pepper
1¾ cups vegetable stock

You will also need:
1 tablespoon sesame oil

Wash the rice under running water until the water runs clear. Drain well. Soak the dried cloud ears in warm water for 30 minutes, then drain, and cut the mushrooms into strips. Blanch the baby corn cobs in boiling salted water, refresh with cold water, and slice into 1¼-inch-long pieces. Wash the choy sum, cut off the tough bottom ends, and chop the vegetable into 2-inch-long pieces. Wash the eggplant, remove the stems, and quarter the flesh. Preheat the oven to 300°F. Heat the vegetable oil in a purpose-made clay pot or another lidded earthenware pot. Add the garlic and sweat until it softens, then stir in the shrimp paste. Briefly sweat together the rice, vegetables, and mushrooms. Season with the vegetarian oyster sauce, the soy sauce, salt and pepper, and add the vegetable stock. Bring to a boil, cover the pot, and place it in the oven for 20–25 minutes. Remove the clay pot from the oven, lift the lid, drizzle the finished dish with sesame oil, and serve in the clay pot.

Cooking in a covered clay pot allows the flavors of the chicken, mushrooms, salted fish, sausage, sauces, and seasonings to penetrate the rice thoroughly. This cooking method also turns purely vegetarian dishes into culinary surprises.

Biriyani rice with lamb
A famous Malayan dish that brings together all the flavors of Southeast Asia

Malayan cuisine is very fond of spices, which thrive in the region's damp, hot climate. They are used fresh, for example aromatic, spicy-hot ginger, lemon grass, and fiery chile peppers. Used in myriad ways and combined with an eye to the other ingredients, they account for the particular character of many local specialties. The special mixture of spices indicated by the name "biriyani," which tastes of cinnamon, cardamom, and cloves, is characteristic of this exceptional rice dish. The preparation method is important too. First, the spices are sautéed in moderately hot ghee (clarified butter) until they begin to give off a pleasant fragrance. Later, the rice is added, and simmered for some time on the stove before it is transferred to the oven to finish cooking gently at a low temperature, then drizzled with saffron-rosewater to add the finishing visual and flavor touches to the dish.

Serves 4–6
For the lamb stew:
2 stalks lemon grass
2 garlic cloves, finely chopped
1 tablespoon small mint leaves, 2 tablespoons cilantro
4 oz tomatoes, 2 red chile peppers
1 lb boneless leg of lamb
3 tablespoons vegetable oil
3 shallots
1½ inch piece fresh ginger root, finely chopped
1 teaspoon curry powder, ¼ teaspoon chili paste
1 tablespoon garam masala
½ cup light cream
1¼ cups lamb stock
juice of ½ lemon, salt
For the rice:
3 cups basmati rice
¼ cup ghee
1 tablespoon finely chopped fresh ginger root
2 garlic cloves, finely chopped
1 shallot, finely chopped
2 cinnamon sticks
8 cardamom seeds, 6 cloves
4½ cups water, salt
a pinch of saffron threads
3 tablespoons rose water

Wash the lemon grass and slice into thin rings. Peel the shallots and cut into rings. Wash the mint and

Stir-fry the cinnamon sticks, cardamom seeds, and cloves in hot fat until the fragrances w...

Add the ginger, garlic, and shallots, and continue to sweat, stirring constantly, allowing the ingredients to color slightly.

Add the washed rice to the spices and stir-fry continuously for 3–4 minutes.

Pour in the water, season with salt, bring to a boil, and simmer until the rice is just barely covered with water.

After 15 minutes' cooking time remove the rice from the oven and drizzle over a spoonful of the saffron-rosewater.

cilantro, pat dry, and chop finely. Blanch, skin, and seed the tomatoes, and dice the flesh. Halve the chile pepper, remove the seeds, and finely chop the flesh. Cut the lamb into ¾-inch cubes. Heat the oil in a ...k and fry the lamb on all sides to seal. Add the sliced shallots and fry for 1 minute until they have browned slightly. Remove the meat and shallots with a perforated spoon and set aside. In the same oil, sauté the diced ginger, lemon grass, garlic, chile peppers, and curry powder until they begin to give off a pleasant aroma. Stir in the herbs and tomato, and continue to sauté with the other ingredients. Next, stir in the chili paste, garam masala, and cream. Pour in the lamb stock and add the reserved browned shallot rings and the cubed lamb. Mix everything well and cook for 10 minutes over a high heat, then reduce the heat and simmer for about 45 minutes, stirring from time to time.

Meanwhile, prepare the spiced rice. Wash the rice until the water runs clear and drain well. Heat the ghee in a flameproof pot and proceed as shown in the first four photos in the sequence opposite. Preheat the oven to 300°F. When the water just barely covers the rice, remove the pot from the stove, cover, and place in the oven for 15 minutes, until done. In a small pot, stir the saffron threads into the rosewater and bring to a boil; simmer for about 1 minute, remove from the heat, and reserve. Proceed as shown in the last photo opposite. Put the rice back in the oven for a further 5 minutes. At the end of the cooking time, take the lamb stew off the stove, stir in the lemon juice, and add salt to taste. Remove the rice from the oven, spoon into bowls, top with a little lamb stew, and serve.

Pilafs

Regardless of whether you call it pilaf, pilafi, pilav, pulao, or pilau, the basic prerequisite is perfectly cooked rice with separate, fluffy grains. Cooks in the regions where pilaf is a classic dish, from Greece to India, are justifiably proud of their mastery of this high art.

So proud, that even plain rice, cooked with almost no further ingredients, and possibly flavored with butter or ghee, a couple of scallions, salt, and spices can be termed pilaf. If an especially strong flavor is desired, the rice can also be cooked in broth or stock.

Occasionally, pilaf masquerades under another name, for it is not just in the Middle and Near East that this style of rice dish is prepared. For example, the Portuguese dish known as *arroz*, which means "rice" pure and simple, is one of the countless variations in the great pilaf family.

That pilaf is ideal for an East–West culinary dialog, and that haute cuisine can acknowledge it proudly is shown by Eckart Witzigmann's pilaf creations in this chapter.

Basic pilaf recipes
Two different cooking methods and an ocean-fresh recipe as an example

Just as with the preparation of risotto, people could argue at great length over the "proper" way to cook pilaf; the question of which national cuisine should be credited with the invention of which cooking method is likewise unresolved. Be that as it may, two basic recipes emerge quite clearly, which for the sake of simplicity we refer to here as the "Turkish" and "Greek" methods, even though a number pilafis in Greece are prepared according to the "Turkish" method and the odd pilav is cooked in Turkey according to the "Greek" method. The most significant differences are how and when the rice is added. In the Turkish method, the long-grain rice is, without further preparation, first stir-fried in fat until translucent, then the liquid is added and the rice cooks in an uncovered pot, similar to a classic risotto. In the Greek method, on the other hand, the rice is first washed until the water runs clear, and then is added to the already boiling cooking liquid and cooked, without stirring, until done.

The technique for producing a pilaf with really fluffy, separate grains is the same for both methods: At the end of the cooking time, take the rice is off the heat, wedge two layers of paper towels between the pot and lid, and allow the rice to rest for 5–10 minutes. Alternatively, wrap the lid in a dish towel and replace it on the pot; in this case, take care to use a dish towel that has not been washed with scented detergent. Both cloth and paper towels absorb the condensation on the pot lid and allow the rice to steam dry without cooling down too quickly.

The "Greek" method:

Thoroughly wash 1½ cups long-grain rice in a strainer under cold running water; drain well.

Melt 4½ teaspoons butter in a large pot, then add 2¾ cups chicken stock.

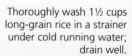

Bring the liquid to a boil. Tip in the washed rice, season with salt, and reduce the heat.

Place the lid on the pot and simmer the rice for 20 minutes. Remove the pot from the heat.

Wedge a cloth or two layers of paper towels between the pot and lid, and allow to steam dry for 10 minutes.

Melt 4½ teaspoons butter. Carefully fluff the cooked rice with a fork and stir in the butter.

The "Turkish" method:

Melt 3 tablespoons butter in a large pot. Add 1½ cups long-grain rice and sweat, stirring, until the grains are translucent.

Add 2¾ cups hot beef stock. Season with salt and bring to a boil. Reduce the heat and cook the rice for 20–25 minutes.

Turn off the heat. In another saucepan, melt 4½ teaspoons butter and allow it to brown slightly.

Stir the butter into the rice and season with pepper. Place two layers of paper towels between the pot and the lid, and allow to steam dry for 5–10 minutes.

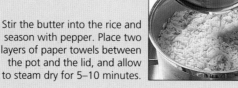

CLAM PILAF

Clams are actually better known in combination with pasta, especially, of course, with spaghetti; but they are also delicious in a pilaf cooked with tomatoes. The pilaf described here is often prepared with mussels instead of clams.

Serves 4
2¼ lb clams
For the court bouillon:
2 tablespoons olive oil, ¾ cup finely chopped onion
1 garlic clove, finely chopped
½ cup white wine, 2¾ cups water
3 parsley stalks
.5 white peppercorns, coarse sea salt
For the pilaf:
1½ cups long-grain rice
2 scallions, 8 oz plum tomatoes
2 tablespoons olive oil, 1 garlic clove, finely chopped
4 teaspoons tomato paste
a pinch of of sugar, salt, freshly ground pepper
3 fl oz white wine
1 tablespoon chopped parsley
½ tablespoon chopped marjoram
You will also need:
1 tablespoon chopped fresh herbs

Scrub the clams under cold running water; discard any that are open. To make the court bouillon, heat the oil in a pot, add the onions and garlic, and sweat them briefly. Pour in the white wine and water, season with parsley, peppercorns, and sea salt, and bring to a boil. Add the clams and boil, covered, until they have opened. Lift the shellfish out of the court bouillon with a slotted spoon; discard any that are still closed. Shell half of the clams and set aside, covered, with the remaining shellfish. Pass the stock through a fine-mesh strainer and reserve it too.

To make the pilaf, wash the rice under cold running water until the water runs clear. Trim the scallions and slice into thin rings. Blanch, skin, and seed the tomatoes, and finely dice the flesh. Heat the oil in a pot, add the scallions and garlic, and sweat them briefly. Add the tomatoes, tomato paste, and seasonings, and continue to sweat. Mix the wine with the shellfish stock, make up to 3 cups with water, and pour this mixture over the tomatoes. Sprinkle in the herbs and bring to a boil. Add the rice, reduce the heat, and simmer, covered, for 15–20 minutes. Remove from the heat; wedge a cloth or two layers of paper towels between the pot and lid, and allow to steam dry for 5–10 minutes. Mix the shelled clams into the rice and adjust the seasoning. Serve the pilaf garnished with the clams in their shells and sprinkled with herbs.

With vegetables
Two traditional pilaf recipes from Greece and Turkey

PILAFI LAHANIKA

In Greece there is actually no definitive recipe for vegetable pilaf; cooks ring the changes with ingredients according to the season. Popular as a main course during Lent, vegetable pilaf is otherwise usually served as an accompaniment. There is a special trick to its preparation: vegetables and rice are cooked in the same pot, layered one on top of the other, not mixed, so that the rice is initially boiled, and then, at the end of the cooking time, steamed.

Serves 4
1½ cups long-grain rice
¼ teaspoon saffron threads, 2 tablespoons hot water
1 onion, 2 leeks
2 carrots, 2 zucchini
7 oz green beans
9 oz tomatoes, 3 tablespoons olive oil

Heat the olive oil in a large pot. Add the onion and leeks, and sweat without allowing them to color.

Add the remaining vegetables, then stir in the steeped saffron, and season with salt and pepper.

Drain the washed rice well and spread evenly over the vegetables.

Add the hot vegetable stock and sprinkle with the herbs and the grated lemon zest.

2¼–2¾ cups vegetable stock
1 tablespoon each chopped dill, parsley, and mint
grated zest of ½ lemon
salt, freshly ground pepper

Wash the rice under cold running water until the water runs clear. Place in a bowl with cold water to cover and soak for 20 minutes. Steep the saffron threads in hot water. Peel, or wash and trim, as appropriate, the onion, leeks, carrots, and zucchini. Slice the onion and leeks into thin rings, and the carrots and zucchini into ⅛-inch-thick rounds. Wash and trim the beans, stringing them if necessary; cut on the diagonal into ¾-inch-long pieces. Blanch, skin, and seed the tomatoes, and dice the flesh. Proceed as shown in the photo sequence opposite. Simmer the pilaf, covered, for 15–20 minutes over a moderately low heat.

IÇ PILAV

Although it too is enriched primarily with vegetables, the Turkish "colorful" or "mixed" pilaf, in contrast to the purely vegetarian and equally popular Greek vegetable pilaf in the preceding recipe, also contains lamb's liver. It is a rather festive accompaniment for lamb or beef dishes.

Serves 4
1 carrot, 1¼ cup podded fresh peas
4 tablespoons olive oil, ¾ cup finely chopped onion
2 tablespoons pine kernels, 1½ cups long-grain rice
1 teaspoon paprika, 1 teaspoon ground cumin
2¾ cups hot meat stock, ¼ cup currants
10 oz lamb's liver, cubed
salt, freshly ground pepper
You will also need:
1 tablespoon chopped dill

Peel the carrot and cut into 2-inch cubes. Blanch the peas in boiling salted water, drain, and refresh in ice water. Heat half the oil in a pot. Add the carrots and onions, and sweat until the onions are translucent. Add the pine kernels and rice, and sauté for 2–3 minutes. Season with salt, sprinkle in the spices, and mix well. Pour in the stock and bring to a boil, then cover, reduce the heat, and simmer for 20–25 minutes.

Meanwhile, plump the currants in a little water for 10 minutes. Heat the remaining oil in a frying pan and sear the liver on all sides; season with salt and pepper. Five minutes before the end of the rice cooking time mix in the peas, liver, and currants. Remove from the heat, place two layers of paper towels or a dish towel between the pot and lid, and allow to steam dry for 5–10 minutes. Sprinkle with the dill and serve.

Spoon half of the rice into the ovenproof dish, spreading the drained garbanzos on top.

Cover with the remaining rice. Cut the ghee into small pieces.

Distribute the cubes of ghee and the onions over the rice.

Drizzle with lemon juice and sprinkle with chopped herbs.

Garbanzo pilaf
An Indian-style vegetarian pilaf finished in the oven

Pulao, pilau, pelao: the Indian cousin of the pilaf is spelled in so many different ways. Just as varied are the ingredients added to this type of rice dish in India. Whether you choose dal (the extremely popular dried, split, and skinned legumes) or vegetables, lamb, poultry, fish or seafood, the most important thing is the right rice. Indian pilaf is always prepared from the best long-grain rice, the preferred variety being aromatic basmati rice, which produces separate, dry grains when cooked. Always included, even in the simplest Indian pilaf, are spices, herbs, and a generous quantity of ghee or melted butter. This recipe is also enriched with golden-brown fried onions and chana dal —- split dried garbanzos. During the slow final cooking in the oven the flavors of the herbs, spices, and onions, the heat of the chiles, and the tang of the yogurt and lemon mingle superbly with the mild-tasting garbanzos and basmati rice.

Serves 4
⅓ cup chana dal, 2 cups basmati rice
½ teaspoon ground turmeric, salt
1 onion
3-inch piece fresh ginger root
1 red chile pepper
4 tablespoons vegetable oil
2 garlic cloves, crushed
⅔ cup full-fat yogurt
3 tablespoons ghee (or clarified butter)
juice of ½ lemon
1 tablespoon chopped cilantro
1 tablespoon chopped mint
3 green chile peppers
½ teaspoon garam masala
You will also need:
butter for greasing the dish
cilantro for garnishing

Wash the chana dal and the basmati rice separately under cold running water, drain, and place in separate bowls with cold water to cover. Soak the garbanzos for 1½ hours and the rice for 1 hour, then drain the rice. Bring the chana dal to a boil in its soaking water with ¼ teaspoon turmeric. Half cover, reduce the heat, and simmer for 25–30 minutes. Pour into a strainer and drain. Bring some salted water to a boil in a large pot; add the rice, reduce the heat, and cook for 10 minutes, until almost done. Drain well. Meanwhile, peel the onion, halve lengthwise and slice into thin rings. Peel and finely grate the ginger. Halve the red chile pepper lengthwise, remove the stem and seeds, and finely chop the flesh. Heat the oil in a frying pan and fry the onions until golden brown and crisp. Remove and drain on paper towels. Sauté the garlic and ginger in the remaining fat until lightly colored. Add the remaining turmeric and 1 tablespoon of the yogurt. Fry, stirring, until the liquid in the yogurt has nearly all evaporated and the mixture begins to turn light brown. Add the remaining yogurt a tablespoon at a time, allowing it to reduce in the same way after each addition. Stir the drained garbanzos and the chopped chile pepper into the yogurt until well blended, and

simmer for 1 minute. Grease a large ovenproof dish with butter. Proceed as described in the photo sequence.

Preheat the oven to 325°F. Halve the green chile peppers, remove the stem and seeds, and finely chop the flesh. Sprinkle over the prepared rice with the garam masala. Cover the dish with foil, place in the oven, and cook the pilaf for 30 minutes, until done. Remove the foil and fork through the rice. Serve in small bowls, garnished with cilantro .

The taste of the sea
Pilafs with seafood and anchovies

SHRIMP PILAF

Although the rice is cooked separately in this pilaf recipe, it is nevertheless saturated with the fine flavor of the shrimp, since a seafood court bouillon is used as the cooking liquid.

Serves 4
1¼ lb raw shrimp
1 small onion
1 garlic clove
1 small carrot
1 celery stalk
5 white peppercorns
1 bay leaf
2 thyme sprigs
salt, ½ cup white wine
For the tomato sauce:
1 lb ripe tomatoes
3 tablespoons olive oil
¾ cup finely chopped onions
1 garlic clove, finely chopped
a pinch of sugar
⅓ cup white wine
salt, freshly ground pepper
For the pilaf:
1½ cups long-grain rice, 2 tablespoons butter
You will also need:
1 tablespoon chopped flat-leaf parsley

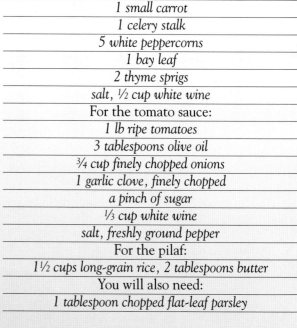

Wash the shrimp under cold running water and set aside. To make the court bouillon, peel the onion, garlic, and carrot, and cut them all into ½-inch pieces. Trim and slice the celery. Place 4½ cups water, the vegetables, peppercorns, bay leaf, thyme sprigs, salt, and white wine in a pot, and bring to a boil. Simmer for 10 minutes, then add the shrimp; let boil briefly, reduce the heat, and simmer for 3–4 minutes. Remove the shrimp from the court bouillon and drain well. Pass the court bouillon through a fine-mesh strainer, reserving 3 cups for later use. Remove the shrimp tails from their shells.

To make the sauce, nick the tomatoes crosswise, then blanch, skin, and seed them, and finely dice the flesh. Heat the oil in a pot, then sweat the diced onion and garlic until the onions are translucent. Add the tomatoes, stir in the sugar, salt, pepper, and white

One variation is to stir the pilaf into the finished shrimp-and-tomato sauce before serving.

wine. Bring to a boil, reduce the heat, cover, and simmer for 10 minutes.

Wash the rice under cold running water. Bring the reserved shrimp court bouillon and the butter to a boil in a pot. Add the rice, reduce the heat, cover, and simmer for 15–20 minutes. Remove the pot from the heat and place two layers of paper towels or a dish towel between the pot and the lid, and allow the pilaf to steam dry for 10 minutes. In the meantime, transfer the shrimp tails to the tomato sauce and warm briefly. Serve the shrimp and sauce in deep dishes with the pilaf, sprinkled with parsley.

HAMSI PILAVI

This Turkish pilaf, which is especially popular on the Black Sea coast, contains freshly caught anchovies; paprika and a red chile pepper give it piquancy.

Serves 4

| 1 lb fresh anchovies |
| 4 tablespoons olive oil |
| 1½ cups finely chopped onion |
| 1 small red chile pepper |
| 8 oz plum tomatoes |
| 1½ cups long-grain rice |
| 2¾ cups hot fish stock |
| 1 teaspoon sweet paprika |
| 1 tablespoon chopped flat-leaf parsley |
| ½ tablespoon chopped mint |
| salt, freshly ground pepper |
| 1 tablespoon olive oil for drizzling |

Slit the bellies of the anchovies with small, sharp scissors, and remove the innards. Wash the fish inside and out under cold running water, then drain well. Heat half of the oil in a pot, add ¾ cup of the onions, and sweat until translucent. Add the anchovies and fry briefly on both sides; season with salt and pepper. Remove the pot from the heat and set aside.

Meanwhile, prepare the rice. Halve the red chile pepper lengthwise, remove the stem and seeds, and finely dice the flesh. Blanch, skin, and seed the tomatoes, and finely dice the flesh. Heat the remaining oil in a pot and sweat the remaining onions without allowing them to color. Add the diced chile pepper and tomatoes and sweat for 2–3 minutes, then add the rice and sauté, stirring, for 3–4 minutes. Add the hot fish stock and stir in the paprika. Bring to a boil, reduce the heat, and simmer the rice for 15 minutes. Preheat the oven to 350°F. Carefully combine the rice mixture and the chopped herbs with the fried anchovies, and season to taste with salt and freshly ground pepper. Drizzle over the oil and finish cooking the anchovy pilaf in the oven for 15 minutes.

Pilafs with poultry
A popular rice dish around the Mediterranean

ARROZ COM FRANGO

The Portuguese are extremely fond of chicken with rice cooked according to the pilaf method, to which not only olives and chile peppers, but a sausage akin to Spanish chorizo lend the right spice. A young vinho verde is the ideal wine to drink with this dish.

Serves 4
1 broiler-fryer chicken (about 2¼ lb)
1 red chile pepper, 1 sweet red pepper
5 tablespoons olive oil, 1 cup finely chopped onion
2 garlic cloves, finely chopped
1½ cups long-grain rice
½ cup white wine (e.g. vinho verde)
2¾ cups hot chicken stock
1½ cups fresh peas
⅓ cup black olives, 7 oz chouriço
salt, freshly ground pepper
1 tablespoon chopped flat-leaf parsley

Wash the chicken inside and out under cold running water, and drain well. Halve the chile and the sweet red pepper, removing the seeds and ribs. Finely chop the chile pepper and cut the bell pepper into ¼-inch dice. Cut the chicken into about 20 pieces and season with salt and pepper. Heat the oil in a large pot and brown the chicken pieces well all over. Add the onion and garlic, and fry briefly. Add the diced chile and sweet pepper as well as the rice, and fry briefly. Pour in the white wine and the hot chicken stock, bring to a boil, reduce the heat, and simmer for about 20 minutes. Meanwhile, blanch the peas in boiling salted water and drain. Cut the chouriço into ⅛-inch rounds. After 20 minutes' cooking time mix the peas, olives, and the chouriço into the rice, and simmer for a further 5 minutes. Adjust seasoning and serve the *arroz com frango* sprinkled with parsley.

QUAIL PILAF

Serves 4

4 ready-to-cook quails (about 7 oz each)

4 tablespoons olive oil, ¾ cup finely diced onions

2 tablespoons tomato paste

2¾ cups hot chicken stock

1¼ cups long-grain rice

¼ teaspoon each ground cinnamon and allspice

8 oz ripe tomatoes

salt, freshly ground white pepper

You will also need:

¼ cup butter, browned; 1 tablespoon chopped mint

Wash the quails inside and out under cold running water, and drain well. Cut each quail into 6 pieces and season with salt and pepper. Heat the oil in a large pot and brown the quail pieces well on all sides, then remove from the pot. Sweat the onion in the remaining oil until it colors slightly. Stir in the tomato paste and sauté, stirring, for 1–2 minutes. Add the hot chicken stock. Bring to a boil, add the rice in a thin, steady stream, reduce the heat, cover, and simmer for 5 minutes. Season with cinnamon, allspice, salt, and pepper. Return the browned quail pieces to the pot and simmer for a further 15–20 minutes.

Meanwhile, blanch, skin, and seed the tomatoes, and finely dice the flesh. After the rice has cooked for 10 minutes, stir in the diced tomatoes. Season the cooked quail pilaf with salt and pepper to taste and serve on warmed plates. Drizzle with the warm browned butter, sprinkle with chopped mint, and garnish to taste with mint leaves.

Browned butter, drizzled over the quail pilaf just before serving, adds the final touch to this dish, which is intriguingly seasoned with allspice and cinnamon. To make the butter, melt the given amount, letting it brown slowly.

Lamb pilaf
Two very popular foods combine to make a favorite dish

Throughout Eastern Europe and the Near East, lamb dishes are frequently accompanied by rice. These two ingredients are combined particularly successfully in lamb pilaf. Two versions of this traditional dish are presented here: In the first recipe, the rice is cooked in the stock with the meat; in the second, the rice is cooked separately in plenty of lamb stock, and is then mixed in with the juicy braised lamb.

LAMB PILAF

Serves 4
7 oz tomatoes, 1 lb boneless lamb shoulder
3 tablespoons butter
1¼ cups finely chopped onion
1¼ cups long-grain rice
salt, freshly ground pepper
1 tablespoon chopped dill

Blanch, skin, and seed the tomatoes, and finely dice the flesh. Cut the lamb into ¾-inch cubes. Melt the butter in a pot and sear the meat on all sides. Reduce the heat slightly, add the onions, and fry briefly. Stir in the diced tomato and cook for a further 5–10 minutes. Pour in 2¼ cups water, bring to a boil, and reduce the heat. Add the rice in a thin, steady stream, season with salt and pepper, and simmer the pilaf until all the liquid has been absorbed. Take the pot off the heat, place two layers of paper towels or a dish towel between the pot and lid, and allow to steam dry for 5–10 minutes. Mix the pilaf well, spoon it onto a platter, sprinkle with chopped dill, and serve.

LAMB PILAF WITH PUMPKIN

Serves 4
1 lb tomatoes, 1 lb pumpkin
1¾ lb boneless lamb shoulder
4 tablespoons olive oil
1¼ cups finely chopped onion
2 garlic cloves, finely chopped
2 tablespoons butter, 1¾ cups long-grain rice
½ cup white wine
2¾ cups hot lamb stock
½ teaspoon ground saffron
2 tablespoons chopped herbs (rosemary and parsley)
salt, freshly ground pepper,

Blanch, skin, and seed the tomatoes, then cut the flesh into ½-inch dice. Peel the pumpkin, scoop out the seeds and the fibrous core, and cut the flesh into ½-inch cubes. Cut the lamb into ¾-inch cubes and season with salt and pepper. Heat the oil in a large frying pan and sear the lamb on all sides. Reduce the heat, add the onions and garlic, and fry briefly. Stir in the tomatoes, cover, and simmer for 30–35 minutes.

Meanwhile, melt the butter in a separate pot and sweat the rice in it until translucent; pour in the wine and the stock. Stir in the saffron, season with salt and pepper, and bring to a boil. Reduce the heat and cook the rice for 18–20 minutes, until done. About 10 minutes before the meat is done cooking, stir in the pumpkin. Mix the meat with the cooked rice, adjust the seasoning, stir in the herbs, and serve.

Venison and rabbit
With short-grain rice and wild rice

BLACK BEAN PILAF WITH RABBIT

Serves 4
½ cup black (turtle) beans, 14-oz saddle of rabbit
2 rabbit legs (8 oz each), 2 tablespoons oil
3 garlic cloves, unpeeled and lightly crushed
⅓ cup diced carrots, ½ cup diced onion
⅓ cup diced leek, ¼ cup diced celery
⅓ cup diced tomatoes, 1 tablespoon tomato paste
· 2 bay leaves, ⅔ cup chicken stock, ½ cup water
salt and freshly ground pepper
For the pilaf:
1 tablespoon oil, 4½ teaspoons butter
¼ cup finely chopped shallot, ¾ cup short-grain rice
1 cup red wine, 1 red chile pepper, 1 bay leaf
1 rosemary sprig, 1¾ cup hot chicken stock, salt
You will also need:
2 large shrimp (about 4 oz each), 5 tablespoons oil
1 bay leaf, 5 oz Jerusalem artichokes, 5 oz chorizo
salt and freshly ground pepper

Soak the beans overnight, then drain. Boil in lightly salted water for 10 minutes, then simmer, covered, over a low heat for 40 minutes; drain and reserve.

Preheat the oven to 350°F. Cut the saddle of rabbit into 4 pieces, tying the belly skin flaps to the back. Season the legs and saddle. Heat the oil in a casserole and brown the garlic and the rabbit pieces on all sides. Brown the vegetables with the other ingredients. Stir in the tomato paste, add the bay leaves, and place in the oven for 30 minutes, adding the water gradually.

Meanwhile, make the pilaf. Heat the oil and butter in a pot. Sweat the shallots, then add the rice and continue to sauté. Add the wine. Stir in the chile pepper, bay leaf, rosemary, and beans. Pour in the stock and cook for 15–20 minutes. Season with salt.

Halve the shrimp lengthwise through the shell, devein, and season lightly. Heat 2 tablespoons of the oil in a frying pan, add the bay leaf and the shrimp, fry for 2 minutes, then set aside. Peel and dice the Jerusalem artichokes. Heat the remaining oil and fry the artichokes until crisp. Drain well and mix into the pilaf. Remove the meat from the casserole and keep warm. Add the stock, reduce the liquid by a third, scraping the bottom to loosen the sediment, and season. Slice the chorizo into rounds and heat with the shrimp. See caption, left, for serving instructions.

Halve the rabbit legs. Mix the sausage and shrimp into the pilaf, place on warmed plates, garnish each portion with a piece of saddle and a halved leg, and drizzle with a little of the unstrained roasting juices.

WILD RICE PILAF WITH VENISON

This recipe must be started a day in advance.

Serves 4

3 lb boneless venison shoulder, 1 lb neck of venison
4 bay leaves, 2 garlic cloves, lightly crushed
1 cup chopped shallot, ¾ cup diced carrot
¾ cup diced celery root, 1 teaspoon juniper berries,
1 teaspoon allspice berries, 5 cloves
4½ cups strong red wine (Merlot), 4 tablespoons oil
2 tablespoons tomato paste
2 tablespoons cranberry sauce, 5 thyme sprigs
salt, freshly ground pepper

For the pilaf:

4 oz smoked bacon, 4 tablespoons oil
¾ cup diced carrots, ½ cup diced celery root
¾ cup diced onion, ½ cup diced celery
4 teaspoons tomato paste, 3 thyme sprigs
6½ cups water, 3–4 bay leaves
⅓ cup sultanas, 3 tablespoons grappa, 1 apple
¼ cup fresh cranberries, 1 cup wild rice

You will also need:

5 oz chanterelles, 5 oz cèpes, 2 tablespoons butter
salt, freshly ground pepper, dash lemon juice
1 tablespoon parsley leaves, stripped from their stalks

Trim the venison shoulder and cut into ½-inch cubes. Chop the neck into 2-inch cubes and place in a bowl with the trimmings. Place the shoulder, bay leaves, garlic, vegetables, and spices on top, add the wine, cover, and refrigerate overnight. Remove the meat, place in a covered container, and refrigerate again. Strain the contents of the bowl and reserve the trimmings and the marinade separately.

Preheat the oven to 350°F. Heat some oil in a deep pan and fry the trimmings, neck, and vegetables. Stir in the tomato paste and fry until dry. Place in the oven, and add the marinade gradually, reducing after each addition. Add the cranberry sauce, thyme, and water, and braise for 2 hours. Strain this stock and season.

To make the pilaf, dice the bacon. Heat the oil in a frying pan, render the bacon, and then fry the venison. Add the vegetables, sweat them briefly, and stir in the tomato paste. Add the thyme, bay leaf, and 2¾ cups of the stock, reduce the heat, and braise for 1½ hours. Meanwhile, plump the sultanas in the grappa for 10 minutes. Peel the apple, chop into ½-inch cubes, and add to the pot with the sultanas and cranberries. Pour in 2 cups stock and sprinkle in the wild rice. Cover the pan with foil, simmer for 20–25 minutes, and adjust the seasoning. Proceed as stated in the caption, right.

Trim the mushrooms; quarter or halve, depending on size, and sauté in melted butter for 2–3 minutes. Season to taste with salt, pepper, and lemon juice, and sprinkle in the parsley. Mix the mushrooms into the pilaf and serve on warmed plates.

Mushroom rice with lamb cutlets and vegetables

With two different sauces: one with the flavor of kaffir lime leaves, the other with cilantro and butter

Serves 4	1 cup red wine, salt, freshly ground pepper
For the lamb cutlets:	**For the cilantro-butter sauce:**
3 lb saddle of lamb	2 shallots, 1 cup white wine
3-inch piece of galangal, ¼ teaspoon curry powder	2 tablespoons chopped cilantro
salt, freshly ground pepper, 4 tablespoons vegetable oil	½ cup ice-cold butter, cubed
For the herb-mushroom rice:	salt, freshly ground pepper
7 oz shiitake mushrooms, 2 red chile peppers	**For the vegetables:**
3 tablespoons butter, 1½ cups Thai fragrant rice	1 large carrot, 5 oz choy sum, 1¾ cups soybean sprouts
about 4½ cups hot chicken stock	3 tablespoons peanut oil, salt, freshly ground pepper
salt, freshly ground pepper	
¼ cup pine kernels, 3 tablespoons chopped garlic chives	First, prepare all the ingredients. Trim the lamb and
For the kaffir lime sauce:	shave the rib bones clean with a knife. Peel the
3–4 shallots, 3 kaffir lime leaves, 1¾ cups lamb stock	galangal. Remove the tough stalks from the shiitake

mushrooms and dice the caps. Halve the chile peppers, remove the stem and seeds, and finely chop the flesh. Peel and cut the shallots for the sauces into thin rounds. Peel and cut the carrot into julienne. Wash the choy sum, drain, and cut into pieces 1½ inches long. Wash the bean sprouts and drain. Crush the galangal to a paste with the curry powder, salt, and pepper, and use it to season the lamb.

Preheat the oven to 400°F. Heat the oil in a large flameproof casserole and sear the meat on all sides. Cover and cook in the oven for 15–20 minutes.

Meanwhile, make the mushroom rice. Melt the butter in a saucepan, and sauté the chopped mushrooms. Add the rice and sweat until translucent. Add the chicken stock, stir in the diced chile, season with salt and pepper, bring to a boil, and then cook, covered, over a low heat for about 15 minutes, until done. Fold in the pine kernels and garlic chives.

To make the lime sauce, place the kaffir lime leaves, shallots, stock, and red wine in a saucepan, bring to a boil and reduce by about three-quarters over moderate heat. Season, strain and keep warm.

To make the cilantro-butter sauce, place the white wine, shallots, and cilantro in a separate saucepan, bring to a boil, then reduce slightly. Strain this sauce, then whisk in the chilled butter cubes and season. To prepare the vegetables, heat the oil in a wok, stir-fry the carrot strips briefly, then add the choy sum and stir-fry for 1–2 minutes. Add the soy sprouts, toss very briefly, then season. When the lamb is done, carve it into 8 double cutlets, as shown in the photo below. Serve the rice on warmed plates with 2 double lamb cutlets per portion, the vegetables, and the sauces.

As they shop at the market, Tony Khoo and Eckart Witzigmann carefully check the produce on offer for freshness and quality.

This dish is characterized by contrasting flavors that harmonize well with each other. It does, however, place a few demands on the cook, since the rice, the vegetables, and the two sauces should not stand around for too long. We therefore recommend that you have all your ingredients assembled and properly prepared before you begin cooking.

Risottos

While some people look on risotto as one of the great culinary achievements of Italy, if not the apex of the much-lauded cuisine of that country, others wonder why so much fuss is made about a plateful of rice with a bit of Parmesan cheese sprinkled on top.

However, any skeptics who ever tasted an authentic, thick and creamy stirred risotto — perhaps with shellfish, radicchio, cèpes, or even truffles — can hardly fail to revise their opinion, switching from the camp of the doubters to that of the enthusiasts. And there, without any fear of exhausting this topic of conversation, they can indulge in practically endless discussions on how to make the ultimate risotto, which variety of rice is the definitive one for which variation, and which is the best wine to serve with it.

Back in 1949, a Radio Turin announcer described the life of the seasonal workers in the rice fields as it was portrayed in Giuseppe di Santis' film *Riso*

amaro (*Bitter Rice*): "The work is arduous and very tough. In water up to their ankles, backs bent, the sun beating down overhead…" Things have changed since those days and, thanks to the use of modern machines, the work is no longer as punishing as it was then. What has remained, and spread around the world, is the Italians' love of rice, and especially of risotto.

Risotto
Rice and cheese belong together in Italy's most famous rice dish

How to cook risotto properly is a question with far-reaching implications in Italy. Each person has his or her own opinion on the matter. Some like it moister, others drier. Some insist on the rice grains being soft, others like them still distinctly *al dente*. Opinions are also widely divided on the question of how vigorously a risotto should be stirred. Nevertheless, there are a few rules that must be followed to ensure success. Most of these are explained in the basic recipe, but first there is the choice of the rice itself.

In good risotto rice part of the starch in the grain, the amylose, dissolves during cooking while the center of the grain remains firm to the bite. From the repeated addition of small quantities of liquid, part of which is absorbed by the rice and part of which evaporates, and from the constant stirring, the rice starch becomes a thickening agent that holds together the individual grains as well as the other ingredients, and makes the risotto so creamy. The best rice for risotto comes from northern Italy. Especially popular are the arborio, baldo, vialone nano, and carnaroli varieties. The large-grained carnaroli, created in 1945 from crossing vialone with a Japanese variety, is not as widely grown and so is generally somewhat more expensive than other varieties. It has a particularly high amylose content, coupled with a low stickiness of the grains. Vialone nano is very similar. Arborio is somewhat stickier, and baldo is very sticky. Just what variety is really the best is a matter of individual taste.

BASIC RECIPE

Risotto rice is not washed before cooking so that the starch is not released prematurely from the grains.

Serves 4

4½–5½ cups meat stock, ¼ cup butter	
½ cup finely diced onion	
2 cups arborio rice, ⅔ cup white wine, salt	
freshly grated hard cheese to taste	

Slowly heat the stock in a casserole and proceed as shown in the photo sequence below.

The classic method:

Melt 4½ teaspoons of the butter in a pot and sweat the onion without allowing it to color, stirring occasionally.

Tip in the rice, stir immediately, and cook over a moderate heat. Do not let the rice stick to the bottom of the pot.

Cook the rice until translucent, stirring constantly, without letting the onions or the rice take on any color.

Add the wine. Continue stirring over a moderate heat until the rice has absorbed most of the liquid.

Pour in a little meat stock, stirring constantly. Add more stock only when the liquid has been mostly absorbed.

Cook the risotto for 12–15 minutes, until done. Season with salt and stir in the remaining butter and the grated cheese.

The quantity of liquid added is variable: some risottos need more, others less. If the stock is used up and the risotto threatens to become too dry, simply add water. The stock or bouillon should be relatively mild and not too salty, as it becomes more concentrated through evaporation. Here, too, it is a matter of finding out for yourself what the "right" flavor and consistency are. Even in Italy there are different rules for preparation. The classic method comes from Lombardy, where the risotto is stirred in an uncovered pot until all the liquid has been absorbed. In the Piedmontese method, after the initial sautéing of the rice, the pot is covered and the rice is left to absorb the liquid without any further stirring. In both cases the risotto stays relatively compact. In the Veneto, by contrast, people like it looser — *all' onda* or "wavy" — and prefer the vialone nano rice variety. The risotto turns out more liquid because the rice is kept moist while it is cooking by the addition of more liquid at various times. This method is especially suitable for variations with tender vegetables or delicate seafood. Sometimes, though not often, olive oil is used instead of butter. Almost anything can then accompany the rice, even fruit in exceptional cases.

The cheese is also very important, since it alone lends many risottos the proper spice. Hard cheeses such as Parmigiano-Reggiano, Grana Padano, or even sheep's milk Pecorino are well suited. Sometimes, though, a slice of Gorgonzola can provide the necessary flavor contrast. Since hard cheese very quickly loses flavor if stored grated, it should always be freshly grated or shaved as needed. Always stir it into the risotto 1–2 minutes before the end of cooking time, so that the melted cheese can completely envelop the rice grains.

Row upon row of heavy Parmesan cheese wheels are stacked to the ceiling in this cellar. The cheeses need to ripen for two to four years in order to develop their full flavor and slightly crystalline texture. The choice of cheese grater is important; the Parmesan cheese mixed into the rice should be neither too floury nor too coarse.

Freshly ground white pepper provides the necessary pungency. With a few twists of the pepper mill, Gabriele Ferron, a famous risotto chef and rice-mill owner from Venetia, puts the finishing touches on this *risotto alla milanese*.

Risotto alla milanese
Beef marrow and saffron are essential for this specialty from Lombardy

Prepared according to the classic Lombardian risotto method, the rice is first sautéed in a *soffritto* of beef marrow, butter, onions, and garlic before the liquid is added. The veal fillet of this recipe is not the classical accompaniment to Risotto alla Milanese, but the thin slices of meat, fried only briefly, go superbly with it. To

prevent the meat from drying out, pan-fry it only when the risotto, stirred to a still-moist doneness, is resting.

Serves 4
For the risotto:
1–2 tablespoons beef marrow
5 tablespoons butter
½ cup finely diced onion
½ garlic clove, finely diced
2 cups arborio rice, ⅔ cup white wine
about ¼ teaspoon saffron threads, salt
4½–6½ cups meat stock
freshly ground white pepper
⅔ cup freshly grated Parmesan cheese
For the veal:
1 lb boneless veal
¼ cup finely chopped shallot
½ garlic clove, finely chopped
2 tablespoons vegetable oil
1 cup marsala, ½ cup veal stock
salt, freshly ground black pepper
You will also need:
curls of butter for the top
¼ cup freshly grated Parmesan cheese
1 teaspoon chopped herbs (rosemary, oregano)

First, prepare the meat. Trim the veal and cut into ¼-inch-thick slices, pound to flatten slightly, and refrigerate. Next, prepare the risotto. Extract the beef marrow from the bones and soak for 10 minutes, then dice finely. Render the marrow with 2 tablespoons of the butter in a sufficiently large pot. Add the diced onions and garlic, and sweat until lightly colored. Tip in the rice and stir until translucent. Add the white wine and allow to reduce slightly. Stir in the saffron threads and salt. Heat the stock and add it a little at a time, cooking the risotto and stirring constantly for 12–15 minutes, until done. Season to taste with salt and pepper, and stir in the grated Parmesan cheese and the remaining butter. Take the risotto off the heat and allow the flavors to blend for a few minutes.

Meanwhile, salt and pepper the slices of veal. Heat the oil in a frying pan and fry the veal briefly on both sides. Remove the meat and set aside. Sweat the shallots and garlic in the remaining oil until lightly colored. Deglaze with marsala and veal stock, and reduce the liquid over a high heat until only about ½ cup of sauce remains. Return the veal to the pan, simmer briefly, and season to taste. Spoon the risotto onto warmed plates; top with curls of butter, and sprinkle with a little grated Parmesan cheese. Drizzle the veal with a little sauce, sprinkle with the chopped herbs, and serve with the risotto.

Probably the most famous of its kind: saffron yellow, and enriched with marrow, butter, and Parmesan cheese, *risotto alla milanese* is a substantial first course as well as an esteemed accompaniment, served, for example, alongside thin slices of pan-fried veal, or, classically, with osso buco.

The quality of Florence fennel can easily be assessed by the state of its fronds: If they are feathery and light, not wilted or dried up where the bulb has been cut, you know you have found a sound specimen.

Fennel risotto
A slice of Gorgonzola complements this dish perfectly

The great blue cheese from northern Italy, of which a number of varieties exist, is the perfect foil for the intense aniseed flavor of the fennel. Gorgonzola comes chiefly from the eastern provinces of Piedmont, or from Lombardy. It is named after the eponymous town northeast of Milan, where the cattle herds grazing in the mountains used to pass the winter, and where a

cheese industry of considerable size developed over the course of time. From the fine range of blue cheeses available, the relatively mild Gorgonzola *dolce* recommends itself for this particular risotto, since a spicier Gorgonzola *piccante* would overpower the taste of the fennel. People who love this vegetable's aniseed flavor should make a point of trying it sometime with wild fennel, if they can find it. It is recognizable by its much smaller, elongate bulbs, which have an even stronger flavor than Florence fennel. A dry white wine from the Piedmont, for example a Gavi di Gavi or a Cortese di Gavi, is the appropriate drink with this delicate dish.

until translucent. Tip in the rice and stir until it too is translucent. Season sparingly with salt and pepper. Add the wine and cook until the liquid is reduced by half. Pour in enough stock to just cover the rice. Simmer, uncovered, for about 15–20 minutes. While the rice is cooking keep topping up with enough stock to keep it barely covered, and stir frequently. Cut the Gorgonzola into 4 slices. Season the fennel risotto to taste with salt and pepper and spoon onto heated plates, topping each immediately with 1 slice of Gorgonzola. The cheese should melt onto the hot rice. Sprinkle the risotto with some chopped fennel fronds and serve.

Serves 4
1 lb fennel bulbs with fronds
6 tablespoons butter, ⅓ cup finely chopped shallot
2 cups avorio rice
salt, freshly ground white pepper
⅔ cup dry white wine, 3½–4½ cups hot vegetable stock
You will also need:
4 oz Gorgonzola
1 tablespoon freshly chopped fennel fronds

Wash and dry the fennel bulbs. Cut off the root end and the green stalks. If necessary, remove the tough outer ribs. Quarter the bulbs lengthwise and slice the quarters diagonally into thin strips. Melt the butter in a large pot and sweat the fennel strips and shallots

Pumpkin and dandelion
Less familiar as risotto ingredients, but nonetheless exquisite

An undemanding crop, pumpkins and squashes flourish worldwide in countless varieties, in a huge range of colors, shapes, and sizes. The species belonging to the genus *Cucurbita* range in color from light yellow through a rich dark green to a reddish orange. Of culinary importance are the widespread robust summer squash *Cucurbita pepo* and the warmth-loving giant pumpkin *Cucurbita maxima*, as well as the smaller winter squash *Cucurbita moschata*. Belonging to the latter species is the Hokkaido pumpkin used here, whose glowing yellow flesh adds optical highlights to the rice. Also used to color the risotto yellow are the petals of the dandelion, a flower once known as the saffron of the poor. *Risotto ai fiori di tarassaco* (risotto with dandelion flowers) is a popular specialty in the Piedmont region. When picking the dandelion flowers, choose plants that do not grow too close to busy roads or on heavily manured meadows.

RISOTTO WITH DANDELION FLOWERS

Serves 4
⅓ leek, 2 tablespoons olive oil
¼ cup finely chopped onion
½ garlic clove, finely chopped
1 bay leaf, 1 small sprig rosemary
1¼ cups arborio rice, 2¾ cups hot veal stock
1 tablespoon dandelion petals stripped from stalks
salt, freshly ground white pepper
You will also need:
⅓ cup freshly shaved Parmesan cheese (optional)

Trim and wash the leek, and dice very finely. Heat the olive oil in a pot and sweat the onion, garlic, and leek

Multicolored squash glow vividly against a background of green vegetables on this market stand, making it hard to choose. The small, orange-colored Hokkaido pumpkin is a good choice for a pumpkin risotto because of its dark yellow, especially tasty flesh.

without allowing them to color. Add the bay leaf and rosemary sprig, tip in the rice, and sauté, stirring, until the grains are translucent. Add ½ cup of the veal stock and allow to reduce, stirring. Mix in the dandelion petals. Add the remaining hot stock a little at a time, simmering for a further 15–20 minutes, and stirring occasionally. Keep topping up with just enough stock to barely cover the rice. Take the pot off the heat, season the risotto with salt and pepper, and mix well. Allow to rest briefly so that the flavors can blend, then spoon the dandelion risotto into heated shallow bowls. Sprinkle with shaved Parmesan cheese if wished, and serve (see photo on page 83).

PUMPKIN RISOTTO

Serves 4
1 lb Hokkaido pumpkin
2 tablespoons olive oil, 1 cup finely chopped onion
6 tablespoons butter
2¼ cups arborio rice
salt, freshly ground white pepper
4½–5½ cups hot veal stock
½ cup freshly grated Parmesan cheese
You will also need:
¼ cup freshly shaved Parmesan cheese
1 tablespoon chopped flat-leaf parsley

Cut the Hokkaido pumpkin (or the same size of a different variety) into sections; scoop out the seeds and the fibrous center with a spoon, peel the pumpkin, and cut the flesh into ¼-inch cubes. Heat the olive oil in a pot with 4 tablespoons (¼ cup) of the butter. Add the diced onion and sweat until translucent. Add the cubed pumpkin and sweat over a moderate heat, stirring, for 5 minutes. Tip in the rice and stir until the grains are translucent. Season sparingly with salt and pepper, and moisten with a little veal stock. Simmer uncovered for 15–20 minutes, stirring frequently and adding just enough hot stock to barely cover the rice. Stir in the remaining butter and the grated Parmesan cheese, mix well, and season to taste. Spoon the risotto onto warmed plates, sprinkle with shaved Parmesan cheese, garnish with parsley, and serve.

Parmesan cheese lends just the right spiciness to the pumpkin risotto, which is actually rather mild. On no account should this hard cheese — ideally, a ripened Parmigiano-Reggiano or a Grana Padano — be bought already grated, or it will dry out too quickly and lose much of its taste. For optimum flavor, grate it or shave it just before use.

With tomatoes and zucchini

Summery light risottos that use only young zucchini and really ripe tomatoes

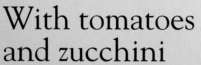

RISOTTO CON ZUCCHINE FIORITE

Serves 4

5 oz zucchini, 10 zucchini flowers

6 tablespoons butter, ¾ cup finely chopped onion

2 cups arborio rice, ⅔ cup white wine

4½–5½ cups hot vegetable stock, salt

⅓ cup freshly grated Parmesan cheese

You will also need:

¼ cup freshly grated Parmesan cheese for sprinkling over the top

Top and tail the zucchini, then cut into sticks about 1 inch long and ⅓ inch wide. Remove the stalk and pistil from the flowers and cut the petals into small pieces. Melt 4 tablespoons (¼ cup) of the butter in a pot and sweat the onions without allowing them to color. Add the rice and sauté, stirring, until translucent. Pour in the wine, reduce, and cook for 12–15 minutes, stirring constantly and adding the vegetable stock gradually. The rice should remain barely covered with liquid. About 8 minutes before the end of cooking time, mix in the zucchini. Add the flowers in the last minute and simmer with the other ingredients. Season with salt and stir in the remaining butter and the cheese. Spoon the risotto onto heated plates and serve sprinkled with Parmesan cheese.

TOMATO RISOTTO

Serves 4
1¾ lb ripe, aromatic tomatoes, 3 tablespoons olive oil
1¼ cups finely chopped onion
2 garlic cloves, finely chopped
6 tablespoons butter, 1½ cups arborio rice
⅔ cup white wine, 3 cups hot veal stock
⅔ cup freshly grated Parmesan cheese
salt, freshly ground white pepper

You will also need:

¼ cup freshly grated Parmesan cheese for the top
1 tablespoon chopped herbs (parsley, basil)

Coarsely dice the tomatoes. Heat the oil in a pot and sweat half the diced onion and half the garlic until they color slightly. Add the tomatoes. Season with salt and pepper, cover, and simmer for about 15 minutes. Push the tomatoes through a strainer, scrape off the purée clinging to the strainer and use it too. Stir and season to taste. Melt half the butter in a large pot and sweat the remaining onion and garlic until the onion is translucent. Tip in the rice and stir until it too is translucent. Season sparingly. Add the wine and cook until the liquid is reduced by half. Pour in the stock a little at a time, stirring constantly. The rice should remain barely covered with liquid. Cook the risotto for 15–20 minutes until done, continuing to stir. Five minutes before the end of cooking time, stir in the tomato purée. Add a little more hot stock if necessary. The tomato risotto should have a relatively liquid consistency. Season to taste, and stir in the grated Parmesan cheese and the remaining butter. Spoon the risotto onto warmed plates, sprinkle with grated Parmesan cheese and the chopped herbs, and serve.

Green asparagus grows on flat beds in full sunlight. Only the lower third of the stalk needs to be peeled. The thin, somewhat more astringent wild asparagus, which is only washed and not peeled at all, is also highly esteemed.

With asparagus and saffron
Rice and asparagus: a delightful combination. Saffron and crayfish lend sophistication.

RISOTTO CON ASPARAGI

Serves 4
14 oz green asparagus
3 tablespoons butter
½ cup finely chopped shallot
1½ cups arborio rice
1 cup dry white wine, 2¼ cups veal stock
salt, freshly ground pepper
⅔ cup freshly grated Parmesan cheese
¼ cup butter, in curls
You will also need:
freshly grated Parmesan cheese for the top (optional)

Cut off the ends of the asparagus, taking off more rather than less. Peel only the lower third of the stalks and cut the stalks into pieces 1–1½ inches long. Cook the asparagus in lightly salted, vigorously boiling water for 10–12 minutes, then lift out and drain well. Reserve 2¾ cups of the cooking water. Melt the butter in a pot, add the diced shallot, and sweat until translucent. Tip in the rice and stir until it too is translucent. Add the white wine and reduce. Meanwhile, mix and heat the veal stock and the asparagus cooking-water. Simmer the rice for 12–15 minutes, stirring frequently and adding the stock mixture gradually to keep the rice barely covered with liquid. Carefully mix in the asparagus and simmer over a low heat for a further 5 minutes, until the rice is done but the center of the grains are still firm to the bite. Depending on the desired consistency — some people prefer the risotto more liquid, others, drier — moisten with a little more liquid (asparagus stock or water) and season with salt and pepper. Gently stir in the Parmesan cheese and the curls of butter. Spoon the risotto onto warmed plates, sprinkle with grated Parmesan cheese if desired, and serve.

RISOTTO WITH SAFFRON

Risotto allo zafferano (see also photo on page 83) is served in Italy either as a *primo piatto* (first course) or an accompaniment — classically, for example, with *osso buco alla milanese*.

Serves 4
2 beef marrow bones
¼ teaspoon saffron threads, about 3½ cups beef stock

¼ cup butter
¼ cup finely chopped onion
½ garlic clove, finely chopped
1½ cups vialone nano rice
½ cup white wine
⅔ cup freshly grated Parmesan cheese, salt

Remove the marrow from the bones, soak well, and cut into small cubes. Steep the saffron threads in a little stock. Melt 4½ teaspoons of the butter in a frying pan and render the cubed beef marrow. Add the onion and garlic, and sweat until lightly colored. Tip in the rice and sauté, stirring, until the grains are translucent. Pour in the wine and reduce slightly. Stir in the salt and the steeped saffron threads. Heat the stock and add it a little at a time, stirring frequently, and keep the rice barely covered with liquid . The risotto will be done after 12–15 minutes. Mix in the grated Parmesan cheese and the remaining butter, allow to rest briefly so that the flavors can blend, then serve the saffron risotto on warmed plates.

SAFFRON RISOTTO WITH ASPARAGUS AND CRAYFISH

Called crayfish or crawfish depending on where you live, these freshwater shellfish look like miniature lobsters and add an elegant touch to risotto.

Serves 4

6 tablespoons butter, ½ cup finely chopped onion
1¼ cups arborio rice
½ teaspoon saffron threads, ½ cup white wine
3½–4½ cups hot vegetable stock
5–6 oz green asparagus tips (about 2 inches long)
16 shelled crayfish tails
salt, freshly ground pepper

Melt 4 tablespoons (¼ cup) of the butter in a casserole and sweat the diced onion without allowing it to color. Tip in the rice, and sauté, stirring constantly, until the grains are translucent, without letting either the rice or the onion color. Mix in the saffron threads, pour in the white wine, and allow to reduce while continuing to stir. Add a little vegetable stock and simmer for 12–15 minutes, stirring frequently and adding the remaining stock a little at a time to keep the rice barely covered with the liquid. Season with salt and pepper. Meanwhile, melt the rest of the butter in a pot, sauté the asparagus tips for 6–8 minutes, then carefully remove them with a slotted spoon and stir them into the rice. Sauté the shelled crayfish tails in the butter remaining in the pot for 2–3 minutes, then season with salt and pepper. Spoon the risotto onto warmed plates, top with the crayfish tails, and serve.

The spinach risotto is lent a certain piquancy by the Gorgonzola, which melts onto the hot rice and is stirred in only just before serving. The risotto should still be absorbing some stock while the cheese is melting; that is, it should be too liquid rather than too dry.

Risottos with leafy vegetables
Spinach-green or radicchio-red, and seasoned with cheese

Fresh baby spinach and radicchio di Trevisiano are the ingredients for these risotto specialties. Radicchio di Trevisiano, which is distinguished from other varieties by its stronger, more bitter flavor, does not form a round head, but rather an open leaf rosette with long, narrow, dark- to wine-red leaves with a characteristic white midrib. Of course, another variety can be used instead, for example the small-headed, red radicchio di Chioggia — the one most commonly available outside of Italy — or radicchio di Treviso, which is very similar in shape to the Trevisiano, but more compact.

RISOTTO WITH SPINACH
Serves 4

14 oz spinach, 3 tablespoons olive oil
⅓ cup finely chopped onion
2 garlic cloves, finely chopped
2 cups vialone nano semifino rice
4½ cups hot vegetable stock
¼ cup freshly grated Parmesan cheese
7 oz Gorgonzola piccante cheese
salt, freshly ground pepper

Trim and wash the spinach, then blanch in boiling salted water. Lift out with a slotted spoon, drain, squeeze thoroughly, and chop finely. Heat the oil in a pot and sweat the onion and garlic until the onion is translucent. Tip in the rice and sauté, stirring, until translucent. Stir in the chopped spinach and sauté briefly with the other ingredients. Pour in the stock a little at a time and simmer the risotto for 15–20 minutes, stirring repeatedly. Season with salt and pepper, stir in the Parmesan cheese, and remove the risotto from the heat. Slice the Gorgonzola and arrange on the top of the rice, cover the pot, and allow

the cheese to melt. Remove the lid, stir in the melted cheese, and serve at once.

RISOTTO AL RADICCHIO

Cooks and chefs in the Veneto depart slightly from the "classic" risotto method when preparing risotto with radicchio. Here, the rice grains are not sautéed in hot oil with the onions and radicchio, but are added to the pot after the wine. One variation would be to stir the risotto as usual, then slice the radicchio into strips and sauté it separately in hot olive oil, mixing it in only when the risotto is done. Either way, the result is exquisite, and the preferred cooking method is purely a matter of personal taste.

Serves 4

14 oz radicchio di Trevisiano, 2 tablespoons olive oil
¾ cup finely chopped onion
1 garlic clove, finely chopped
¼ cup butter, ⅔ cup red wine
1½ cups arborio rice, 3½ cups veal stock
a pinch of sugar, ¼ cup freshly grated Parmesan cheese
salt, freshly ground white pepper

You will also need:

¼ cup freshly grated Parmesan cheese
2 tablespoons coarsely snipped chives

Trim and wash the radicchio. Slice it diagonally into thin strips and reserve. Heat the olive oil and 2 tablespoons of the butter in a pot and sweat the onion and garlic without allowing them to color. Add the sliced radicchio and sauté for 2 minutes. Moisten with the wine and reduce the liquid, stirring. Tip in the rice and simmer briefly, stirring repeatedly. Heat the veal stock in a separate pot. Pour a little boiling stock into the rice and simmer the rice, uncovered, for a further 15 minutes or so, stirring constantly. Keep adding just enough stock to keep the rice barely covered with liquid. Season the risotto with salt, pepper, and sugar, and stir in the grated Parmesan cheese and the remaining butter. Remove from the heat and spoon the risotto onto warmed plates. Sprinkle with Parmesan cheese and chives, and serve.

Risotto with brown rice
Brown rice is especially high in vitamins

It is chiefly in whole-food cuisine that brown (that is, unmilled) rice plays an important role. Nutritionally , whole-grain rice is very valuable, as the bran layer still adhering to the grain, which is removed in processing to make white rice, contains large amounts of vitamins, minerals, and fiber. The oil-containing germ is also present in the grain, and because it turns rancid after a while, brown rice has a shorter shelf life than white rice. When short-grained brown rice is used for risotto, it needs to cook for longer than milled rice — about 40–50 minutes in all — and also needs more liquid because the bran forms a sort of shield against heat and moisture.

Other sorts of brown rice and other varieties of rice are less well suited to this preparation method, as they do not have the typical risotto characteristics. Thus, for example, red rice from the Camargue and Canadian wild rice must be soaked overnight or they will not cook through at all. Even then, they have a much longer cooking time than long-grain brown rice;

you should allow at least 2 hours. This means that a great deal of liquid — especially veal or vegetable stock — must be used, and that, despite vigorous stirring, the grains will not produce that creamy thickening typical of the Italian short-grain varieties, and characteristic of a risotto.

The nutty taste of short-grain brown rice harmonizes perfectly with the flavors of all sorts of vegetables, so it is particularly well suited to vegetarian risottos. The best example of this is the savoy cabbage risotto given below.

SAVOY CABBAGE RISOTTO

Smoked bacon and spicy *salsiccia*, or, failing this, a coarse salami, go very well with savoy cabbage, which should be as young and delicate as possible.

Serves 4

10 oz savoy cabbage,
1 oz raw smoked bacon
4½ tablespoons butter
½ cup finely chopped onion
1 garlic clove, finely chopped
2 cups short-grain brown rice
½ cup white wine
about 7 cups hot veal stock, salt, freshly ground pepper
5 oz salsiccia, ¼ cup freshly grated Parmesan cheese

Quarter the savoy cabbage and cut out the hard core. Remove the dark-green outer leaves, slicing just the light leaves into thin strips. Cut the bacon into small dice. Melt half of the butter in a casserole and sweat the onion, garlic, and bacon until the onion is translucent. Tip in the brown rice and stir until the grains are glazed. Moisten with the white wine and allow to reduce until most of the liquid is gone. Ladle in a little hot veal stock — the rice should always be barely covered with liquid — and season with salt and pepper. Reduce the heat and simmer the rice for 30–40 minutes, stirring occasionally, and adding the remaining stock a little at a time. Mix in the cabbage and cook for a further 20 minutes. Meanwhile, skin the *salsiccia* and cut into rounds. At the end of cooking time, stir the sausage into the rice until heated through, season to taste, and sprinkle with the grated Parmesan cheese. Dot the hot risotto with the remaining butter and serve at once.

VEGETABLE RISOTTO

A tasty, purely vegetarian affair: A variety of vegetables are mixed in with the rice, which is cooked in a light vegetable stock.

Serves 4
6 tablespoons butter, ½ cup finely chopped onion
2 cups short-grain brown rice
about 7 cups hot vegetable stock
freshly grated nutmeg
¾ cup diced carrots, 1 cup chopped leek
2 stalks celery, finely chopped
salt, freshly ground pepper
You will also need:
½ cup freshly shaved Parmesan cheese
1 tablespoon chopped flat-leaf parsley

Melt half of the butter in a casserole and sweat the onion until translucent. Add the rice and sauté, stirring, until it is glazed. Moisten with a little vegetable stock and allow to reduce. Reduce the heat and cook the rice for 30–40 minutes, stirring occasionally and adding the remaining stock a little at a time so that the rice remains just covered with liquid. Season with salt, pepper, and nutmeg. Meanwhile, melt the remaining butter in a frying pan. Add the carrot, leek, and celery, and sweat briefly. Remove from the heat and set aside. At the end of the cooking time for the rice, stir in the vegetables and cook together for a further 20 minutes. Remove the risotto from the heat, adjust the seasoning, sprinkle with shaved Parmesan cheese and chopped parsley, and serve.

In France pigs as well as dogs search for the valuable black truffles that grow in the Périgord, usually under dwarf oaks. In Italy these luxurious mushrooms with the black, finely wrinkled skin, which can sometimes reach the size of an orange, are named after a small town in Umbria and sold as Norcia truffles.

aphrodisiac. In this especially luxurious version of a truffle risotto, the strong flavor of the white truffle is further intensified by a classic *sauce périgueux*. The black truffles used in the sauce come from the Périgord, that region of France renowned for its culinary specialties, or from the Italian provinces of Piedmont and Umbria.

Truffle risotto
Risotto al tartufo, a luxurious and delicious delicacy from the Piedmont

In Italy the rare, highly aromatic white truffle grows chiefly in the environs of Alba. In November and December, therefore, this little old town becomes a mecca for gourmets. The often-spherical fruiting bodies of the white truffle are smooth on the outside and whitish or ocher in color. Their flesh, chestnut to dark brown in color, is streaked with small white veins, which give this truffle its characteristic marbled appearance. They give off a highly beguiling fragrance, which probably goes some way toward explaining the truffle's longstanding reputation as a powerful

Serves 4
For the truffle sauce:
1 black truffle (about 2 oz)
¼ cup butter
¼ cup finely chopped shallot
¼ cup dry red Port wine, 1 cup veal stock
2 teaspoons Cognac
salt, freshly ground pepper
For the risotto:
1 white truffle (about 2 oz), 1½ cups vialone rice
2 tablespoons butter, ¼ cup finely chopped shallot
2¾ cups hot vegetable stock
salt, freshly ground pepper
You will also need:
freshly grated Parmesan cheese (optional)

One or two days before you make the risotto, carefully brush the white and black truffles to remove any dirt clinging to them. Place both truffles in a tightly sealed container with the rice. Storing the rice and truffles together will impart the latter's distinctive flavor to the grain.

To make the sauce, thinly peel the black truffle and make a stock out of the parings. To do this, chop the truffle peelings very finely or pound them in a mortar. Melt 2 teaspoons of the butter in a saucepan and sweat the shallots in the butter without allowing them to color. Add the truffle peelings to the shallot and sweat together briefly. Deglaze with the Port wine and reduce until almost all the liquid has evaporated. Pour in the veal stock and reduce again by half. Strain through a piece of cheesecloth, season with a little salt and freshly ground pepper, and cool. Remove the butter that has congealed on the surface; this is most easily done by laying a paper towel on top once or twice to absorb it.

Melt 2 teaspoons of the butter in a saucepan, and place the remaining butter in the refrigerator until needed. Slice the black truffle into thin strips and sweat slowly in the melted butter. Deglaze with the Cognac and then add the truffle stock. Reduce the liquid by half.

To make the risotto, melt the butter in a pot and sweat the shallots until lightly colored. Add the rice and a little salt, and sweat together for 2–3 minutes, stirring, until the rice is translucent. Add the hot vegetable stock a little at a time and simmer the rice for about 15 minutes, stirring frequently. Add a little more stock if the risotto becomes too compact in texture. Remove the truffle sauce from the heat and add the remaining butter — it should be ice-cold — to the sauce in curls, whisking constantly. Season to taste. Pile the risotto onto warmed plates, shave the white truffle finely over the top, and sprinkle with freshly grated Parmesan cheese if wished. Serve with the truffle sauce.

Risotto with spicy mushrooms
With fresh morels or porcini, an incomparable pleasure

Mushrooms are extremely popular in Italy. In the season, up to 200 varieties come on the market, chiefly in Trentino. Apart from the very costly *tartufi*, *porcini* (also called cèpes) and morels are top of the popularity stakes. Dried mushrooms further enhance the flavor of a risotto. Not all varieties are as suitable for drying as porcini, whose powerful flavor is intensified by drying. The dried porcini are soaked for 10 minutes in lukewarm water, then cut up small, before they are added to the rice.

MOREL RISOTTO

Like cèpes, morels grow only in the wild; they cannot be cultivated. As early as March, this coveted mushroom, with its yellow, gray, or brownish, spherically ribbed cap, is to be found in wooded meadows or parklands, especially near ash trees. It is available on the market until into June. If you've missed the morel season, you can make this dish with dried morels instead. In this case, reduce the quantity to 1 ounce. Soak the dried mushrooms in lukewarm water for 20 minutes, then wash very thoroughly to get rid of all the sand. Squeeze out all excess water and cut the soaked morels into small pieces.

Serves 4 as an accompaniment
4 oz small fresh morels, ¼ cup butter
⅓ cup finely chopped shallot
1 cup vialone nano rice
⅔ cup white wine, ½ cup light cream
1¾ cups hot veal stock, salt, freshly ground pepper
¼ cup freshly grated Parmesan cheese
You will also need:
1 tablespoon chopped flat-leaf parsley

Wash the morels thoroughly and drain well. Cut off the tip of the stems and halve the larger mushrooms. Melt 2 tablespoons of the butter in a casserole and sweat the shallots until they take on a little color. Add the rice and sauté, stirring, until translucent. Add the white wine and reduce slightly. Pour in the cream and season with salt and pepper. Add the heated stock a little at a time, stirring frequently. Cook the risotto for 12 minutes. Melt the remaining butter in a frying pan and sweat the well-drained morels for 1 minute. Season with salt and pepper. Fold the morels into the risotto and simmer for 3–4 minutes more. Lastly, mix in the grated Parmesan cheese. Spoon the morel risotto onto heated plates, sprinkle with parsley, and serve immediately.

Young fresh cèpes, or porcini, are a delight for the mushroom hunter. If you have the good fortune to come across superb specimens like these during a walk in the woods, you really must try the risotto recipe opposite. Otherwise, try to find them fresh on the market during the right season.

PORCINI RISOTTO
Serves 4

⅓ oz dried porcini, 10 oz fresh porcini

4½ tablespoons butter, 1⅛ cup finely chopped onion

1½ cups carnaroli rice

⅔ cup white wine, about 3½ cups hot veal stock

½ teaspoon ground saffron

¼ cup freshly grated Parmesan cheese

2 tablespoons olive oil, 1 tablespoon chopped parsley

salt, freshly ground pepper

Soak the dried porcini in lukewarm water for 10 minutes. Meanwhile, trim the fresh mushrooms, thinly slice lengthwise, and set aside. Squeeze all excess liquid from the soaked porcini and chop finely. Melt 3 tablespoons of the butter in a pot, add the chopped mushrooms and ¾ cup of the onion, and sweat until lightly colored. Tip in the rice and stir over a high heat until the grains are translucent, but not colored. Add the wine and reduce slightly, stirring. Pour in the stock gradually, stirring constantly. Add the saffron, season, and cook for a 12–15 minutes, until done. Mix in the remaining butter and the Parmesan cheese, and remove from the heat. Heat the oil in a frying pan and sweat the remaining onion until translucent. Add the fresh porcini and sauté for 1–2 minutes. Season, and sprinkle with the parsley. Spoon the risotto and the mushroom ragout onto warm plates, and serve.

For many mushroom lovers, saffron-yellow rice with a ragout of fresh porcini is simply the greatest. The morel risotto here is intended as an accompaniment, for serving with, say, veal or poultry dishes, or else with fine game such as venison. If you wish to serve it as a separate course, simply double the ingredients.

Risotti con pesce e frutti di mare

Rice with fish and seafood, always an impressive combination

EEL RISOTTO

Some dishes are associated with special occasions, as is the case with this one. Rice with eel is the traditional start to the festive menu for Christmas Eve — at least in Venetia. The preparation of this risotto, for which it is best to use a river eel weighing about 2¼ pounds, differs slightly from the classic risotto method, as the rice is not first sweated until translucent, but is added directly to the court bouillon.

Serves 4
2¼ lb eel, skinned and ready to cook
2 tablespoons olive oil
2 tablespoons butter
½ cup finely chopped onion
1 garlic clove, finely chopped
1 cup finely chopped celery,
about 3 cups fish stock, 1 tablespoon lemon juice
1½ cups carnaroli rice
1 bay leaf, 2 tablespoons chopped parsley
salt, freshly ground pepper,

Cut the eel into pieces about 2 inches long. Heat the oil and butter in a pot, and fry the eel pieces on all sides. Add the onion, garlic, and celery, and sauté briefly. Moisten with 1 cup fish stock, stir in the lemon juice, and season with salt and pepper. Cover the pot and cook the eel over a low heat for about 20 minutes. Lift the eel out of the court bouillon and allow to cool slightly. Remove the bones as well as the gray skin, and reserve the eel. Pour the rice into the remaining stock, stir, and add the bay leaf. Pour in the remaining hot fish stock a little at a time and cook the rice over a low heat for 15–18 minutes, until done. Mix in the chunks of eel and the parsley in the last 5 minutes of cooking time, adjust the seasoning, and serve.

SEAFOOD RISOTTO

Serves 4
1½ lb monkfish, 1 lb clams, 1 lb mussels
2 carrots, 2 stalks celery
1 bay leaf, 5 white peppercorns, 8 scallops
3 tablespoons butter, ½ cup finely chopped onion
1 garlic clove, finely chopped
1½ cups vialone nano rice, ½ cup white wine
1 tablespoon chopped parsley
salt, freshly ground white pepper

Bone the monkfish and cut into 1-inch chunks. Wash the clams and mussels under cold running water, and discard any open ones. Pull the beards off the mussels. Peel the carrots, trim the celery, and cut both into chunks. Bring 5½ cups of water to a boil with the bay leaf, vegetables, peppercorns, and a little salt. Reduce the heat, add the fish, and simmer for 5 minutes. Lift out and reserve. Bring the court bouillon back to a boil, add the mollusks and cook until they open. Remove, discarding any that remain closed. Strain the court bouillon, reserving 3 cups.

Clean the scallops thoroughly. Holding each one firmly in a cloth, slice through the inner muscle with a sturdy, pointed knife and lift off the flat upper shell. Loosen the scallop with a knife at the gray edge of the flesh. Pull off the gray edge, and carefully separate the white flesh, known as the noisette, from the orange-colored roe, or coral. Cut the white flesh in half crosswise. Melt the butter in a casserole, and sauté the scallops and corals for 1 minute on each side. Lift out and set aside. Sweat the onion and garlic in the butter until the onion is translucent. Tip in the rice, and sauté until it too has become translucent. Add the white wine and reduce, stirring. Season with salt and pepper, and pour in the reserved stock a little at a time, stirring. The rice will be done after 18–20 minutes. Shell all but a few of the clams and mussels, and reserve the unshelled ones for a garnish. Mix the fish pieces, clams, mussels, and scallop meat and coral into the risotto during the last few minutes of cooking time to heat through. Sprinkle in the parsley, adjust the seasoning, garnish with the clams and mussels still in their shells, and serve from the casserole.

Monkfish, mollusks, and *moscardini*
Risottos with the bounteous harvest from the sea: freshly caught fish and delicate seafood

RISOTTO OF MONKFISH WITH SEAFOOD

Serves 4
12 medium-sized shrimp, shelled
9 oz baby squid, 7 oz boneless monkfish
1 lb small clams, 1 lb mussels
6 tablespoons olive oil, ½ cup finely chopped onion
1 garlic clove, finely chopped
½ cup white wine, 1 thyme sprig, dash lemon juice
2 tablespoons chopped parsley
1 tablespoon basil in thin strips
salt, freshly ground pepper,
For the risotto:
½ cup finely chopped onion
1 garlic clove, finely chopped
10 oz tomatoes, 2 tablespoons olive oil
1½ cups carnaroli rice, ½ cup white wine
1 bay leaf, 1 red chile pepper, 4½ cups hot fish stock
salt, freshly ground pepper
You will also need:
basil leaves to garnish

Cut half of the shrimp into ½-inch pieces. Wash the baby squid and pull off the skin. Pull the tentacles completely out of the body and, using a sharp knife, cut them off from the head just above the eyes so that they remain joined by a narrow band. Squeeze out the beak and remove the translucent quill. Carefully wash the bodies inside and out, and slice into ½-inch-wide rings. Cut the monkfish crosswise into ½-inch-thick slices. Carefully scrub the clams and mussels under cold running water, removing all traces of sand and lime. Dicard any open ones. Pull the beards off the mussels. Heat 2 tablespoons of the olive oil in a pot and sweat the onion and garlic until lightly colored. Add the clams and mussels, moisten with the wine, cover, and cook until the mollusks have opened. Remove from the heat. Shuck two-thirds of the mussels, discarding any closed ones, and set aside with the others. Strain the court bouillon and reserve.

To make the risotto, blanch, skin, and seed the tomatoes, and finely dice the flesh. Heat the oil in a pot and sweat the diced onion and garlic without allowing them to color. Tip in the rice and sauté, stirring, until translucent. Add the tomatoes and sweat for 1–2 minutes, then pour in the wine and reduce, stirring, over a high heat. Add the bay leaf and the whole chile pepper, then pour in the court bouillon and the hot fish stock gradually. Season, and cook for 12–15 minutes, stirring frequently.

Heat 2 tablespoons of the oil in a frying pan, add the thyme sprig, and sauté the shrimp pieces, squid rings, and monkfish for 2–3 minutes. Season with salt, pepper, and lemon juice. Sprinkle in 1 tablespoon

chopped parsley and the basil strips. One minute before the rice has finished cooking, mix the contents of the frying pan carefully into the risotto with the shucked mussels. Clean out the pan, heat the remaining oil, and sauté the whole shrimp and the squid tentacles for 2 minutes. Add the unshelled clams and mussels, and heat briefly. Season with salt and pepper, and sprinkle with the remaining parsley. Spoon onto warmed plates, topping the risotto with the shrimp, squid tentacles, clams, and mussels. Garnish with a few whole basil leaves and serve.

RISOTTO WITH HOP SHOOTS AND MOSCARDINI

Young hop shoots are sometimes available on the market, at least in Italy. Otherwise, hops grow wild, or as a climbing plant in gardens. If you are harvesting them yourself, cut off the uppermost, still tender shoots into lengths of about 3 inches.

Serves 4

10 oz moscardini or other small squid
¾ cup finely chopped onion, 5 oz young hop shoots
7 tablespoons butter, 2 tablespoons olive oil,
1½ cups vialone nano rice
about 4½ cups hot veal stock
1 tablespoon chopped parsley
salt, freshly ground white pepper
You will also need:
½ cup freshly grated Parmesan cheese (optional)

First prepare the *moscardini*: Pull the skin off the bodies. Pull the tentacles out of the bodies and, using a sharp knife, cut them off from the head just above the eyes so that they remain joined by a narrow band. Squeeze out the beak and remove the translucent quill. Carefully wash the bodies inside and out. Bring plenty of salted water to a boil, drop in the *moscardini*, and cook for 1 minute. Lift out, drain, and set aside.

Meanwhile, wash and chop the hop shoots. Heat 3 tablespoons of the butter in a casserole with the oil and sweat ½ cup of the onion without allowing it to color. Sauté the hops, stirring, for about 8 minutes. Tip in the rice and stir until the grains are translucent. Season lightly, pour in a little hot stock and simmer for 15–20 minutes, stirring several times and gradually adding the remaining stock; the rice should always be covered with liquid. Melt the remaining butter in a frying pan and sweat the remaining onion until lightly colored. Add the *moscardini* and continue to sauté, stirring, for about 10 minutes. Season, and sprinkle with parsley. Mix half of the squid into the risotto, spoon onto heated plates, garnish with the remaining moscardini, sprinkle with Parmesan cheese, and serve.

Remove the quill by carefully prising apart the squid along the cut edges. The ink sac is located at the lower end of the cuttlefish's body.

Remove the innards: Reach into the body with your thumb and carefully push or pull them out. Be careful not to damage the ink sac.

Using your thumb and index finger, squeeze the ink out of the sac into a bowl and set it aside for later use.

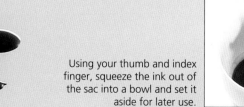

Risotto nero
This risotto owes its unusual color to cuttlefish ink

People who overcome their initial uncertainty about the jet-black rice and try this risotto for the first time will be rewarded by the intense flavor experience. The ink is responsible more for the color than for the taste, while the cuttlefish themselves provide the flavor. If cuttlefish are unavailable, the dish can be prepared with another cephalopod, such as squid or octopus. In order to get hold of the dye without damaging the ink sac, you must handle fresh cuttlefish carefully. If you use ready-prepared frozen cuttlefish or squid, the ink sac will have been removed, and you will have to buy it separately. It is available in Italian or Spanish delicatessens, labeled *nero di seppia* and *tinta de calamar*, respectively.

Serves 4
1¼ lb cuttlefish
7 tablespoons olive oil
¾ cup finely chopped shallot
1 garlic clove, finely chopped
½ cup dry white wine
4½ cups fish stock
1½ cups arborio rice
3 tablespoons chopped flat-leaf parsley
¼ cup butter
salt, freshly ground pepper

To make the *risotto nero*, first prepare the cuttlefish. Using a sharp knife, cut off the heads with the tentacles. If the ink is to be used, the cuttlefish must be carefully cut open lengthwise. Pull out the quill, as described in the first photo on the left, and proceed as shown in the photo sequence. Cut off the tentacles from the head so that they remain joined together by a narrow band of flesh. Wash thoroughly. Pull the skin off the cuttlefish bodies, wash the bodies well, and drain. Cut the bodies into very thin strips and set aside with the tentacles for later use. Heat the olive oil in a sufficiently large pot and sweat the diced shallot and garlic until the shallot is translucent. Add the strips of cuttlefish and stir-fry for several minutes. Season with salt and pepper, add the wine, and cook for 1 minute. Stir in the cuttlefish ink and simmer for a further 10 minutes, stirring from time to time. In a separate pot, heat the fish stock. Tip the rice into the cuttlefish mixture and cook, stirring, for several minutes, until only a little liquid remains in the pot. Pour in a little hot stock and continue to stir until the rice has absorbed the liquid. Repeat this process until the rice is done; it should take about 15 minutes. Stir the chopped parsley and the butter into the risotto, adjust the seasoning, and serve immediately.

With scampi and gilt-head sea bream
Italian cuisine is famous for its imaginative treatment of seafood

RISOTTO AGLI SCAMPI

Scampi (*langoustines* in French, also known in English as Dublin Bay prawns or Norway lobsters) turn risotto into a luxury. Native to the cooler waters of the North Atlantic as well as the Mediterranean, scampi, along with lobster, figure among the most coveted of crustaceans. Fresh scampi are distinguished by their pink color and their translucent flesh; if in doubt, the smell test is decisive. So that their delicate flesh remains beautifully tender, the scampi are not cooked with the rice for the whole of the latter's cooking time, but are added to the pot only in the last 5 minutes. If scampi are not available, substitute jumbo shrimp.

Serves 4

¾ cup diced mixed root vegetables (onion, carrot, leek)
1 bay leaf
12 scampi or jumbo shrimp (about 3 oz each)
½ cup finely chopped onion
1 garlic clove, finely chopped
3 tablespoons butter, 1½ cups vialone nano rice
½ cup white wine, 8 saffron threads
salt, freshly ground pepper

You will also need:

1 tablespoon chopped flat-leaf parsley

Bring 4½ cups of water to a boil in a large pot with the coarsely diced vegetables and bay leaf. Add the scampi, reduce the heat, and simmer for 2 minutes. Lift the scampi out with a slotted spoon and strain the court bouillon into a bowl — there should be about 3½ cups remaining — and reserve. Grasp each scampi by the head in one hand, holding the tail in the fingers of the other hand, and twist off the tail. Discard the head. Squeeze the shell of the tail hard between your thumb and index finger until it cracks. Break open the shell completely, remove the flesh, halve lengthwise, devein, and refrigerate.

Melt the butter in a pot and sweat the diced onion and garlic until lightly colored. Tip in the rice and sauté, stirring, until the grains are translucent. Pour in the white wine and reduce. Sprinkle in the saffron threads and season with salt and pepper. Reduce the heat and simmer the risotto, stirring occasionally, for 8–20 minutes, adding the scampi court bouillon very gradually to keep the rice always just covered with liquid. In the final 5 minutes of cooking time, add the halved scampi and mix in carefully. Season to taste with salt and pepper, spoon onto warmed plates, sprinkle with chopped parsley, and serve.

RED-WINE RISOTTO WITH SEA BREAM

Serves 4
1 gilt-head sea bream (ocean sunfish) (about 1½ lb)
½ cup finely chopped white onion
1 small garlic clove, finely chopped
¼ cup butter, 1½ cups arborio rice
1 cup red wine, 3–3½ cups hot veal stock
2 tablespoons olive oil
salt, freshly ground white pepper
You will also need:
nasturtium flowers to garnish

Either have your fish seller bone the fish, leaving the skin on, or lift off the fillets yourself. To do this, grasp the tail of the fish firmly with a cloth and cut off the fins, working toward the head. Scale the fish, slit open its belly, and remove the innards. Wash inside and out under cold running water. Remove the fillets from the bones and refrigerate. Melt 2 tablespoons of the butter in a pot and sweat the diced onion and garlic without allowing them to color. Tip in the rice and sauté, stirring constantly, until the grains are translucent. Moisten with the red wine and reduce, stirring, until very little liquid remains. Pour in the hot veal stock a little at a time, stirring constantly — the rice should always remain just covered with liquid — and cook for 12–15 minutes, until done. Season, and remove from the heat. Slice the fish diagonally into ½-inch-wide strips and season with salt and pepper. Heat the olive oil and the remaining butter in a frying pan and brown the pieces of fish on both sides. Lift out and either gently mix the fish strips into the rice during the final 2–3 minutes of cooking, or serve separately with the finished risotto. Spoon the risotto onto warmed plates, top with the fried strips of fish if applicable, garnish with nasturtium flowers, and serve.

Soups

Banish the memory of tasteless, lifeless grains in a bland liquid. The culinary possibilities offered by soups with rice are impressively demonstrated by the recipes in this chapter. Here rice is combined with fish, shellfish, freshwater crayfish, mushrooms, poultry, and vegetables, from young and tender to firm and

crunchy in flavorful clear consommés and hearty soups to produce delicious light dishes that are both satisfying and easy to digest.

   To get the most flavorful results it is essential that the rice either cooks with the other ingredients in the dish, just to the point of perfection, or, if cooked rice is being used, that it simmers only very briefly in the stock or soup. In some cases it is added to the tureen or bowls only right before serving, and then just moistened with the hot liquid. In this way, the rice is heated sufficiently without being allowed to swell excessively.

The rice soups in this chapter are ideal either as a meal on their own or as a first course. When they are presented as attractively as, for example, the pumpkin soup, or in as sophisticated a fashion as the crayfish soup, even the most dyed-in-the-wool skeptic will be seen reaching for a spoon.

Clear soups
With cooked rice as a very simple but impressive garnish

LAMB CONSOMMÉ WITH RICE AND VEGETABLES

It may seem somewhat extravagant to prepare a special bouillon from lamb and bones for an apparently simple recipe such as this one, but the result is definitely worth the effort.

Serves 4
For the consommé:
1 shoulder of lamb on the bone (about 2¼ lb)
1 carrot, 1 white onion
1 leek, 1½ stalks celery
2 tablespoons vegetable oil
5 peppercorns, 3 parsley sprigs
For the garnish:
¾ cup long-grain rice
1–2 young carrots, 1 stalk celery
½ white onion, 1 leek, salt
You will also need:
1 tablespoon chopped parsley

To make the consommé, place the lamb in a large pot with cold water just to cover and bring to a boil. Trim or peel the vegetables for the *mirepoix* as appropriate and cut into ¾-inch pieces. Heat the oil in a frying pan and sweat the vegetables until they color slightly. Add the vegetables to the pot, season with salt, and toss in the peppercorns and parsley sprigs. Bring to a boil again, reduce the heat, and simmer for 70–80 minutes, skimming several times. Remove the meat from the stock and strain the liquid. Measure and reserve 5½ cups of the stock; use the remainder in other dishes.

The lamb consommé makes this soup a hearty first cousin of the Italian minestrone. Here, however, rice, rather than pasta, is the filling garnish.

Sprinkle the rice into the stock, bring to a boil, reduce the heat, and simmer for 15–20 minutes. Meanwhile, peel or trim the vegetables for the garnish. Cut the carrots into thin rounds, the celery into fine slices, the onion into ½-inch dice, and the leek into thin rings. Add the vegetables to the stock during the last 10 minutes of cooking time and simmer with the other ingredients. Season to taste. Remove the lamb meat from the bones, cut into ½-inch chunks, return to the stock, and reheat. Serve the soup in heated shallow bowls, sprinkled with parsley.

BEEF BOUILLON WITH RICE, LEAF SPINACH, AND PARMESAN STRACCIATELLA

Make this soup in the spring, when baby spinach is in season. The leaves are so tender that they can be cooked simply by ladling hot stock over them, and they are also good eaten raw in salad.

Serves 4

¼ cup long-grain rice

1 cup trimmed baby spinach

2 oz baby carrots

4½ cups strong beef bouillon

freshly grated nutmeg, salt

For the Parmesan stracciatella:

2 eggs

¼ cup grated Parmesan cheese

You will also need:

parsley leaves

chives

Boil the rice in lightly salted water for about 15 minutes, strain, and keep warm. Meanwhile, wash the leaf spinach and drain well. Peel the carrots and cut into julienne. Bring the beef bouillon to a boil and reduce the heat. Season to taste with salt and nutmeg. Add the julienned carrot and simmer for 3–4 minutes. To make the Parmesan stracciatella, beat the eggs in a bowl, whisk in the Parmesan cheese, combining thoroughly, and pour into the gently simmering bouillon, stirring constantly with a fork. Divide the spinach among heated soup cups. Add the hot rice, whole parsley leaves, and chives, then ladle the hot stock on top and serve.

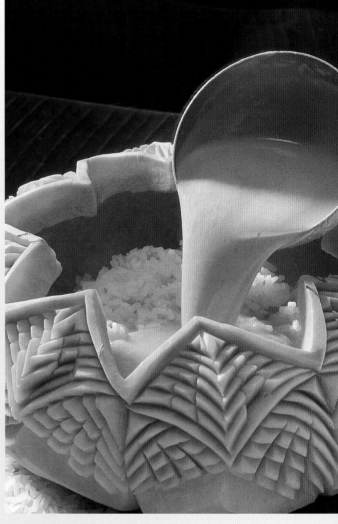

In Thailand loving attention is paid not only to the preparation but also to the artistic presentation of foods. Our chef's refined carving technique turns a splendid specimen of the Cucurbitaceae family into an elegant tureen for pumpkin soup.

Pumpkin soup
With an unusual garnish of crisp-fried baby eggplants

This pumpkin soup is given a decidedly piquant twist by the Thai green curry paste. Condiments of this sort, which are occasionally infernally hot, are prepared in Thailand for each dish according to a separate recipe. As a rule, though, most variants contain chiles — usually dried — as well as shrimp paste, coriander, cumin, lemon grass, galangal, garlic, shallots, pepper, turmeric, and lime zest as basic ingredients. These ingredients are pounded in a mortar or processed in a blender to a firm but spreadable paste. The variety required here gets its color from fresh green chile peppers, optionally intensified by cilantro. It is used mainly in poultry dishes.

Thai baby eggplants, no bigger than olives, are only seldom available. Here, you may substitute other Asian baby eggplants, halved or quartered, depending on size.

Serves 4
1 small pumpkin, about 12 oz
1–2 leeks, 1½ stalks celery
2 oz baby bananas, peeled
1 red chile pepper
3 stalks lemon grass, 2 tablespoons butter
1 garlic clove, halved
1 tablespoon finely chopped galangal
3¼ cups chicken stock
⅓ cup light cream, ⅓ cup coconut milk
1 teaspoon Thai green curry paste
salt, freshly ground white pepper
For the substantial garnish:
10 oz boneless, skinless chicken breast
2 teaspoons finely chopped galangal

| 2 kaffir lime leaves |
| 2 teaspoons Thai green curry paste |
| 2 tablespoons butter |
| For the final garnish: |
| 4 Thai baby eggplants, 1 tablespoon vegetable oil |
| 2 red chile peppers |
| ¾ cup cooked Thai fragrant rice |
| Thai basil |

Using a tablespoon, remove the seeds and fibrous core from the pumpkin. Peel the pumpkin with a sharp knife and cut the flesh into small pieces. Trim and wash the leek and the celery. Cut the leek, celery, and bananas into small pieces. Halve the chile pepper lengthwise. Slice the lemon grass into thin rounds. Melt the butter in a large pot and sweat the pumpkin flesh, leek, celery, bananas, chile pepper, lemon grass, garlic, and galangal for 5–6 minutes. Reserve 1 tablespoonful of this vegetable mixture for the final garnish. Heat the chicken stock and stir into the vegetables in the pot, together with the cream,

coconut milk, and curry paste. Season with salt and pepper, and simmer the soup over a moderate heat for 15–20 minutes. Remove the halved chile pepper and discard. Purée the soup in a blender or food processor, or with a hand-held blender, and strain.

To make the substantial garnish, cut the chicken breast into ½-inch-wide strips. Slice the kaffir lime leaves into thin strips. Mix the chicken strips with the curry paste, lime leaves, and galangal. Melt the butter in a frying pan. Add the strips of chicken and the spice mixture, and sauté briefly. Reheat the strained pumpkin soup and adjust the seasoning. Add the sautéed chicken strips and simmer for 1–2 minutes.

To make the final garnish, trim the baby eggplants. Heat the oil in a pan and sauté the eggplants briefly. Halve the chile peppers and remove the seeds. To serve, spoon the rice into a prepared pumpkin tureen or a heated soup terrine and ladle the hot soup, with the strips of chicken, on top. Add the reserved vegetables, the sautéed eggplants, and the halved chile peppers, and garnish with Thai basil.

With mushrooms and caviar
Rice as a substantial garnish, and then as a crisp-fried accompaniment

MUSHROOM SOUP WITH RICE

Serves 4
10 oz mixed mushrooms (chanterelles, cèpes, pio-pini)
2 tablespoons butter, ½ cup finely chopped shallot
½ cup short-grain rice
4½ cups hot beef bouillon
1 tablespoon chopped parsley, salt, freshly ground pepper
You will also need:
2 tablespoons crème fraîche, chopped parsley

Trim the mushrooms. Halve the smaller ones and cut the larger ones into slices. Melt the butter in a pot and sweat the shallots until lightly colored. Tip in the rice and sauté, stirring, until translucent. Add the mushrooms and sauté for 2 minutes. Pour in the hot bouillon and simmer the soup over a low heat for 12–15 minutes, until the rice is done. Adjust the

seasoning and sprinkle in the chopped parsley. Ladle the soup into warmed bowls, add a dollop of crème fraîche, sprinkle with chopped parsley, and serve.

VICHYSSOISE WITH CAVIAR AND RICE CRACKERS

Inspired by the classic recipe from the Ritz-Carlton in New York, this cold potato soup is enriched with cream and served with quail's eggs and caviar.

Serves 4
For the Vichyssoise:
1 lb floury potatoes
¼ cup lukewarm milk, 1½ tablespoons butter, melted
a pinch of freshly grated nutmeg
3¼ cups well-flavored beef bouillon
2 tablespoons crème fraîche
⅓ cup heavy cream, whipped to soft peaks
1 tablespoon chives, salt, freshly ground white pepper
For the rice crackers:
⅓ cup long-grain rice, 1 egg white
2 tablespoons chopped chives
2 tablespoons vegetable oil, 1½ tablespoons butter
salt, freshly ground pepper

You will also need:
8 quail's eggs, 1 oz osetrova caviar

Peel and dice the potatoes, and boil in slightly salted water until soft. Pour off the water and leave the potatoes to steam dry. While still warm, put them through a ricer over a bowl. Whisk in the milk, butter, nutmeg, salt, and pepper. Bring the bouillon to a boil, whisk in the whipped potatoes and crème fraîche, and simmer over a low heat for 10 minutes. Take off the heat and allow to cool, stirring frequently, or place the pot in a bowl of ice water and stir until cold.

To make the crackers, cook the rice in slightly salted water for 20 minutes; strain, refresh under cold water, and drain well. Mix with the egg white, chives, salt, and pepper. Heat the oil and butter in a frying pan. Form the rice mixture into about 20 crackers 1 inch in diameter, and fry on both sides until crisp.

Boil the quail's eggs for 7 minutes, refresh under cold water, then shell and halve them lengthwise. Whip the chilled soup until foamy. Gently fold in the cream and sprinkle in the chives. Ladle the soup into bowls. Garnish each portion with 4 egg halves, top with caviar, and serve with the rice crackers.

In Thailand each diner seasons his or her own shrimp-rice soup to taste at the table with fish sauce, nam prik, and garlic oil. To make the garlic oil, place 6 peeled, halved garlic cloves in a bottle, then fill with 2¼ cups vegetable oil. Seal tightly and allow to steep in a sunny spot for 2–3 weeks.

Sea harvest
Here, rice is accompanied by fish, shrimp, squid, and fresh seaweed

RED-SNAPPER BROTH WITH RICE

Serves 4
3 tablespoons butter
4 garlic cloves, chopped
½ cup white wine
10–15 saffron threads
3–4 stalks lemon grass, cut in thin rounds
5½ cups fish stock
1 lb boneless red-snapper
2¾ cups cooked Thai fragrant rice
salt, freshly ground black pepper
You will also need:
8 green asparagus, cooked
8 cherry tomatoes, 1 cup fresh seaweed

Heat the butter in a pot and sweat the garlic until lightly colored. Moisten with the white wine and add the saffron, lemon grass, and fish stock. Simmer

for 10 minutes. Season the fish with salt and pepper, and cut into pieces diagonally. Add to the broth, reduce the heat, and simmer for 2–3 minutes. Cut the asparagus lengthwise into thin slices and halve the cherry tomatoes diagonally. Add the seaweed to boiling water and simmer for 5 minutes. Spoon the rice into a bowl or tureen, top with the red-snapper pieces, and ladle the hot stock on top. Top with the asparagus and tomatoes, and garnish with the seaweed.

RICE SOUP WITH SHRIMP

Serves 4
For the soup:
17 oz squid, 7 oz medium-sized shrimp
4 air-dried Chinese pork sausages
2 pints water or chicken stock, ½ teaspoon salt
¾ cup Thai fragrant rice, 3–4 scallions
4 eggs, 1 tablespoon cilantro
For the nam prik sauce:
4 garlic cloves, finely chopped
¼ cup finely chopped shallot
1 tablespoon shrimp paste, ¼ teaspoon salt
1 tablespoon palm (or brown) sugar
8 Thai red chiles, juice of 2 limes

You will also need:
fish sauce and garlic oil

To make the nam prik sauce, pound the garlic and shallots to a paste in a mortar with the shrimp paste, salt, and sugar. Halve the chile peppers and remove the seeds. Purée the chiles in a blender with the lime juice. Add the paste and blend very briefly; thin with a little chicken stock if wished.

To make the soup, wash the squid and pull off its skin. Pull the tentacles out of the body and cut off just above the eyes so that they remain joined by a narrow band. Grasp the band from below in the center, and pop out and remove the beak. Remove the translucent quill from the body sac. Wash the tentacles and body. Cut the body into ¼-inch-wide rings. Peel and devein the shrimp. Cut the sausage into 1-inch-long pieces. Wash the rice. Bring the water or stock to a boil with the salt, add the rice, cover, and simmer over a low heat for 20 minutes. Add the squid, shrimp, and sausage for the final 10 minutes. Trim the scallions and slice into thin rings. Ladle the soup into bowls. Crack open the eggs one at a time and slip one into each bowl. Sprinkle with the scallions and cilantro. Hand round the sauces and the garlic oil separately.

With fresh crustaceans
And stock made from their shells

BISQUE DE LANGOUSTINES

If langoustines, also called scampi and Dublin Bay prawns, are not available, use jumbo shrimp instead.

Serves 4

8 langoustines (about 5 oz each) or 2 lb jumbo shrimp
½ leek, ½ carrot, 1 stalk celery, 1 small onion
1 shallot, 2 small garlic cloves,
3 tablespoons olive oil, 2 tablespoons butter
¼ cup long-grain rice, 2 tablespoons tomato paste
½ cup white wine, ½ cup Noilly Prat vermouth
2 tablespoons cognac, 5½ cups fish stock
1 sprig each tarragon, parsley and basil
pinch cayenne pepper, salt
⅓ cup heavy cream, whipped to soft peaks
For the garnish:
1 leek, 1 stalk celery, pinch cayenne pepper, salt
1½ tablespoons butter, 2 tablespoons olive oil
4 small tarragon sprigs, 1 tablespoon chopped tarragon

Grasp each langoustine by the head in one hand, holding the tail in the fingers of the other hand, and twist off the tail. Break open the shell completely, remove the flesh, and devein. Cover the shelled tails and refrigerate. Halve the heads lengthwise, wash them out thoroughly, and chop all the cleaned shells. Trim or peel the vegetables for the *mirepoix* as appropriate and cut into ¼-inch dice. Heat the olive oil and butter in a large pot and stir-fry the chopped shells for 10 minutes. Add the vegetables and sauté for 5 minutes, then stir in the rice. Add the tomato paste and sweat for a further 2–3 minutes. Deglaze with the wine, add the vermouth and cognac, and reduce by half. Pour in the stock, add the herbs, bring to a boil, and simmer for 20–25 minutes.

Meanwhile, make the garnish. Wash and trim the leek and celery, and cut into julienne. Blanch in slightly salted water, then drain well. Strain the soup into a pot, pressing the ingredients hard against the strainer with the back of a wooden spoon to extract all the juices. Season to taste with salt and cayenne pepper, and keep warm. Season the chilled langoustine with salt and cayenne pepper. Heat the butter and olive oil for the garnish in a frying pan and sweat the tarragon sprigs. Add the langoustine and sauté on all sides until golden brown, then sprinkle with the chopped tarragon. Stir the soup briefly and fold in the cream. Divide the langoustines and julienned vegetables among warmed soup cups, ladle the soup on top, garnish with a fried tarragon sprig, and serve.

SPICY CRAB SOUP

Exotic mangrove crabs from the Indopacific are, unfortunately, seldom available, but blue crabs or Dungeness crabs make an admirable substitute.

Serves 4

2 crabs (about 14 oz each)
3 small green and 3 small red chile peppers
1 stalk lemon grass, 6-8 kaffir lime leaves
3 oz enoki mushrooms, 3 oz fresh straw mushrooms
3¼ cups chicken stock
1½ tablespoons chopped galangal
2 tablespoons fish sauce, 3 tablespoons kaffir lime juice
¼ teaspoon palm (or brown) sugar
the white meat from 16 scallops
You will also need:
1 cup cooked Thai fragrant rice, cilantro to garnish

Boil the crabs, and — except for the claws — shell them as described on page 210. Crack the claws with the blade of a heavy knife. Halve the chile peppers and remove the seeds. Slice the lemon grass into thin rounds and the lime leaves into thin strips. Trim all the mushrooms, halving any larger ones. Bring the stock to a boil. Add the chiles, lemon grass, lime leaves, galangal, fish sauce, lime juice, and palm sugar. Simmer over a low heat for 10 minutes. Add the mushrooms and the scallops, and cook for a further 3 minutes. Reheat the crab claws and crab meat in the soup. Ladle into soup bowls, add ¼ cup cooked rice to each portion, and serve garnished with cilantro.

CRAYFISH SOUP

Serves 4
4½ lb crayfish
For the stock:
12 oz tomatoes, 4 tablespoons vegetable oil
2½ cups coarsely chopped onion
2 tablespoons tomato paste, 5 garlic cloves, halved
¼ cup finely chopped celery
1 bay leaf, 5 white peppercorns
11 cups water, ½ teaspoon salt
For the soup:
7 tablespoons vegetable oil, 2 tablespoons flour
1 large green pepper, ¾ cup long-grain rice
2¼ cups finely chopped onions
2 garlic cloves, finely chopped
1 cup finely chopped celery, 6 scallions, dash Tabasco
2 tablespoons chopped parsley
salt, freshly ground pepper

Preheat the oven to 400°F. Bring a pot of water to a rolling boil, add the crayfish one at a time, and cook for 3–4 minutes. Remove and refresh in cold water.

Separate the tails from the heads by twisting apart. Remove the meat from the tails and devein. Cover the crayfish meat and refrigerate. Halve the heads lengthwise, wash out the shells carefully, and drain well. Roast the shells in the oven for 1 hour.

Meanwhile, finely chop the tomatoes. Heat the oil in a pot, sweat the onions, and sauté the crayfish shells. Add the tomatoes, tomato paste, celery, and garlic, and cook gently. Drop in the bay leaf and peppercorns, pour in the water, add the salt, and bring to a boil. Reduce the heat and simmer for 1½ hours, skimming several times. Line a strainer with cheesecloth and strain the stock.

To make the soup, heat 4 tablespoons of the oil in a pot, stir in the flour, and brown lightly, stirring constantly. Gradually add the crayfish stock, stirring well, and bring to a boil. Lower the heat and reduce to 6½ cups, stirring occasionally, then strain. Meanwhile, core, seed and dice the green pepper. When the soup is done, stir in the rice and simmer for 10 minutes. Heat the remaining oil in a frying pan and sweat the garlic and onions without allowing them to color. Add the celery and diced peppers, and sauté for 5 minutes. Stir the vegetables into the soup and simmer for 10 minutes. Season with salt and pepper. Cut the scallions into thin rings, stir into the soup with the crayfish tails, and cook for another 5 minutes.

Before serving, season the crayfish soup to taste with Tabasco and sprinkle liberally with chopped parsley.

Snacks and appetizers

People around the world use rice in making tasty snacks and appetizers. For example, rice balls, croquettes, and stuffed vine leaves are popular in Europe, the Near East, and North Africa. But it is Japanese cuisine that has produced the most varied and the most esthetically demanding rice snacks in the world.

This culinary world of wonders can be summed up in a single word: sushi. The most popular sorts can be broken down into two groups. The first group comprises the individually made canapés, such as *nigiri-zushi* (in compound expressions, "sushi" begins with a "z"), elongated rice cakes topped with raw or marinated fish, seafood, or an omelet. If the topping is not entirely slip-proof, like roe for example, a strip of nori seaweed is wrapped around the rice before the topping is put in place. This produces *gunkan-maki*, which means, in essence, "sushi in the form of a battleship." The second type of sushi are *maki-zushi* or *nori-maki*. To make these, the rice is rolled up tightly in nori leaves and encloses a filling of vegetables or seafood.

Sushi are in and of themselves a delight to the eye. Therefore they are only very modestly garnished, if at all. The band of nori around *nigiri-zushi*, for example, may be seen as a garnish, although its primary purpose is to hold the rice and topping together. Much more important in terms of opulent decoration is the artistic arrangement of the canapés on the platter.

A great deal of practice and experience are needed to become a sushi chef, or *itamae* (literally, "the one standing before the chopping board"). A feel for rice quality is as important as the proper knack for filling and shaping.

For dipping
Spicy sauces are the ideal accompaniment for both sushi and baked rice balls

SUSHI RICE

The most important ingredient for all types of sushi is short-grain rice. An experienced *itamae*, or sushi chef, will not only distinguish between the different

To make nigiri-zushi:

Place the topping across the fingers of your left hand. Take a portion of rice the size of a ping-pong ball in your right hand, or vice versa.

Spread a little wasabi (Japanese horseradish) onto the topping, still holding the rice in the fingers of your right hand.

To make maki-zushi:

Place a sheet of nori on a bamboo rolling mat. Spread rice on top to a depth of ½ inch, leaving a strip free at the top. Place the filling in the center.

Place the rice on the topping and press it down with your right index finger.

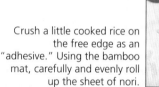

Crush a little cooked rice on the free edge as an "adhesive." Using the bamboo mat, carefully and evenly roll up the sheet of nori.

Continue rolling evenly up to the top edge. Pull out the bamboo mat and press the roll onto the "adhesive" strip.

The hollow is clearly visible. With the fingers of your left hand, keep squeezing the sushi together at the sides.

Wrap the roll in the bamboo mat and press flat evenly on all four sides. This gives the roll a rectangular cross-section.

Round off the ends of the sushi with your thumb and index finger. Dip your fingers in water repeatedly during the shaping process.

Remove the mat again and slice the roll in 4–6 pieces, dipping the knife in vinegar water between each cut.

Turn the sushi over and serve with soy sauce, wasabi, and *benishoga* (paper-thin slices of red pickled ginger).

varieties of rice, but also between fairly recently harvested rice and rice that has been stored for longer and therefore has lost more of its moisture. Sushi chefs often use customized mixtures of rice in order to obtain quite specific qualities. Whatever the mix, sushi rice is always flavored with vinegar, salt, and sugar in varying proportions, depending on the type of sushi and one's personal taste.

Dark soy sauce is served as a dip with all kinds of sushi, and grated green wasabi root (known as Japanese horseradish or Japanese mustard) is used as a condiment. Japanese green tea is the appropriate drink with sushi.

1½ cups Japanese short-grain rice, 1½ cups water
4 tablespoons rice vinegar, 1½ teaspoons sugar
1½ teaspoons salt

Wash the rice in a strainer under cold running water until the water runs clear. Drain for 1 hour. Bring the water and rice to a boil in a pot. Reduce the heat, cover, and cook over a low heat for 15 minutes. Remove from the heat, wedge two layers of paper towels between the pot and the lid, and let the rice rest for 10–15 minutes. Meanwhile, mix the vinegar, sugar, and salt, and warm gently until the sugar dissolves. Spoon the rice into a shallow wooden bowl and gradually work in the vinegar mixture with a wooden spoon by cutting into it alternately to the left and the right rather than stirring. Cover the rice with a damp dish towel until you are ready to proceed.

BAKED RICE BALLS

Although spicy-hot *sambal oelek* can be bought ready-made, it tastes better homemade. Stored in the refrigerator, it will keep fresh for 1–2 weeks.

Makes 20

For the rice balls:
1¾ cups steamed Thai fragrant rice
1 egg, 2 tablespoons chopped cilantro
1 stalk lemon grass, finely chopped
grated zest of ½ kaffir lime
1–2 teaspoons sambal oelek, 1 tablespoon fish sauce
1 tablespoon chopped Thai basil
2 tablespoons vegetable oil
For the *sambal oelek*:
20 Thai red chiles
vinegar or tamarind juice, 1½ teaspoons salt
For the *nam pla* sauce:
2–3 scallions, 2 red chile peppers, 1 kaffir lime leaf
½ teaspoon palm (or brown) sugar,
juice of 1 kaffir lime

4 tablespoons fish sauce, 3 tablespoons water
2 teaspoons finely chopped fresh ginger root
1 garlic clove, finely chopped
1 tablespoon chopped cilantro

First prepare the *sambal oelek*. Remove the stems from the chiles and place the chiles in a blender. Add just enough vinegar or tamarind juice to keep the blades turning, and blend. Season with salt, pack into sterilized jars, and refrigerate.

To make the rice balls, thoroughly mix the fragrant rice with the egg, cilantro, lemon grass, lime zest, *sambal oelek* to taste, fish sauce, and basil. Cover and refrigerate for 30 minutes. Preheat the oven to 400°F. Wet your hands and form the mixture into about 20 balls. Grease a baking sheet with some oil, place the rice balls on it, and carefully brush them with a little oil. Bake for about 20 minutes, until golden yellow.

To make the *nam pla* sauce, trim the scallion and slice into fine rounds. Cut the chile peppers into rings, removing the seeds as you do so. Slice the lime leaf into very thin strips. Stir together the sugar, lime juice, fish sauce, and water until the sugar dissolves. Mix in the scallion, ginger, garlic, chile rings, lime leaf, and cilantro. Lift the rice balls from the baking sheet and serve with the sauce.

From Europe and the Far East
Rice, pan-fried till crunchy or gently steamed in the wok

WILD RICE GALETTES

Serves 4
½ cup Canadian wild rice, 1 tablespoon butter
1 cup water, a pinch of salt, 1 egg yolk
1 teaspoon crème fraîche, 2 tablespoons vegetable oil
For the garnish:
2¼ cups water, 2 tablespoons fruit vinegar
12 quail's eggs, well chilled
¼ cup crème fraîche, cayenne pepper
dash lemon juice, 2 oz osetrova or sevruga caviar
chive flowers, salt
You will also need:
parchment paper
1 smooth round cutter 3 inches in diameter

Wash the wild rice and soak overnight in cold water. The next day drain well. Preheat the oven to 350°F. Melt the butter in a pot and sweat the rice briefly. Pour in the water, add salt, and bring to a boil. Cover and cook in the oven for 20–25 minutes. When done, pour off the excess water, and leave to cool. Mix in the egg yolk and crème fraîche Place the cutter on top of a sheet of parchment paper and fill with ⅛ of the wild rice mixture, leveling the top. Remove the ring and repeat with the remaining rice mixture. Cover the *galettes* with plastic wrap and chill in the refrigerator.

To make the garnish, bring the water and vinegar to a simmer. Crack open the quail's eggs one by one, and poach for 1 minute. Lift out the eggs and trim any trailing bits of egg white. Place the eggs in lukewarm salted water until needed. Season the crème fraîche with cayenne pepper, lemon juice, and salt, and refrigerate. Heat the vegetable oil in a heavy-based pan and fry the *galettes* until crispy on both sides. Place 2 *galettes* on each warmed plate. Garnish with 3 quail's eggs, a little seasoned crème fraîche and caviar, and sprinkle with the chive flowers.

RICE ROLLS WITH GINKGO NUTS AND HOT SAUCE

Serves 4
4 oz shiitake mushrooms, 3 oz straw mushrooms
4 tablespoons light soy sauce, 3 tablespoons sake
3 tablespoons mirin
5 oz skinless, boneless chicken breast, diced
1 cup finely chopped carrots, 3 cups nishiki rice
15–20 canned ginkgo nuts, 3½ cups chicken stock, salt

marinated ingredients and the ginkgo nuts. Pour in the stock, bring to a boil, add salt, and simmer for 15 minutes. Sprinkle in the Japanese parsley. Divide the mixture into four. Scald fresh vine leaves with boiling water and refresh in cold water, or rinse preserved leaves in cold water; drain well. Proceed as shown in the photo sequence below. Wrap the rolls in foil, place in the steaming basket, and cover. Place the basket in a wok and steam for 15 minutes. Remove the foil, slice the rolls into pieces, and serve with the sauce.

Arrange vine leaves on a rolling mat, overlapping as you go. Spread a quarter of the rice mixture over the bottom edge, leaving a ½-inch edge free on the left and right.

With the aid of the bamboo mat, shape into a firm roll, repeatedly rolling the mat back behind the roll in order to press the filling down firmly.

At the end of the rolling process, press the rice roll together again firmly with the folded mat. Make 4 rolls in this manner.

| 2 tablespoons chopped Japanese parsley (mitsuba) |
| 1 lb vine leaves (fresh, or preserved and drained) |
| For the sauce: |
| 1 garlic clove, ½ cup finely chopped onion |
| 2 red chile peppers, 3 tablespoons mirin |
| 2 tablespoons light soy sauce, 1 tablespoon lemon juice |
| 1 teaspoon chopped wasabi (Japanese horseradish), salt |
| You will also need: |
| 1 wood-and-raffia steaming basket |
| 1 bamboo rolling mat (10 x 10 inches), kitchen foil |

Trim and slice all the mushrooms. Mix the soy sauce, sake, and mirin in a bowl. Add the chicken, carrots, and mushrooms, cover, and place in the refrigerator for 15 minutes. Place the rice in a pot and mix with the

To make the sauce, finely pound the garlic, onion, and chile flesh in a mortar, and stir well to combine with the remaining ingredients.

Press the fish fillets in the green rice on the skin side only.

Entrées with zing
Rice here as a crunchy coating, there as a salad ring

RED SNAPPER IN A RICE CRUST
Serves 4

12 red snapper fillets with their skin (about 2 oz each)

2 egg whites, lightly beaten; ¼–⅓ cup green rice

4 tablespoons olive oil, cilantro, salt, freshly ground pepper

For the sauce:

¼ cup chopped scallions, ¼ cup butter

generous pinch each saffron threads and curry powder

½ teaspoon pounded coriander seed

4 teaspoons Noilly Prat vermouth

3 tablespoons white wine, ⅓ cup fish stock

dash lemon juice, salt, freshly ground pepper

To make the sauce, sweat the scallions in 1½ tablespoons of the butter (chill the rest). Add the saffron, curry powder, coriander, vermouth, and wine, and reduce by half. Add the stock and simmer for 2 minutes. Whisk in the remaining butter in flakes, add lemon juice, and season. Season the fish, dip the skin side in the egg white, and coat with rice as shown above left. Heat the oil and fry the fish on the coated side for 2–3 minutes. Whisk the sauce again, pour some on each plate, arrange 3 fillets on top, and garnish with cilantro .

RICE-SALAD RING WITH CRAYFISH

Serves 4
4 cooked crayfish tails (about 5 oz each)
1 red chile pepper, 2 tablespoons vegetable oil
½ cup finely chopped white onion
1 tablespoon Champagne vinegar
1 tablespoon chopped parsley
2 tablespoons butter, salt, coarsely ground pepper
For the rice salad:
1¼ cups long-grain rice, 10 oz tomatoes
1 red chile pepper, 1 tablespoon vegetable oil
½ cup finely chopped onion
1 garlic clove, finely chopped, ½ cup finely diced carrot
2 teaspoons chopped fresh ginger root,
2 tablespoons chopped herbs (parsley, chives)
2 hardboiled eggs, finely chopped
salt, freshly ground pepper
For the curry sauce:
2 teaspoons finely chopped ginger in syrup
½ cup mayonnaise, ½ teaspoon curry powder
¼ cup heavy cream, whipped to soft peaks
dash lime juice, salt, freshly ground white pepper
You will also need:
four 1-cup ring molds 5 inches in diameter
oil for greasing the molds, mixed salad leaves

Halve the crayfish tails lengthwise and devein. Chill 4 halves. Shell and chop the remaining crayfish. Cut the chile pepper into rings and remove the seeds. Heat the oil and pan-fry the chopped crayfish briefly. Add the onion and chile, and sauté briefly. Season with salt, drizzle with vinegar, sprinkle with parsley, and leave to cool.

Boil the rice in slightly salted water for about 20 minutes, then drain. Blanch, skin, and seed the tomatoes, and finely dice the flesh. Halve the chile pepper, remove the seeds, and thinly slice the flesh. Heat the oil in a frying pan and sweat the onion and garlic until lightly colored. Add the carrots and sweat for 3–4 minutes, followed by the tomatoes, ginger, and chile strips, sautéing for 2 minutes. Mix the rice, vegetables, herbs, and eggs, and season. Oil the ring molds, press in the rice mixture, and leave to cool.

To make the sauce, mix the ginger, mayonnaise, and curry powder. Fold in the cream and add lime juice, salt, and pepper to taste. Melt the butter in a frying pan, then briefly sauté the halved crayfish tails, cut surface downwards. Unmold the rice rings onto plates, spoon the marinated crayfish meat into the center, and pour a little curry sauce on top. Place one sautéed crayfish tail to the side and sprinkle with pepper. Garnish with the mixed salad leaves.

Paellas

The paella is one of the delights of Spanish cuisine. To make it, you need Spanish rice; a heavy, flat, two-handled pan called a *paellera* and ideally made of wrought iron; and a strong, rich stock. The other ingredients can be more or less sumptuous, depending on the season and on individual taste.

Bacon, white beans, and slices of piquant chorizo are recommended for cold days. A paella containing nothing but vegetables in addition to the rice makes an ideal summer dish. Fish and seafood paellas are particularly popular; the freshly caught fruits of the sea are sold on the market daily in the *zona de arroces*, the "area of rice dishes" around Valencia and along the Ebro delta.

Paellas were originally cooked over an open fire, and even nowadays this style of preparation, which was traditionally the province of men only, still has its charm. No other method produces the *socarrado*, a golden-brown crust on the base of the pan, fiercely coveted by all diners. It is certainly easier to

prepare on the stove, however, where the paella is cooked until the rice is dry.

There are no hard and fast rules for either the preparation of or ingredients for this colorful rice dish. The proof of its flexibility are the countless regional variations: Each paella has a unique quality and never fails to surprise and delight through its own special flavor.

Rice from the pan
Usually with a few saffron threads and some flat-leaf parsley; and always with garlic

Although Spanish short-grain rice looks like the Italian variety and the preparation of paella would at first glance appear to be similar to that of risotto, the two dishes actually have little in common. The rice grains of the paella should never be creamy in texture, and therefore the amount of liquid added must be gauged so that the rice just absorbs it. The basic rule is to add about twice as much liquid as rice. When cooked, the rice grains should be dry and separate. For this reason, the paella is not stirred after the grains are sweated. Occasionally, the paella is just parboiled on the stove and then transferred to the oven to finish cooking. In any case, the rice should always be covered with aluminum foil and left to rest in the pan for a little while before serving.

ARROZ A BANDA

For this dish, the rice is cooked *a banda*, that is, separately, from the fish and shrimp. In Spain it is served separately, too, as a first course before the fish. It has a delicious seafood flavor from simmering in saffron-flavored fish stock.

Fish stock is easy to prepare: just make sure that the trimmings used are from freshly caught, lean white fish, such as turbot, sole, or John Dory. In addition, simmer the stock gently for no more than 20–30 minutes — any longer and it will become cloudy and gluey, and hence unusable.

Alioli is the Spanish term for the sauce the French call *aioli*!

Serves 4
For the stock:
2¼ lb fish trimmings (heads, tails, skin, and bones)
3 tablespoons vegetable oil
1 cup coarsely chopped onion
3 garlic cloves, coarsely chopped
¾ cup coarsely chopped green bell peppers

7 oz ripe tomatoes, coarsely chopped
9 cups water
1 bay leaf, 3 parsley sprigs, 10 white peppercorns

Heat the oil in a *paellera* of about 12-inch diameter and sweat the chopped garlic without allowing it to color.

Tip in the unwashed rice all at once and continue to sauté, stirring constantly, until the grains are translucent.

Pour in half of the reserved stock-wine mixture, add salt, and simmer for 10 minutes.

Pour in the remaining stock-wine mixture and simmer for 10 minutes. Add 2¼ cups of the potato cooking water to the pan.

Simmer the rice for a further 10 minutes, remove from the heat, cover with foil, and leave to rest for 10 minutes.

For the *alioli*:

6–8 garlic cloves, ½ teaspoon coarse sea salt
2 slices white bread, crusts removed, soaked in milk
1 egg yolk, 1 cup olive oil, a little lemon juice

For the fish:

1 mullet weighing about 3 lb, gutted
12 shrimp tails in their shells
14 oz small waxy new potatoes
1 teaspoon saffron threads, 1 cup white wine, salt

For the rice:

2 tablespoons olive oil, 2 garlic cloves, finely chopped
2 cups short-grain rice, salt

First prepare the fish trimmings. Remove the gills, the fins or fin edges in the case of flat fish, and chop coarsely. Transfer to a bowl and rinse for 20 minutes under cold running water, until the water runs clear, then drain. Heat the oil in a large pot and sauté the trimmings for 3–4 minutes, turning constantly. Add the chopped onion, garlic, peppers, and tomatoes, and sweat for a few minutes, turning them repeatedly. As soon as they begin to simmer, pour in the water. Add the seasonings, bring to a boil, and skim off the scum several times. Reduce the heat and simmer the stock for 30 minutes. Line a strainer with cheesecloth and ladle in the stock; there should be 5¼ cups.

To make the *alioli*, peel and halve the garlic cloves and pound them to a paste with the salt in a mortar. Squeeze the bread dry and mix it into the garlic with the egg yolk. Stir to a smooth paste. If it becomes too thick, stir in a little warm water until creamy. Let it rest, then stir vigorously and transfer to a bowl. Whisk in the oil, drop by drop at first, then in a thin stream. Season with a few drops of lemon juice.

Grasping the mullet firmly at the tai! end in a cloth and working toward the head, cut off the fins and scrape off the scales. Cut off the head and wash the mullet inside and out under cold running water. Cut into chunks 1¼ inches wide. Peel the shrimp down to the last tail joint, and devein. Peel the potatoes and halve lengthwise. Dissolve the saffron in 3 tablespoons of the fish stock. Heat the remaining stock with the wine, stir in the dissolved saffron, and reserve 2¾ cups of this liquid for the rice. Season the remaining stock with salt and boil the potatoes in it for about 10 minutes. Remove from the heat. Prepare the rice as shown in the photo sequence on the left. Reheat the potatoes in the remaining stock, add the fish chunks, and simmer for 5 minutes. The stock should only just cover the fish and potatoes; if necessary, add a little more water or wine. Add the shrimp and simmer for 3–4 minutes. Serve the rice as a first course, then ladle the fish, shrimp, and potatoes onto warmed plates, and pass round the *alioli*.

Vegetable paellas
Colorful and packed with vitamins

These recipes use a few small cubes of air-dried *serrano* ham browned in the pan to enhance the flavor. If you prefer a vegetarian paella, simply leave out the ham.

PAELLA DE VERDURAS

Serves 4
2–3 young carrots, 2 small white turnips
1 red bell pepper, 1–2 zucchini
2 oz snow peas, 5 oz tomatoes, 1 quart vegetable stock
⅔ cup white wine, 3 tablespoons extra-virgin olive oil
¾ cup finely chopped onion
2 garlic cloves, finely chopped
¾ cup finely diced serrano ham
1 tablespoon chopped parsley
2 cups Spanish short-grain rice
salt, freshly ground white pepper
You will also need:
1 tablespoon chopped flat-leaf parsley

Peel the carrots and turnips, and cut into ½-inch chunks. Halve, core, and seed the red pepper, and cut the flesh into strips. Top and tail the zucchini, halve them lengthwise, and slice into half-moons. Cut the snow peas in half diagonally. Blanch, refresh, and skin the tomatoes; cut into quarters, seed, and cut the flesh lengthwise into strips. Bring the stock to a boil with

the wine. Heat the oil in a *paellera* and sweat the onions and garlic until lightly colored. Add the ham and sauté for 2–3 minutes. Sprinkle in the parsley and rice, and stir-fry for 3 minutes. Pour in one-third of the stock. Mix in the carrots and turnips, and season. Reduce the heat, simmer for 15 minutes, and mix in the red pepper. Pour in another third of the stock and simmer for 10 minutes, then add the zucchini, snow peas, tomatoes, and remaining liquid. Mix well, season, and simmer for 8–10 minutes without stirring. When the rice is done, remove from the heat, cover with foil, and leave to rest for 10 minutes to absorb the remaining liquid. Sprinkle with parsley and serve.

PAELLA WITH WILD RICE AND PEPPERS

Serves 4
2 red and 2 green bell peppers
1 red and 1 green chile pepper
¾ cup diced serrano ham, 3 tablespoons olive oil
1 cup finely chopped onion
2 garlic cloves, finely chopped
1 cup Spanish medium-grain rice
4½ cups vegetable stock
1 cup white wine, 1⅜ cups wild rice, salt
You will also need:
1 tablespoon chopped flat-leaf parsley

Preheat the oven to 425°F. Roast the bell peppers until the skin blisters. Remove from the oven and rest under a damp cloth or in a plastic bag. Skin, halve, core, and seed the peppers, and dice the flesh. Seed the chile peppers and finely dice the flesh. Heat the oil in a *paellera* and sweat the onion, garlic, chiles, and ham for 2–3 minutes. Add the white rice and stir-fry for about 3 minutes. Mix the stock with the wine; pour one-third of it into the rice, and simmer for 10 minutes. Mix in the wild rice and the bell peppers, pour in another third of the stock mixture, season, and simmer for 10 minutes. Pour in the remaining liquid and simmer for 15 minutes without stirring. Remove from the heat, cover with foil, and leave to rest for 10 minutes. Sprinkle with the parsley and serve.

Paella de mar
Two versions with fresh seafood,
one dry, one moist

ARROZ CALDOSO

Caldo means "broth" or "sauce" in Spanish, and it is
this word that gives *arroz caldoso* its name, since this
delicious Catalan rice dish, first cousin to the paella, is
meant to be soupy in texture.

Serves 4
1 lobster (about 1½ lb)
10 oz carpetshells
10 oz squid
5 tablespoons olive oil
¾ cup finely chopped onion
2 garlic cloves, finely chopped
1 cup finely diced sweet red pepper
4 teaspoons Jerez brandy
1 cup sieved tomatoes (passata)
4½–5½ cups fish stock
1¼ cups Spanish short-grain rice
1 teaspoon saffron threads
salt, freshly ground pepper

The *arroz caldoso* cooks over a high heat on the stove, the rice
absorbing additional flavor from the shellfish, squid, and lobster
pieces cooked with it. The degree of "soupiness" desired, and
therefore the exact amount of fish stock needed, varies, but it is
important that the dish does not become too dry.

Clean the lobster under cold running water, scrubbing
with a brush if necessary. Cook for 2 minutes in fast-
boiling water and lift out. Halve the lobster lengthwise
with a large knife, cut through both halves between
the tail and body, and remove the stomach sac. Set the
lobster pieces aside.

Thoroughly wash the carpetshells, removing any
traces of sand and lime clinging to them, and discard
any open ones. Wash the squid and peel off the skin;
pull the tentacles right out of the body sac and cut off.
Remove the beak and quill. Wash the tentacles and
bodies of the squid again, inside and out, cut into ¾-
inch pieces, and drain well. Heat the oil in a *paellera*
and briefly sweat the diced onion, garlic, and red
pepper. Add the carpetshells, the sliced squid, and the
lobster pieces, and sauté for 5 minutes. Deglaze with
the brandy, stir in the sieved tomatoes and then the
fish stock. Sprinkle in the rice, stir in the saffron
threads, and season with salt and pepper. Cook over a
high heat for 15–20 minutes. Remove from the heat
and serve the *arroz caldoso* in the pan.

PAELLA DE MARISCOS

A variety of fresh shellfish are featured in this popular paella, and once again saffron is responsible for the beautiful golden color.

Serves 4

| 2¼ lb mixed mollusks (e.g. mussels, periwinkles, and carpetshells) |
| 4 jumbo shrimp |
| 4½–5½ cups fish stock, 1 teaspoon saffron threads |
| 4 tablespoons olive oil, 1 cup finely chopped onion |
| 3 garlic cloves, finely chopped |
| 2 stalks celery, finely sliced |
| 2 cups Spanish short-grain rice |
| 9 oz tomatoes, salt, freshly ground pepper |
| You will also need: |
| 1 tablespoon chopped flat-leaf parsley |

Carefully wash the mollusks under cold running water, removing any traces of sand and lime adhering to them. Discard any open ones. Pull the beards off the mussels. Bring some water to a boil in a large pot, add the mollusks and 1 jumbo shrimp, and boil until the

mollusks have opened. Discard any that remain closed. Shuck the mollusks, leaving a few in their shells for a garnish, and refrigerate them and the cooked shrimp.

Heat the fish stock in a casserole, sprinkle in the saffron threads, and steep for 10 minutes in the hot stock. Heat 3 tablespoons of the oil in a *paellera*, and briefly sweat the onion, garlic, and celery without allowing them to color. Tip in the rice and sweat briefly, stirring. Pour the fish stock over the rice, add salt, and simmer for about 15 minutes. Meanwhile, preheat the oven to 400°F. Blanch, refresh, skin, and seed the tomatoes, and finely dice the flesh. Twist the tails off the 3 remaining jumbo shrimp. Cut the unpeeled tails in half lengthwise with a serrated knife and devein. Scatter the diced tomatoes, shucked mollusks, and halved jumbo shrimp tails over the rice, drizzle with the remaining oil, and season sparingly. Transfer the paella to the oven and cook for 10 minutes, until done. Garnish with the mollusks in their shells and the one reserved jumbo shrimp 2 minutes before the end of cooking time. Remove the *paellera* from the oven, sprinkle the pàella with the chopped parsley, and serve in the pan.

Gloriously colorful and packed with flavor, jambalaya is a delight even in purely visual terms. The colorful Creole rice dish owes its superb taste above all to the freshly caught lobster.

Jambalaya
Seafood with bacon, rice, and fiery-hot scotch-bonnet chiles

Jambalaya appears in numerous guises on tables in the South and throughout Central America. Constants of the recipe are tomatoes and crustaceans, which can be combined according to personal taste and what is available, as well as (usually) ham or bacon. A certain heat, achieved by the addition of chiles and crushed black pepper, is indispensable. The seeds of the chiles should be removed before cooking, however, to avoid too much of a good thing.

Serves 4
2 medium-sized lobsters (about 1¼ lb each)
2 scotch-bonnet chiles
4 tablespoons vegetable oil, ½ cup diced smoked bacon
½ cup finely chopped shallot, 1 garlic clove, crushed
¾ cup long-grain rice
2¼ cups fish stock
a few saffron threads, crushed black pepper
½ teaspoon chopped thyme, 1 tablespoon lime juice
14 oz tomatoes, 9 scallions
3 oz air-dried ham, sliced thinly
salt, freshly ground pepper
You will also need:
1 tablespoon chopped flat-leaf parsley

Bring plenty of water to a boil in a large pot, add the lobsters headfirst, and boil for 3 minutes. Lift out and refresh in ice water. Crack open the tails and cut each

into 8 pieces. Halve the scotch-bonnet chiles lengthwise, remove the seeds, and slice the flesh into thin strips lengthwise. Heat half of the oil in a large frying pan — a high-sided iron pan is ideal — and sauté the bacon till very brown. Add the diced shallot and crushed garlic cloves, and sauté for 2 minutes. Sprinkle in the rice and sweat, stirring constantly, until the grains are translucent. Pour in the fish stock. Season with the saffron threads, 1 teaspoon salt, crushed black pepper, thyme, lime juice, and the chile strips, and simmer over a low heat for about 20 minutes, until the rice is done. Meanwhile, blanch skin, and seed the tomatoes, and finely dice the flesh. Trim and wash the scallions and cut diagonally into ½-inch pieces; blanch in boiling water for 2 minutes and refresh in ice water. Cut the ham slices into wide strips and mix into the rice with the diced tomato and the sliced scallions. If the mixture becomes too dry,

pour in a little more fish stock and simmer for an additional 5 minutes. Sear the lobster pieces on both sides in the remaining oil and mix into the rice. Season to taste, and sprinkle with parsley. Garnish with the lobster's head, and serve in the pan.

From the wok

The wok (the Cantonese word for "pan") is probably the most important utensil in an Asian kitchen. Stir-frying, the method usually associated with it, is a Chinese invention. No other cooking method produces such crunchy vegetables, or allows ingredients to absorb seasonings more quickly.

What's more, when food is stir-fried at a high temperature for only a few minutes, vitamins are largely preserved. A wok can be used for a great deal more than just stir-frying, however. Special bamboo inserts can be used for steaming foods, including rice. The high sides of the wok also allow food to be boiled or deep-fried, and you can even smoke foods in it.

Originally made of cast-iron , and now available in various metals, the shape of the wok is designed for optimum use of energy. Only the round base of the wok is heated directly, and the warmth then diffuses to the walls of the pan. The constant stirring means that all the ingredients cook evenly.

The preparation for stir-frying usually requires more patience than the cooking itself, for all the food must be cut up by the time the oil in the wok is hot. The aim is to achieve harmony and balance, so the more delicate the ingredients, the larger the pieces. Seasoning is also very important in stir-frying. Among the spices generally used are fresh ginger, lemon grass, and chiles.

Eckart Witzigmann and his colleague, a chef at The Mansion, the Thai restaurant in the Kempinski Hotel in Bangkok, in action at the stove: He takes care of the "heat" by stirring in the Thai curry paste, a spoonful at a time; she makes sure that nothing catches and burns.

Crunchy vegetables
Cooked to a turn in the wok

The uniformly cut vegetables, some of them blanched before cooking, are added to the wok one after another, beginning with the ingredients that need the longest time, and adding those with the shortest cooking time at the end. It is important to slice or chop all the ingredients: the bite-sized morsels of food are done in a flash, thus saving energy and preserving valuable nutrients. And, of course, they are then suitable for eating with chopsticks, which cannot be used to cut up food. The vegetables, fish, or meat must be absolutely fresh. If individual ingredients in a dish are meant to be stir-fried only briefly or to be deep-fried, lift them out with a slotted spoon as soon as they are cooked. The wok is not normally rinsed between the individual stages of preparing a dish, but may be cleaned with a special wok brush. The ideal wok has a rounded base, and can be used with a stabilizing ring on gas ranges. Models with flattened bases, designed specially for electric ranges, are also available.

CHICKEN-VEGETABLE RICE

Serves 4
2¼ lb chicken thighs, 7 oz baby corncobs
3 oz shiitake mushrooms,
3 oz snow peas, 3 scallions
4 tablespoons oil, 3 garlic cloves, sliced
½ cup finely diced sweet red pepper
1½ cups cooked long-grain brown rice
2 tablespoons each oyster sauce and fish sauce
pinch palm (or brown) sugar
salt, freshly ground pepper
You will also need:
1 teaspoon chopped celery leaves for garnishing

Take the chicken meat off the bones. Remove any sinews and slice the meat. Blanch the corn cobs in boiling salted water and refresh under cold water. Remove the hard stems from the shiitake mushrooms, and halve or quarter the caps according to size. Trim the snow peas and scallions, cutting the latter into ¾-inch-long pieces. Heat 3 tablespoons of the oil in a wok. Add the sliced chicken and stir-fry over a high heat until crispy, then lift out. Sweat the garlic in the oil remaining in the wok, stirring. Then add, successively, the corncobs, mushrooms, red pepper, scallions, and snow peas. Stir-fry the vegetables for a total of about 4 minutes — they should still be crunchy — and remove. Heat the remaining oil in the wok and stir-fry the rice for 2–3 minutes. Mix all the vegetables and the chicken into the rice, then stir in the sauces and season with palm sugar, salt, and pepper. Stir-fry for a further 1–2 minutes and serve the dish sprinkled with celery leaves.

VEGETABLE CURRY WITH RICE

Ready-made curry paste, which is used in a variety of ways in Thai cooking, is available in specialist Asian groceries in green, red, and yellow versions.

Serves 4

4½ cups coconut milk
2 oz fresh or 1 cup canned straw mushrooms
4 oz yard-long beans, 4 oz asparagus, 8 oz green beans
5 scallions, white part, with only a little green
2 oz snow peas, 2 oz winged beans
3-inch piece lotus root, 5 oz potatoes, 4 oz carrots
5 oz taro root, 2 red chile peppers
4 tablespoons Thai green curry paste
6 tablespoons light soy sauce, pinch of sugar
2 kaffir lime leaves
handful Thai basil, whole or chopped
You will also need:
1 cup Thai long-grain rice

Make the coconut milk yourself , as described on page 227, from 2 fresh coconuts weighing about 1 lb each or buy it canned. If using fresh straw mushrooms, trim them. Whether fresh or canned, halve the mushrooms. Trim the yard-long beans, cut into 6-inch-long sections, and make a loose knot in each section. Trim the asparagus and the green beans, and cut both into 1-inch-long pieces. Trim the scallions and halve them

lengthwise. Trim the snow peas. Pod the winged beans and slice the pods. Slice the lotus root into rounds. Peel the potatoes, carrots, and taro root, and cut into sticks. Remove the stems and slice the chile peppers into strips diagonally. Blanch the potatoes, carrots, taro root, and lotus root in boiling salted water for 3 minutes, lift out, and drain. Cook the rice in boiling water for 12–15 minutes. Bring the coconut milk to a boil in a wok, stir in the green curry paste, simmer for 1–2 minutes, and proceed as shown below. Strain the rice, spoon onto warmed plates, ladle the vegetable curry on top, and serve.

Simmer the halved mushrooms, sliced lotus root, and podded wing beans in the hot coconut milk.

Mix the asparagus, the sliced wing-bean pods, and the green beans into the coconut milk.

Add the carrot and potato sticks and the sliced taro root, mix well, and simmer briefly.

Add the scallions, snow peas, and the yard-long beans, and simmer briefly.

Stir in the chile-pepper strips and season the dish with soy sauce and sugar.

Add the lime leaves and simmer for 10–12 minutes. Lastly, stir in the Thai basil.

To make the fried curry rice, heat the oil in a wok until smoking hot and distribute it evenly, up the sides of the wok as well as on the base.

Add the shallots, garlic, lemon grass, and curry powder, and stir-fry for 1–2 minutes.

Add the cubed pork and chicken to the hot wok and stir-fry for 2 minutes.

Add the shrimp and stir-fry for 1 minute. Whisk the egg in a small bowl.

Push the contents of the wok to one side. Pour in the beaten egg, allow to set briefly, and mix everything together.

Add the cooked rice and stir-fry for 5 minutes, until all the ingredients are hot and the dish gives off an appetizing aroma.

Fried curry rice
A mixture of meat, fish, and seafood flavors

Fried rice can be made successfully only with rice cooked the previous day, so for the following recipes you will need to prepare the rice a day in advance of the meal. The choice of curry powder for fried curry rice is also important, and the particular combination of spices needs to be especially well suited to meat. The fresh aroma and taste of lemon grass contribute an important flavor nuance, along with the heat of the chiles and the assertive cilantro.

Serves 4

| 1¼ cups Thai long-grain rice |
| 2¼ cups water |

5 oz shrimp
4 oz boneless, skinless chicken
2 oz boneless pork
1 fresh red chile pepper
3 tablespoons vegetable oil
¼ cup finely chopped shallot
2 garlic cloves, finely chopped
½ stalk lemon grass, sliced into thin rings
1 teaspoon curry powder for pork, 1 egg
zest of ½ lime, 1 tablespoon chopped cilantro,
1½ teaspoons sugar, 1 tablespoon fish sauce
salt, freshly ground white pepper
You will also need:
Bombay duck and cilantro for garnishing

Wash the rice under cold running water until the water runs clear, then drain. Bring some salted water to a boil in a pot, tip in the rice, cover, and cook over a low heat for about 20 minutes. Remove from the heat, allow to cool, and refrigerate for use the following day.

The next day prepare the other ingredients. Shell the shrimp, cut open the back with a sharp knife, and devein. Wash the shrimp well and drain. Cut the chicken and pork into ½-inch cubes. Slice the chile pepper into thin rings and remove the seeds. After all the ingredients have been prepared, proceed as shown in the photo sequence on the left. When all the ingredients are cooked, stir in the lime zest, cilantro, sugar, and chile rings, and add salt to taste. Season the fried curry rice with the fish sauce and pepper, and stir-fry for a further 1–2 minutes. Spoon the fried rice into bowls, garnish with a few very quickly fried Bombay duck and fresh cilantro, and serve.

At Asian markets like the one here in Bangkok, rice is sold loose, or even by the sack; 1- or 2-pound boxes like those sold in America are uncommon.

Fried rice
Fruity with pineapple and shrimp, piquant with vegetables and egg

FRIED RICE IN PINEAPPLE

Serves 4
1 pineapple (about 3 lb), 10 oz peeled shrimp
4 tablespoons vegetable oil, ½ cup finely chopped shallot
3 garlic cloves, finely chopped

½ teaspoon ground turmeric
½ teaspoon curry powder, ½ teaspoon shrimp paste
2¼ cups day-old cooked jasmine rice, salt, sugar
You will also need:
whole cilantro leaves for garnishing

Cut the pineapple in half lengthwise so that the crown of leaves remains on one half. Peel the other half and cut out the "eyes" and the hard inner core. Dice the pineapple flesh. Hollow out the half with the leaves, leaving an edge about ½-inch thick, then dice the scooped-out fruit and set aside. Devein the shrimp and cut them into ½-inch pieces. Preheat the oven to 350°F. Heat the oil in a wok and sauté the shallot and garlic until the shallot is translucent, then remove. Add the shrimp to the wok and fry on all sides for about 1 minute, then remove them too. Add the turmeric, curry powder, and shrimp paste to the wok and stir-fry briefly, then tip in the cooked rice and stir-fry for a few minutes. Add the pineapple cubes and sauté. Mix in the shrimp, shallots, and garlic, and season with salt and sugar. Pile the mixture into the hollowed-out pineapple half and bake for about 10 minutes. Serve garnished with cilantro leaves.

Fried rice tastes superb with fried shrimp and pineapple chunks, especially when served as decoratively as it is here, in a hollowed-out pineapple half.

VEGETABLE FRIED RICE WITH EGGS

Serves 4

| 4 eggs, 2 red chile peppers, 4 scallions |
| 7 oz green beans, 5 oz carrots, 9 oz tomatoes |
| 5 tablespoons vegetable oil |
| 3 cups day-old cooked basmati rice |
| ½ cup finely chopped shallot |
| 2 garlic cloves, finely chopped |
| 1 tablespoon finely chopped fresh ginger root |
| 2 stalks celery, sliced; ½ cup vegetable stock |
| 2 tablespoons vegetarian oyster sauce |
| 3 tablespoons light soy sauce |
| ½ teaspoon ground turmeric |
| ⅓ cup candlenuts, chopped and roasted |
| grated zest and juice of ½ lime |
| ½ teaspoon palm (or brown) sugar |
| salt, freshly ground pepper |
| You will also need: |
| cilantro for garnishing |

Boil the eggs for about 8 minutes, refresh under cold water, then shell and keep warm in tepid water. Slice the chile peppers into thin rings, removing the seeds and stem. Trim the scallions and cut into rings. Trim the beans and snap into 1-inch-long pieces. Peel the carrots and cut into thin sticks 1½ inches long. Blanch, refresh, skin, and seed the tomatoes, and cut the flesh into ½-inch dice. Heat 2 tablespoons of the oil in a wok and stir-fry the rice for 2–3 minutes. Remove and set aside. Heat the remaining oil and stir-fry the shallots, garlic, and ginger for 1 minute. Add the scallions, beans, carrots, chiles, and celery, and stir-fry for 3 minutes. Pour in the stock and simmer for 5 minutes. Add the tomatoes and simmer for 2 minutes, then season with the sauces, salt, pepper, and turmeric. Stir in the candlenuts, lime zest and juice, palm sugar, and rice, mixing together gently. Dry and halve the eggs. Spoon the vegetable rice into bowls, arrange 2 egg halves on top, garnish with cilantro, and serve.

Brown vegetable rice
A Thai brown-rice specialty, crowned with half a giant river shrimp

In Asia the giant blue freshwater shrimp used in this recipe are sold fresh and whole, with their long, pincer-shaped claws still attached. Elsewhere they may be sold frozen as jumbo shrimp tails, with the head and claws removed. Another ingredient, the cilantro root, may prove difficult to find. If you grow your own herbs, though, you can harvest the slender roots from your garden. The green part of the plant cannot be used as a substitute in this recipe, since the flavor of the roots and leaves is not the same.

Serves 4
¾ cup long-grain brown rice
5 oz tomatoes
½ cup diced carrot, ½ cup diced onion
½ cup diced celery
4 oz Thai green asparagus, trimmed and diced
¾ cup diced pumpkin, 4 oz baby corncobs, diced
1½ cups diced broccoli florets
1½ cups diced cauliflower florets
2 giant river shrimp (about 12 oz each)
7 tablespoons vegetable oil
½ teaspoon palm (or brown) sugar
3 eggs
2 tablespoons fish sauce, 3 tablespoons soy sauce
salt, freshly ground pepper
For the spice paste:
3 small red chile peppers
3 tablespoons vegetable oil
3 cilantro roots, finely chopped
3 garlic cloves, finely chopped

Wash the rice under cold running water, then place in a bowl with cold water to cover, let stand until any particles of dirt have risen to the surface, and drain.

A certain amount of strength and, above all, a heavy, sharp knife are needed to cut up this splendid giant river shrimp expertly, as demonstrated here by Eckart Witzigmann.

Stir-fry the blanched vegetables in the hot wok for 1–2 minutes. Season with sugar and pepper, then add the tomatoes.

Crack open the eggs, one after another, into the wok, stirring immediately. Season sparingly with salt, fish sauce, and soy sauce.

Stir the cooked rice into the vegetable-egg mixture. Mix thoroughly and season to taste with salt and pepper.

Preheat the oven to 400°F. Transfer the rice to an ovenproof pot and cover with 2¾ cups water, salt lightly, bring to a boil, then reduce the heat and simmer, uncovered, for 10 minutes. Remove from the heat, cover the pot, and cook in the oven for about 20 minutes, until done. Skin, quarter, and seed the tomatoes. Blanch all the diced vegetables in boiling salted water for about 4 minutes; pour off the water, and drain thoroughly.

To make the spice paste, halve the chile peppers, remove the seeds, and chop the flesh very finely. Stir the chile peppers, garlic, and cilantro roots with the oil to form a paste, and set aside. Next, halve the jumbo shrimp lengthwise and devein them. Heat 3 tablespoons of the oil in a wok and fry the shrimp, cut surface upwards, for about 6 minutes. Turn, fry for another minute, then lift out and keep warm. Clean the wok, then heat the remaining oil in it and proceed as shown on the left. Arrange the fried shrimp on the rice and serve, passing the spice paste separately.

The halved jumbo shrimp makes a spectacular impression in the wok with its long, slender claws lying on a bed of brown rice, lots of vegetables, and eggs. If smaller, peeled shrimp are used, the visual impact of this rice dish is not as dramatic, but the flavor is not compromised.

Spiced fish rice
Tender fillet of yellowtail kingfish
and rice, with the full flavor of
exotic spices and seasonings

If kingfish is not available, use sturgeon or bonito

Serves 4–6

2½ cups basmati rice, 7 tablespoons vegetable oil
5 cardamom seeds, 4 cloves, ¼ cinnamon stick
1 onion, sliced into rings; 3½ cups water
1 garlic clove, slightly crushed; ¼ onion, sliced
10 oz fillet from a yellowtail kingfish
¼ cup coconut milk
salt, crushed black pepper
For the spice paste:
7 oz tomatoes, ¾ cup diced onion
5 garlic cloves, chopped
2 tablespoons chopped fresh ginger root
2 tablespoons chopped cilantro
juice of ½ lime, 5 teaspoons ground turmeric
5 teaspoons ground cumin seed, ½ cup fish stock
You will also need:
3 tablespoons rose water, a few saffron threads
cashew nuts, roasted and halved

Rinse the rice under cold running water until the water runs clear, then drain. Heat 3 tablespoons of the oil in a pot and stir-fry the spices. Reduce the heat, add the onion rings, and stir-fry briefly. Add the rice and stir-fry for 2 minutes. Pour in the water, cover, and simmer for 20–25 minutes. Allow to cool thoroughly. To make the spice paste, skin and seed the tomatoes, and dice the flesh. Purée the onions, garlic, and ginger in a blender with the tomatoes (reserving a few) and the remaining ingredients. Cut the fish into 1-inch pieces. Heat 3 tablespoons of the oil in a wok and gently fry the fish. Stir in the spice paste and coconut milk, season, simmer for 5 minutes, and transfer to a bowl. Clean the wok and heat the remaining oil in it. Stir-fry the garlic and onion over a high heat until brown, lift out, then briefly stir-fry the rice. Fold in the fish. Bring the rose water to a boil with the saffron threads, then drizzle over the rice. Sprinkle with cashew nuts and the reserved tomatoes, and serve.

Pumpkin custard rice
Rice mixed with eggs, coconut milk, and pumpkin flesh, and cooked in the pumpkin shell

Pumpkin custard rice is a popular choice in Thailand and other Asian countries as an accompaniment for fowl and other meat dishes.

The pumpkin enjoys great popularity in many Asian cuisines, the delicate-fleshed vegetables providing a pleasantly mild, light taste and texture. In this recipe, which is surprisingly easy to prepare, you do not have to cut up myriad ingredients into painstakingly small pieces, as is generally the case for Far Eastern dishes. Here, the rice is cooked first. It is then mixed with a few other ingredients and spooned into the pumpkin.

The fairly small Hokkaido pumpkins, weighing about 2¼ pounds each, are especially suitable for stuffing. You need only cut off a lid from the pumpkin and scoop out its flesh to obtain an extremely attractive and completely natural container for serving this rice dish. Because of its ability to cope with high temperatures, the Hokkaido pumpkin, whose lovely orangey-yellow color stems from its high carotene content, is the most widespread species of pumpkin in the tropics of both hemispheres. Provided it is not cut into, it will keep for weeks, even months. The other ingredients are easily obtainable. Coconut milk, for example, may be bought in cans in the supermarket, or in powdered form in specialist Asian groceries. You can, however, make it yourself quite easily (see page 227). Steaming, the particularly gentle cooking method used here, prevents the destruction of vitamins and preserves all the taste of the individual ingredients used. (It is important to use a steaming basket or steamer insert that is an exact fit for the wok.) The different flavors harmonize beautifully, rendering the addition of other seasonings almost completely unnecessary.

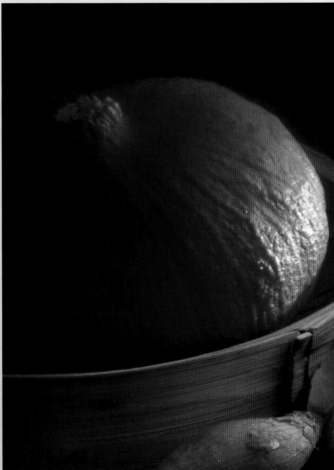

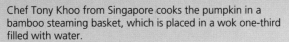
Chef Tony Khoo from Singapore cooks the pumpkin in a bamboo steaming basket, which is placed in a wok one-third filled with water.

Serves 4

| 1¼ cups glutinous rice |
| 2 Hokkaido pumpkins (about 2¼ lb each) |
| 3 tablespoons vegetable oil |
| 2 shallots, sliced into thin rings |
| 3 eggs |
| 1⅛ cups coconut milk |
| 1 teaspoon salt |
| You will also need: |
| *kitchen string for tying the pumpkins shut* |

Wash the rice under cold running water until the water runs clear, then drain well. Transfer the rice to a bamboo steamer, place in a wok, and put the lid on the steamer. Fill the wok one-third full with water. Bring the water to a boil, reduce the heat, and steam the rice for 15 minutes. Meanwhile, thoroughly wash the pumpkins, then dry them and cut off the top portion to form a lid, as shown in the photo below. Remove the seeds and fibrous insides with a spoon. Scoop out the pumpkin flesh, leaving an even edge of about ¾ inch, and cut into small dice of about ¼ inch. Heat the oil in a wok and stir-fry the shallot rings until golden brown. Add the diced pumpkin and stir-fry for 1–2 minutes. In a large bowl, whisk the eggs with the coconut milk and salt. Add the steamed rice, the shallot rings, and the diced pumpkin, and mix thoroughly. Spoon the rice-pumpkin mixture into the hollowed-out pumpkins, replace the lids, and tie the pumpkins tightly shut with kitchen string so that the lids do not slip off. Fill the wok one-third full with water and place the steaming basket in the wok. Transfer the pumpkins to the steamer and replace the steamer lid. Bring the water to a boil, reduce the heat, and steam the pumpkins for about 1½ hours until soft, taking care that the water never evaporates completely; add a little hot water from time to time if necessary. At the end of the cooking time lift both pumpkins out of the steaming basket, remove the string, and bring the whole pumpkins to the table while still hot.

The small, beautifully colored Hokkaido pumpkins make absolutely ideal containers for this dish, imparting just the right consistency to the coconut-custard rice as it cooks, and producing a particularly delicate result that does not dry out. If you do not have a wok and bamboo steaming basket, you can use a steamer insert and a normal pot of the appropriate size.

With artistic flair
Stuffed, carved, and draped: fine Far Eastern gastronomy

POHPIA — STUFFED RICE LEAVES

If you cannot find round rice leaves (see page 55), adapt the recipe to use egg-roll wrappers.

Serves 4
3 garlic cloves, 5 tablespoons vegetable oil
1 cup finely chopped scallion
6 tablespoons chopped herbs (Thai basil, cilantro, Vietnamese lemon balm)
½ cup Thai long-grain rice, 1 red chile pepper
7 oz jumbo shrimp, peeled and deveined
7 oz Chinese cabbage, ½ cup finely diced shallots
2 teaspoons finely chopped fresh ginger root
½ cup finely diced carrot, ¼ cup finely chopped celery

The sweet-and-sour sauce complements the *pohpia* superbly. To make it, briefly stir-fry 2 finely chopped garlic cloves and 1 cup finely chopped scallion in 1 tablespoon oil. Stir in 3 cups finely cubed pineapple and ¼ cup ketchup. Season with salt, pepper, and 1 tablespoon rice vinegar, and simmer for about 5 minutes.

½ cup finely diced tofu, 1 cup soybean sprouts
4 tablespoons ketjap asin, 1 tablespoon ketjap manis
24 rice leaves (7–8 inches diameter)
1 egg white, salt, freshly ground pepper
You will also need:
1 cup vegetable oil for deep-frying

Chop 1 garlic clove finely. Heat 1 tablespoon of the oil in a wok and sauté the scallions and chopped garlic until lightly colored. Reduce the heat, add the herbs, and stir-fry for 1 minute. Salt lightly, remove from the wok, and leave to cool. Clean the wok. Cook the rice in lightly salted water for about 12 minutes, then drain well. Finely dice the remaining garlic cloves. Cut the chile pepper into thin strips and remove the seeds. Cut the shrimp into ¼-inch dice. Cut the Chinese cabbage into very thin strips. Heat the remaining oil in a wok and sauté the garlic, shallots, and ginger for 1 minute. Add the chiles, carrots, celery, and tofu, and stir-fry for 2–3 minutes, then remove from the wok. Stir-fry the shrimp for 3–4 minutes and remove. Fry the Chinese-cabbage for

1 minute, add the bean sprouts, and fry for 1 minute. Add the rice and stir-fry for 2 minutes. Mix with the previously stir-fried ingredients and season with the sauces. Add salt and pepper if needed and allow to cool slightly. Soften the rice leaves in cold water one at a time, placing two on a dry dish towel. Spread the herb mixture over half of one leaf. Place the second leaf on top and fold both into a semicircle over the filling. Spread some filling on one half of the semicircle and fold in half. Brush the edges with egg white and press firmly to seal. Fill the remaining rice leaves in this way. Heat the oil in a wok and fry each parcel for 2 minutes on each side. Remove, drain on paper towels, and serve with sweet-and-sour sauce (see caption page 196).

FRIED VEGETABLE NOODLES

Serves 4
7 oz narrow rice noodles
2 oz fresh straw mushrooms, 2 oz shiitake mushrooms
2 oz green beans, 2 oz white cabbage sprouts
6 tablespoons oil, ¼ cup finely diced tofu
6 garlic cloves, finely chopped
½ cup finely chopped shallots
3 tablespoons finely chopped galangal, 2 eggs
1 teaspoon tamarind paste, 4 tablespoons fish sauce
pinch of palm (or brown) sugar
½ cup chopped scallion, ½ cup shredded carrot
¾ cup soybean sprouts
2 oz garlic chives, 2 cups celery leaves
¼ cup roasted peanuts and ¼ cup gingko nuts, chopped
4 teaspoons dried shrimp, 2 teaspoons lime juice, salt
For the sauce:
2 teaspoons tamarind paste, 6 tablespoons fish sauce
½ teaspoon palm sugar

Boil the rice noodles in lightly salted water for 3–4 minutes, refresh under cold running water, and drain. Trim and finely dice the mushrooms. Trim the beans and cut into ⅓-inch-long pieces. Cut the white cabbage sprouts, or failing these, baby white-cabbage leaves, into strips. Heat the oil in a wok and sauté the tofu, garlic, shallots, galangal, mushrooms, and beans. Whisk the eggs in a bowl, pour into the wok, stir until set. Stir-fry the noodles, tamarind paste, fish sauce, sugar, scallions, carrots, cabbage and soybean sprouts, garlic chives, celery leaves, nuts, and dried shrimp for 4 minutes over a high heat. Add salt if necessary and stir in the lime juice. Combine the ingredients for the sauce, stir in a little water until smooth and pass separately to accompany the vegetable noodles.

Stuffings

Originally, stylishness was not the main aim when rice-stuffed dishes were placed before diners. Instead, the most varied cuisines throughout the world made clever use of rice to "stretch" expensive ingredients or to improve the nutritional value of less nourishing foods.

That some truly interesting dishes arose from these imperatives is proven by numerous examples of vegetables, meat, and seafood with delicious stuffings, from purely vegetarian creations to delicate mixtures containing meat, with flavor nuances ranging from the Mediterranean-inspired to the exotic and spicy.

Rice-filled creations achieve the status of high culinary art when they are prepared by a master chef such as Eckart Witzigmann. A wild-rice-stuffed trout becomes a lavish main course, a mangrove crab is a feast for the eyes and palate, and a truffled chicken makes the heart of any gourmet beat faster.

When planning a menu, it is important to remember that the preparation of these *chefs d'oeuvre* takes some time, as well as a certain amount of practice. However, the results will justify the effort.

Portobello mushrooms
Stuffed with a mixture of vegetables, rice, and cheese

Portobellos are the fully mature form of the crimino, a variety of the common cultivated white mushroom. The large cap makes them ideal for stuffing. The dark gills must be removed first, however, as they would otherwise make the entire dish dark brown. In addition, the mushrooms must not be left standing for long, as they begin to discolor immediately. Other large-capped mushroom varieties can also be used.

Use a knife to skin the mushrooms, starting each time at the edge of the cap and pulling the skin off in strips toward the center.

With the aid of a pointed knife, cut all around the stem to detach it from the cap, or carefully twist it off by hand.

Scrape off the gills on the underside of the cap. This is best done with a melon baller or a teaspoon.

STUFFED AND BAKED PORTOBELLOS

Serves 6
6 portobello mushrooms
For the stuffing:
1 small red chile pepper, 8 oz portobello mushrooms
2 tablespoons butter, 1/2 cup finely chopped shallot
1/2 cup finely chopped carrot
3/4 cup finely chopped zucchini,
1 1/2 cups avorio rice, 1/2 cup light cream
2 3/4 cups hot veal stock
1 tablespoon chopped flat-leaf parsley
1/2 cup grated medium-mature Gouda
salt, freshly ground pepper
You will also need:
butter for greasing, 2/3 cup veal stock

To make the stuffing, halve the chile pepper, remove the stem and seeds, and finely chop

the flesh. Prepare the 8 ounces of portobello mushrooms as shown in the photo sequence on the left, and finely dice the caps and stems. Melt the butter in a pot and sweat the shallot until translucent. Add the chile, carrot, and zucchini, and continue to sweat for 1–2 minutes. Tip in the rice and cook, stirring, until translucent. Add the cream and the veal stock a little at a time, stirring occasionally. After 10 minutes mix in the diced mushrooms and simmer for a further 5 minutes. Season with salt and pepper, stir in the parsley and the cheese, and remove from the heat.

Preheat the oven to 350°F, and grease an ovenproof dish with butter. Prepare the portobello mushrooms for stuffing as shown on the left. Finely dice the stems and mix into the rice-vegetable mixture. Divide the mixture evenly among the prepared mushroom caps, place the caps in the greased dish, pour in the veal stock, and bake the stuffed mushrooms for 15 minutes.

STUFFED AND BREADED PORTOBELLOS

Serves 4

8 portobello mushrooms

¹/₂ recipe Stuffed and Baked Portobellos stuffing

You will also need:

2 eggs

4¹/₂ teaspoons flour

1¹/₂ cups fresh white breadcrumbs

salt, freshly ground pepper

oil for frying

First make the stuffing described in the previous recipe using half the amount of all the stuffing ingredients. Prepare the portobello mushrooms for stuffing as shown in the photo sequence on the left. Place 4 mushroom caps gill-side up on a work surface and divide the vegetable-rice mixture evenly among them. Place the remaining mushroom caps gill-side down on top to cover, and press together lightly. Whisk the eggs in a shallow bowl with salt and pepper, and place the flour and breadcrumbs on separate plates. Dredge the stuffed mushrooms in flour, then dip them in egg, and coat them in the breadcrumbs. Heat the oil in a large, high-sided pan and fry the breaded mushrooms over a moderate heat for 4–5 minutes on each side. Lift out, drain on paper towels, and serve. A mixed salad goes well with this dish.

Classic
Vegetables with a rice stuffing

STUFFED EGGPLANTS WITH TOMATO SAUCE

Serves 4
2 eggplants (about 8 oz each)
For the stuffing:
1/3 cup wild rice, 2 tablespoons vegetable oil
1/2 cup finely chopped onion
1 garlic clove, finely chopped
1/2 cup diced carrot, 3/4 cup long-grain rice
1 3/4 cup vegetable stock
1/2 cup each diced red and green bell peppers
1 tablespoon chopped flat-leaf parsley
salt, freshly ground pepper
For the tomato sauce:
1 lb tomatoes, 2 tablespoons butter
3/4 cup finely chopped onion
1 garlic clove, finely chopped
a pinch of sugar, 1 tablespoon basil, cut into strips
salt, freshly ground pepper
You will also need:
2 tablespoons vegetable oil, 1/2 cup vegetable stock

Soak the wild rice overnight in cold water, then drain. Heat the oil in a pot and sweat the onion and garlic until lightly colored. Add the carrots and long-grain rice, and sauté, then stir in the wild rice and pour in the stock. Bring to a boil, reduce the heat, and simmer for about 10 minutes. Add the peppers and simmer for a further 10 minutes, then season and mix in the parsley. Cook the eggplants for 3–4 minutes in fast-boiling water, lift out, and cool in a bowl of cold water. Preheat the oven to 400°F. Dry the

eggplants, then halve them lengthwise and scoop out the flesh with a teaspoon, leaving a ¹/₂-inch edge all around. Finely dice the flesh, mix into the rice, and divide the stuffing among the eggplant halves. Transfer these to an oiled ovenproof dish, drizzle with a little oil, pour in the stock, and bake for 15–20 minutes.

To make the sauce, skin and seed the tomatoes, and dice the flesh. Melt the butter in a saucepan and sweat the onion and garlic until lightly colored. Add the tomatoes and sugar. Simmer for 10 minutes, season, and add the basil. Serve with the eggplants.

TURKISH STUFFED PEPPERS

Serves 4
4 light-green bell peppers (3–4 oz each)
For the stuffing:
¹/₄ cup currants, 2 tablespoons olive oil
¹/₂ cup finely chopped onion
1 garlic clove, finely chopped
1 cup long-grain rice, ¹/₄ cup pine nuts
1³/₄ cups vegetable stock, 1 tablespoon chopped mint,
1 tablespoon chopped flat-leaf parsley
salt, freshly ground pepper

For the sauce:
2 tablespoons olive oil, ¹/₄ cup finely chopped onion
1 garlic clove, finely chopped
3 cups diced sweet red peppers, 2 thyme sprigs
¹/₂ cup white wine, ³/₄ cup vegetable stock
salt, freshly ground pepper

To make the stuffing, plump the currants in warm water for 10 minutes. Heat the oil in a pot and sweat the onion and garlic without letting them color. Add the rice and sweat briefly, stirring. Drain and squeeze dry the currants and mix into the rice with the pine nuts. Pour in the stock, season, and simmer over a low heat for 15–20 minutes. Add the herbs and set aside.

To make the sauce, heat the oil and sweat the onion and garlic until lightly colored. Add the diced peppers, fry briefly, add the thyme sprigs, and season. Deglaze with the wine and stock, simmer for 20 minutes, then purée. Preheat the oven to 350°F. Place the bell peppers on their sides and cut off a piece to form a lid. Remove the core and seeds. Fill the peppers with the rice, replace the lids, transfer to an ovenproof dish, pour in the sauce, and bake for 15–20 minutes.

Dolma is the Turkish name for peppers used for stuffing. Their thin walls and skin mean that they cook more quickly than other varieties, making them especially well suited for stuffing.

Mediterranean and Caribbean
The stuffed zucchini are a purely vegetarian dish, but the chayotes have a kid-meat-and-rice stuffing

ZUCCHINI STUFFED WITH RED RICE

The exotic flavor of the stuffed chayotes comes from a special seasoning mixture. The Jamaican curry powder, freshly mixed especially for this dish, lends a piquant touch to both kid-meat and chayotes. The Caribbean spiciness is provided by a piece of fiery-hot scotch-bonnet chile. The red rice with its slightly nutty flavor – the main ingredient of the stuffing for the zucchini – is a specialty from the Camargue in the south of France. The remaining ingredients of this dish have an equally Mediterranean flavor: spicy herbs and black olives.

Camargue red rice is always sold unpolished, and thus counts as a whole-grain rice variety.

Serves 4

4 zucchini (about 5 oz each)
For the stuffing:
1 cup Camargue red rice, 1 green bell pepper
7 oz tomatoes, 10 black olives, pitted
2 tablespoons vegetable oil, 1/2 cup finely chopped onion
1 garlic clove, finely chopped
2 1/4–2 3/4 cups vegetable stock
1 tablespoon chopped herbs (thyme, basil, oregano, and parsley), salt, freshly ground pepper

You will also need:

olive oil for drizzling, 2/3 cup vegetable stock
1/4 freshly grated hard cheese (Parmesan, Sbrinz or Cantal)

To make the stuffing, rinse the rice under cold running water. Transfer to a bowl, cover with cold water, and leave to soak overnight. The next day, drain the rice. Quarter the green pepper, remove the core and seeds, and cut the flesh into strips. Blanch, skin, and seed the tomatoes, and dice the flesh. Halve the olives. Heat the oil in a large pot, add the onion and garlic, and sweat without letting them color. Stir in the rice and stock, season, and bring to a boil. Reduce the heat and simmer for 20–25 minutes, mixing in the diced pepper and tomatoes after 15 minutes. Stir in the olives and chopped herbs, adjust the seasoning, and set aside.

Preheat the oven to 400°F. Wash the zucchini, halve them lengthwise, and scoop out the flesh with a spoon, leaving a thin shell. Finely dice the scooped-out flesh and mix into the rice. Mound the stuffing in the zucchini halves and place these in an ovenproof dish. Drizzle the zucchini with oil, pour in the stock, and bake for 15–20 minutes. Halfway through the cooking time, sprinkle with grated cheese.

Freshly grated Parmesan or another hard cheese provides the delicate crust for a stuffing packed with vegetables and nutritious whole-grain rice.

STUFFED CHAYOTES

Chayotes, or mirlitons or christophenes, as they are also known, belong to the gourd family. Their firm, slightly sweetish flesh can be prepared like a potato's, and they are also well suited to stuffing. Depending on the variety used, however, they must be peeled beforehand – ideally under cold water, since they ooze a very sticky juice. Thinner-skinned varieties do not need peeling. Bear in mind also that the rice for the stuffing must be cooked before you begin preparing this dish.

Serves 4

2 chayotes (9–10 oz each)

For the curry powder:

$^1/_2$ teaspoon ground turmeric

good pinch cayenne pepper

$^1/_4$ teaspoon coriander seeds

$^1/_4$ teaspoon fenugreek seeds

$^1/_4$ teaspoon cumin seed, 5 black peppercorns

$^1/_2$ star anise, $^1/_4$ teaspoon yellow mustard seeds

$^1/_4$ teaspoon freshly grated nutmeg, 10 allspice berries

For the filling:

1 lb kid-meat off the bone (e.g. from the leg)

2 tablespoons vegetable oil

$^3/_4$ cup finely chopped onion

$^1/_4$ scotch-bonnet pepper, seeded and finely chopped

1 thyme sprig, 1 cup water or veal stock

$^1/_2$ cup diced green bell pepper

$1^1/_2$ cups cooked long-grain rice, salt

You will also need:

butter for greasing, 1 cup veal stock

2 tablespoons melted butter

Peel the chayotes if using a thick-skinned variety; halve them lengthwise and remove the pits. Scoop out the flesh, leaving a $^1/_2$-inch-wide edge, and dice finely. Finely crush all the ingredients for the curry powder in a mortar. Cut the kid meat into $^1/_2$-inch cubes. Heat the oil in a large pot and brown the meat. Add the onions and the curry powder, and sauté for 1–2 minutes. Stir in the chile, thyme sprig, and water or stock, and simmer. After 10 minutes, stir in the green pepper and the diced chayote, and cook for another 10 minutes. Remove from the heat, stir in the rice, and season with salt. Preheat the oven to 350°F. Mound the stuffing in the chayote halves and transfer these to a buttered ovenproof dish. Pour in the stock and bake the chayotes for about 50 minutes, drizzling them at regular intervals with melted butter. Halfway through the cooking time, cover the dish with foil. Serve hot.

Lamb chops
Topped with an onion-and-rice mixture and served with a summery vegetable ragout

This is a rather lavish dish, whose well balanced Mediterranean flavors more than repay the effort invested in making it. Rosemary and thyme develop their intense aroma and flavor beautifully when pan-fried, and a *soupçon* of garlic complements the tender lamb chops. Light-fleshed summer truffles, which are indigenous to Central Europe, lend an additional accent to the whole. If the long rib bones are to remain on the chops, as they are meant to in this recipe, tell butcher when you buy the meat, as they are normally cut off.

Serves 4

8 lamb chops with long rib bones (about 3 ½ oz each)
¼ cup butter, 1 cup finely chopped white onion
½ cup arborio rice, ¼ cup white wine
1 ½ cups chicken stock
pinch freshly grated nutmeg
⅔ cup freshly grated Parmesan cheese, 1 egg yolk
3 tablespoons olive oil
2 garlic cloves, lightly crushed
3 thyme sprigs, 1 rosemary sprig
1 teaspoon moderately hot mustard
salt, freshly ground black pepper
For the truffle vinaigrette:
2 oz summer truffles, 9 tablespoons extra-virgin olive oil
4½ tablespoons balsamic vinegar
3 tablespoons beef stock
pinch salt, ½ teaspoon sugar, pinch grated nutmeg
For the vegetables:
1¾ lb small artichokes, lemon juice
14 oz cherry tomatoes, 4 tablespoons olive oil
2 garlic cloves, 2 thyme sprigs
salt, freshly ground black pepper
You will also need:
1 oz summer truffle, shaved, 4 small thyme sprigs

Scrape clean the bottom third of the long rib bones of the lamb chops, and refrigerate the meat until

Brown the lamb chops, garlic, and herbs in the hot fat for 1 minute.

Turn the lamb chops and brown on the other side for 1 minute. Cook all 8 chops in this manner, 2 at a time.

Place the lamb chops on a board and spread evenly with the rice-and-onion mixture. Smooth the stuffing and return to the frying pan.

Spread mustard on the meat on the rib bones, and sprinkle the rice-and-onion mixture with the remaining Parmesan cheese.

required. Melt half the butter in a casserole and sweat the onion until lightly colored. Tip in the rice and sweat, stirring, until the grains are translucent. Pour in the wine and reduce until it has largely evaporated. Add the chicken stock gradually and cook the rice for 18–20 minutes, stirring several times. Remove from the heat and allow to cool a little. Then season with salt, pepper, and nutmeg, stir in half the Parmesan cheese and the egg yolk, and allow to cool completely.

Meanwhile, make the truffle vinaigrette. Carefully brush off all the earth from the summer truffles. Where this is not possible because of deep cracks, peel the truffles. Rinse briefly under running water only if absolutely necessary. Cut the truffles into very small dice. Heat 4 tablespoons of the olive oil in a casserole and sweat the truffles for 10 minutes over a moderate heat. Deglaze with the vinegar, remove from the heat, stir in the beef stock and the remaining oil, season with salt, sugar, and nutmeg, and allow to cool.

To make the vegetable accompaniment, remove the hard outer leaves of the artichokes, cut off the tips, and halve the artichokes lengthwise. Scoop out the hairy choke with a small spoon and place the artichokes in plenty of water acidulated with lemon juice to prevent them from discoloring. Blanch, skin, quarter, and seed the cherry tomatoes. Heat the olive oil in a frying pan and sauté the garlic, thyme, and the well-drained artichokes over a moderate heat. Add the tomatoes and sauté for a further 3–4 minutes, then season and set aside.

Preheat the oven to 400°F. Salt and pepper the lamb chops. Heat the oil and the remaining butter in a large frying pan and fry the lamb chops as shown in the first three photos of the sequence on page 206. Roast the lamb chops with their rice topping for 10 minutes, then remove from the oven. Proceed as described in the final photo, then place the chops briefly under a hot broiler to melt the cheese. Place the chops on warmed plates. Deglaze the pan with 1/3 cup water, bring to a boil, and strain. Reduce a little and adjust the seasoning. Divide the sauce, truffle vinaigrette, and vegetables among the plates with the lamb chops, and sprinkle with thinly shaved truffle. Garnish each plate with a thyme sprig and serve.

The lamb chops stay tender and juicy under the onion-and-rice topping, which is sprinkled with Parmesan cheese and broiled. The meat is served with a vegetable ragout made from small artichokes and aromatic cherry tomatoes. Rounding out the whole beautifully is the vinaigrette of summer truffles, with a few paper-thin truffles shaved over the top intensifying the mushroom flavor even further.

Rice-stuffed poultry
Tender poultry and rice
harmonize superbly

STUFFED ROCK CORNISH HENS
WITH CARIBBEAN SAUCE

Serves 4

4 oven-ready Rock Cornish hens (about 1 lb each), salt

For the stuffing:

³/₄ cup long-grain rice, 9 oz tomatoes

2 tablespoons vegetable oil, ³/₄ cup finely chopped onion

1 garlic clove, finely chopped

¹/₂ cup diced carrot, ¹/₂ cup diced green pepper

1 strip lemon zest, finely chopped

2 tablespoons chopped mint, salt, freshly ground pepper

For the chile sauce:

2 tablespoons vegetable oil

1 cup finely chopped onion,

1¹/₄ cups diced mango, 1 cup diced carrot

1¹/₃ cups diced pumpkin, 6 allspice berries

5 black peppercorns, 2 thyme sprigs

2 tablespoons chopped fresh ginger root

1 small scotch-bonnet pepper, seeded and finely chopped

¹/₃ cup sugar, ¹/₃ cup cider vinegar, ¹/₃ cup poultry stock

You will also need:

oil for brushing

Wash the Rock Cornish hens inside and out, pat dry, and salt inside and out. Cook the rice for 15 minutes in boiling salted water, and drain. Blanch, skin, and seed the tomatoes, and finely dice the flesh. Heat the oil and sweat the onion and garlic until the onion is translucent. Add the diced carrot and green pepper, and continue to sweat for 2–3 minutes. Mix in the lemon zest, cooked rice, tomatoes, and mint, and season. Preheat the oven to 400°F. Loosely fill the stomach cavity of the hens with the stuffing a tablespoonful at a time; do not fill too full as the stuffing will expand as it cooks. Close the cavity and secure with toothpicks or skewers and string, and tie the legs together at the joints. Brush all over with oil and roast in an ovenproof dish for 40–45 minutes, brushing several times with oil.

Meanwhile, make the sauce. Heat the oil and sweat the onions without allowing them to color. Add the mango, carrot, pumpkin, allspice, pepper, thyme, and ginger, and sweat for 5 minutes over a moderate heat. Add the chile and sugar, allowing the sugar to caramelize. Pour in the vinegar and stock, reduce the heat, and simmer for 15 minutes. Purée the sauce in a blender, press through a fine-mesh sieve into a pitcher to serve.

TRUFFLED CHICKEN WITH RICE STUFFING

Serves 4
1 oven-ready chicken with giblets (about 3 lb)
2¹/₂ oz summer truffles, 2 tablespoons butter
¹/₂ teaspoon sweet paprika, 1 teaspoon salt
2 teaspoons Cognac
3 oz baby carrots, 1¹/₂ stalks celery, 5 garlic cloves
6–8 scallions, white part only
1 bay leaf, a little chopped celery leaf
²/₃ cup chicken stock, freshly ground pepper, oil for greasing,
For the rice stuffing:
³/₈ cup basmati rice, 1 small onion, ¹/₂ bay leaf, 1 clove
1 tablespoon olive oil, 3 tablespoons butter
1 cup chicken stock, ¹/₄ cup peas
¹/₂ cup diced green beans, ¹/₄ cup diced carrot
¹/₄ cup diced celery, ¹/₄ cup diced fresh asparagus
¹/₄ cup diced scallion, 4 teaspoons Madeira
¹/₂-inch slice goose-liver parfait
salt, freshly ground pepper
For the giblet stuffing:
2 teaspoons butter
¹/₂ garlic clove, finely chopped
¹/₄ cup finely chopped shallot
1 teaspoon thyme leaves, 1 teaspoon chopped sage
salt, freshly ground pepper

Push the truffle slices between the skin and flesh of the chicken, distributing it as evenly as possible over the breast and legs.

Place the giblet stuffing in the stomach cavity, then fill with the rice-vegetable mixture, taking care not to stuff the bird too tightly. Close the opening with toothpicks or skewers and string.

Roast the chicken for 60–70 minutes. Halfway through the cooking time, add the vegetables, bay leaf, and celery leaves to the baking dish.

Place the cooked chicken and the vegetables on a heated platter, removing the bay leaf. Pass the sauce separately.

Reserve the giblets, and wash the chicken inside and out, and pat dry. Push back the skin at the neck, cut the neck off at the breastbone, remove the wishbone, and refrigerate the chicken until needed. Carefully clean the summer truffles, washing or peeling only if necessary. Finely dice half of the truffles and set aside.

To make the rice stuffing, wash the rice in hot water and drain well. Preheat the oven to 400°F. Peel and halve the onion; finely chop one half and stud the other with the bay leaf and clove. Heat the oil and 1 tablespoon of the butter in an ovenproof pot and sweat the diced onion until translucent. Add the rice and sweat briefly. Pour in the stock, season, add the spice-studded onion, cover, and cook in the oven for about 20 minutes. Blanch the peas and beans in lightly salted water for 3 minutes, refresh, and drain. Blanch the carrots, celery, and asparagus for 2 minutes, refresh, and drain. Melt 2 teaspoons of the butter and sweat the beans and peas, then mix them into the rice with the remaining vegetables and the scallions. Melt the remaining butter and sauté the diced truffle for 2 minutes. Deglaze with the Madeira, season, and mix the diced truffles into the rice. Dice the goose-liver parfait and mix into the cooled rice.

To make the giblet stuffing, dice the heart and liver very finely. Melt the butter and briefly sweat the garlic and shallot, then add the heart and liver, and sauté for 1 minute. Season, sprinkle in the herbs, and leave to cool. Using a truffle plane, shave the remaining truffle into paper-thin slices, sauté briefly in melted butter, then season with salt and pepper.

Ensure that the oven is still at 400°F, and proceed as shown in the first two photos above. Pull the neck skin taut over the opening and secure to the back. Mix together the paprika, salt, and Cognac, and rub all over the chicken. Truss the bird. Trim or peel the vegetables and cut into fairly large pieces. Oil an ovenproof dish, place the chicken in it, and roast as indicated in the third photo. Remove the cooked chicken and vegetables from the baking dish, deglaze the roasting juices with the stock, strain the sauce, reduce slightly, and season to taste. Serve the chicken as shown in the final photo.

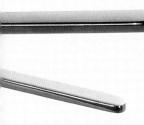

Sprinkle the Rock Cornish hens with chopped mint 5 minutes before the end of cooking time. Remove the string before serving and pass the sauce around separately to accompany the birds.

To make the aromatic basil oil, sweat 1¹/₂ cups fresh basil leaves, ¹/₄ cup chopped shallot, 2 chopped garlic cloves, and 10 peppercorns in some oil, top up with a scant ¹/₂ cup olive oil and simmer for 20 minutes over a low heat.

Seafood
Stuffed or with rice salad

STUFFED CRAB

Serves 4
4 blue or Dungeness crabs (14 oz each)
4 scallops with coral, shelled; 1 tablespoon vegetable oil
1¹/₄ cups cooked long-grain rice, cooled
1 cup finely diced apple, 1¹/₂ cups diced mango
¹/₄ cup chopped scallion, ¹/₂ cup diced celery
¹/₂ cup each diced red and green bell pepper
4 tablespoons basil oil, 20 drops chile oil, juice of 1 lime
1 teaspoon each lemon grass and cilantro, chopped
1 small celery heart, finely chopped
2 tablespoons pine nuts, salt, freshly ground pepper
2 tablespoons dried, roasted shrimp

Lower the live crabs one at a time into fast-boiling water, and lift out after 15 minutes. Keeping the legs intact, crack open the underside and remove the innards. Lift out the meat, cut it up, and set aside with the shell and legs. Finely dice the scallops. Heat the oil and very briefly sauté the scallops. In a bowl, mix the rice, apple, mango, scallion, celery, and peppers. Add the basil and chile oils, lime juice, herbs, celery heart, salt, and pepper, and mix well. Dry-fry the pine nuts in a heavy-based frying pan, and mix into the rice with the dried shrimp, scallops, and crab meat. Wash out the shell thoroughly. Arrange the shell with its legs on a plate as pictured above, stuff with the rice salad, and serve.

STUFFED BABY SQUID

Serves 4
¹/₂ cup long-grain brown rice
1 lb baby squid, 6 tablespoons olive oil, 1 cup fish stock
10 oz mussels, ¹/₄ cup finely chopped onion
1 garlic clove, lightly crushed, 2 thyme sprigs

¹/₃ cup white wine, 1 cup diced zucchini
¹/₃ cup diced sweet red pepper, ¹/₂ cup chopped leek
10 oz tomatoes, 3 tablespoons butter
salt, freshly ground pepper
For the sauce:
10 oz clams, 2 tablespoons oil, ¹/₄ cup chopped onion
1 garlic clove, lightly crushed, ¹/₃ cup white wine
¹/₃ cup chopped shallot, 1 garlic clove, chopped
¹/₂ teaspoon tomato paste, 1¹/₈ cups sieved tomatoes (passata)
1 thyme sprig, 1 rosemary sprig, salt, pepper,
For the pesto:
1 garlic clove, finely chopped; 2 teaspoons pine nuts,
1 cup fresh basil leaves, torn into strips
¹/₄ cup freshly grated Parmesan cheese
¹/₂ cup olive oil, salt, freshly ground pepper

Wash the rice, soak overnight in cold water, and drain. Wash the squid and pull the tentacles out of the body sac together with the innards. Cut off the tentacles just above the eyes so that they remain joined together. Remove the beak and quill, and wash out the body sac. Heat 1 tablespoon of the oil in a pot and sweat the rice. Pour in the stock, salt lightly, and bring to a boil. Reduce the heat and simmer for 20 minutes. Clean the mussels, pull off the beards, and discard any

open shells. Heat 2 tablespoons of the oil in a frying pan and sweat the onion and garlic. Add the mussels and thyme, deglaze with the wine, and simmer until the mussels have opened. Shuck the mussels, discarding any that remain closed. Blanch, skin, and seed the tomatoes, and finely dice the flesh. Heat 1 tablespoon of the oil and sweat the zucchini, red pepper, and leek for 2 minutes. Mix in the tomatoes and rice, season, and simmer until all the liquid has evaporated. Allow to cool and mix in the mussel meat.

To make the sauce, clean the clams, discarding any open ones. Heat 1 tablespoon of the oil, sweat the onion and garlic, add the clams, deglaze with wine, and simmer until the clams have opened. Strain, reserving the stock. Shuck two-thirds of the clams and set aside. Heat the remaining oil and sweat the shallot and garlic until the shallot is translucent. Stir in the tomato paste and stock, and reduce by half. Mix in the sieved tomatoes, season, add the herbs, and simmer for 15–20 minutes. Heat the shucked clams in the sauce.

Preheat the oven to 350°F. Spoon the stuffing into a pastry bag with a large, round tip and pipe loosely into the squid, and insert the tentacles in the opening. Heat the butter and remaining oil in a frying pan and fry the squid. Transfer to the oven and cook for 10–12 minutes. To finish, see the caption above right.

To make the pesto:

Grind the garlic, pine nuts, and salt to a paste in a mortar. Mix in the basil and the Parmesan cheese. Pour in the olive oil in a thin stream, season, and mix well. Serve the squid in the tomato sauce, garnished with basil leaves and clams in their shells, and drizzled with pesto.

Wild rice and smoked salmon
A very impressive combination

STUFFED BELL PEPPERS

Serves 4
2 green peppers (about 6 oz each)
16 thin slices of smoked bacon, 1/2 cup vegetable stock
1 recipe Stuffed Trout stuffing (opposite)
butter for greasing
For the tomato sauce:
1 1/4 lb ripe tomatoes, 1 red chile pepper
2 tablespoons olive oil
3/4 cup finely chopped white onion
1 garlic clove, finely chopped; 1 teaspoon thyme
salt, freshly ground pepper,

Preheat the oven to 375°F. Halve the peppers lengthwise, remove the core and seeds, and fill both halves with the stuffing. Cover each with 4 strips of bacon, arrange in a buttered ovenproof dish, pour in the stock, and bake for about 30 minutes.

Meanwhile, make the sauce. Blanch, skin, and seed the tomatoes, and finely dice the flesh. Remove the stem from the chile pepper and slice into thin rings, removing the seeds. Heat the oil in a pot and sweat the onion and garlic until the onion is translucent. Add the tomatoes and chile, reduce the heat, and simmer for 5 minutes. Season and stir in the thyme leaves. Take the peppers out of the oven, arrange each half on a plate with the tomato sauce, and serve.

STUFFED TROUT

A trout for stuffing should be left whole rather than having its belly slit, so it is gutted through the gills. This should pose no problems if you follow the method given here. If you are still doubtful, though, you could ask your fish seller to do it for you. If you buy trout that have been gutted in the conventional way, sew their bellies shut before stuffing them.

Serves 4
2 sea trout (about 1 lb each)
3 oz air-dried bacon, thinly sliced
a few parsley sprigs
3/4 cup butter, 3 tablespoons vegetable oil
4 garlic cloves, lightly crushed
5 juniper berries, 2 bay leaves, 1 rosemary sprig
2 dill stalks
salt, freshly ground pepper
For the stuffing:
2 tablespoons butter
3/4 cup finely chopped celery
1/2 cup finely chopped scallion
3 oz smoked salmon, 1 tablespoon chopped dill
1 1/2 cups cooked wild rice
salt (fleur de sel), black pepper

For the sauce:

⅓ *cup Noilly Prat vermouth*
⅓ *cup white wine,* ⅔ *cup fish stock*
4 finely chopped juniper berries
6 tablespoons ice-cold butter
3 tablespoons gin, juice of ½ *lime*
salt, cayenne pepper
You will also need:
cotton thread, aluminum foil
cooking-grade sawdust, oil for brushing

Scale the sea trout. Using a sharp, pointed knife, make a small slit at the ventril opening and loosen the flesh. Fold down the gill coverings and, using a small pair of scissors, cut off the exposed gills first at the top, attached end, then at the bottom end, and pull out the gills. Reach into the gill opening with your thumb and index finger and pull out the contents of the stomach. Carefully rinse out the trout inside and out, and drain.

To make the stuffing, melt the butter in a frying pan and sweat the celery and scallions for 3–4 minutes, then leave to cool. Finely dice the smoked salmon. In a bowl, mix the vegetables, salmon, dill, and cooked wild rice, and season to taste.

Lightly salt and pepper the trout and proceed as shown in the first photo below. Notch the trout along the backbone with a sharp knife. Wrap the fish in the bacon strips and tie loosely with cotton thread. Place a parsley sprig in each gill opening. Line the base of a wok with aluminum foil, then cover with cooking-grade sawdust to a depth of 1¼ inches. Wrap a suitable sized rack in foil, brush with oil, punch a few holes in it, and place in the wok. Place the wok on the

Remove the strings from the pan-fried trout and bone the fish as follows: First, carefully loosen the crispy skin with a knife and fold down to the side.

Next, season with coarsely crushed black pepper and *fleur de sel*. Carefully lift off the top fillets on both sides and serve separately.

Detach the central bone with a knife and carefully lift out in a single movement together with the attached abdominal bones, taking care not to leave any bones behind in the fish.

stove, switch on the heat, and proceed as shown in the second photo below. Then heat the butter and oil in a large frying pan and add the garlic, seasonings, and herbs. Fry the trout for about 8 minutes on each side.

To make the sauce, bring the vermouth, wine, stock, and juniper berries to a boil in a saucepan, and reduce to about 5 tablespoons. Whisk in the ice-cold butter in flakes, and season with gin, lime juice, salt, and cayenne pepper. Bone the fried fish as shown in the photo sequence above, drizzle with the sauce, and serve in the pan.

Stuffing and boning the trout:

Spoon the rice mixture into a pastry bag with a large round tip, and pipe the stuffing into the fish, taking care not to fill it too full.

When the wok begins to smoke, place the trout on the foil-covered rack and cover the wok with its lid. Smoke the trout for 5 minutes. Remove from the heat, and allow to sit in the smoke for another 5 minutes.

Heat 2 tablespoons of the oil in a wok and stir-fry the pork for 2 minutes. Add the shrimp and stir-fry for a further 2 minutes. Lift out the pork and shrimp.

Heat the remaining oil and briefly stir-fry the garlic, scallion and chile-pepper rings, and ginger. Add the snow peas and stir-fry for 2 minutes.

Add the mushrooms, stir-fry for 1 minute, and mix in the rice. Stir in the soy sauce and the cooked meat and shrimp.

Pour a little batter into the pan, tilting to distribute evenly. Cook for 2 minutes, then place 2 tablespoons of filling on one half of the crêpe.

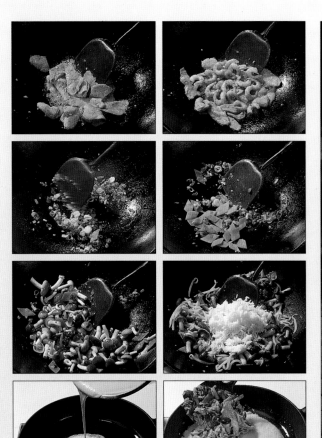

Crêpes
Rice-flour crêpes, fried till crisp and filled in the Vietnamese style

Shrimp, pork, and vegetables as well as rice are used to stuff the crêpes, which can be made several hours in advance; they are then simply reheated briefly in the pan before they are filled.

Serves 4
For the batter:
¹/₈ cup dried yellow mung beans
1³/₄ cups coconut milk, 1 cup rice flour, 1 egg
¹/₄ teaspoon ground turmeric, pinch sugar, salt
For the filling:
4 garlic cloves, 5 tablespoons fish sauce, pepper
pinch palm (or brown) sugar, 4 oz pork loin
9 oz deep-sea shrimp in their shells
²/₃ cup jasmine rice, 2 oz snow peas, 3 scallions
1 red chile pepper, 5 oz pio-pini or shiitake mushrooms
1 cup fresh bean sprouts, 4 tablespoons vegetable oil
1 tablespoon chopped fresh ginger
2 tablespoons light soy sauce
1 tablespoon chopped Vietnamese cilantro (rau ram)
1 tablespoon garlic chives
For the radish sauce:
¹/₄ teaspoon palm sugar, 3 tablespoons fish sauce
3 tablespoons light soy sauce
1 red chile pepper, juice of ¹/₂ kaffir lime
¹/₄ cup very thin strips of white radish (daikon)
¹/₄ cup very thin strips of carrot
For the nam prik sauce:
4 garlic cloves, finely chopped
¹/₄ cup finely chopped shallot

1 tablespoon shrimp paste, ¼ teaspoon salt
1 tablespoon palm (or brown) sugar
8 Thai red chiles, juice of 2 limes
You will also need:
4 tablespoons vegetable oil for frying, rau ram, chives

Soak the mung beans in cold water for 30 minutes, then drain and purée in a blender with the coconut milk. Transfer to a bowl and mix well with the rice flour, egg, ground turmeric, sugar, and salt. Strain and refrigerate for 2 hours.

To make the filling, peel and finely chop 2 garlic cloves and mix with 3 tablespoons of the fish sauce, pepper, and palm sugar. Cut the pork into thin slices and rinse the shrimp. Place in separate shallow bowls, pour the spicy sauce on top, cover, and chill for 30 minutes. Bring the rice to a boil with 1¾ cups lightly salted water, reduce the heat, and simmer for 15 minutes. Drain, refresh under cold running water, and drain again. Peel and finely chop the remaining garlic. Trim the snow peas and scallions. Cut the snow peas into diamond shapes with about a ½-inch edge, and slice the scallions into rings. Cut the chile pepper into thin rings, removing the stem and seeds. Trim the mushrooms, cutting a bit off the bottom of the stems

(remove the stems from the shiitake completely), and halve the larger ones. Wash the bean sprouts, drain well, and proceed as shown in the first six photos on page 214. Stir-fry the mixture for 2 more minutes, sprinkle in the herbs, and remove from the wok.

To make the radish sauce, halve the chile pepper, remove the stem and seeds, and finely chop the flesh. Mix the palm sugar with the fish and soy sauces until the sugar has dissolved. Stir in the chile pepper, lime juice, and radish and carrot strips, and allow the flavors to blend for 10 minutes.

To make the nam prik sauce, pound the garlic and shallots in a mortar with the shrimp paste, salt, and sugar to as fine a paste as possible. Halve the chiles, remove the stem and seeds, and purée in a blender with the lime juice. Add the garlic paste and blend. For a thinner sauce, stir in a little chicken stock.

Make the crêpes. Preheat the oven to its lowest setting. Heat 1 tablespoon oil in a 7-inch crêpe pan, but do not allow it to become too hot. Proceed as shown in the last two photos on page 214. Then cover, reduce the heat, and cook for 3–4 minutes, until the underside of the crêpe is slightly browned and crispy. Fold over the filling and keep warm in the oven. Make the remaining crêpes in the same way.

Arrange the stuffed crêpes on warmed plates, garnish with rau ram and garlic chives, and serve with the sauces. Pass around any leftover filling.

Desserts

Many culinary traditions around the globe agree on one point at least: Sweet rice is usually served as a glorious finale to a meal, with aromatic fruits often providing a flavor counterpoint. In the choice of cooking liquid and rice and fruit varieties, however, there are differences.

In America, Europe, the Near East, and North Africa, short-grain rice is usually cooked in milk to make sweet rice dishes. There are many desserts in addition to rice pudding. Some can be eaten warm, others cold; some are presented as dumplings and soufflés, others are served molded or even baked like a cake. Most are served with fruit, ranging from apples to pomegranates.

Asian-inspired recipes prove that long-grain rice can be transformed into fine desserts too. These, however, are cooked in coconut milk, or water mixed with fruit juice or fruit pulp, rather than in milk. Pineapple, papaya, or mango, for example, can then contribute an additional refreshing fruit note.

Of course, a rice dessert does not have to be prepared from cooked rice. Puffed rice cereal, for example, which provides a surprising crunchy effect in delicately melting, cool parfaits, offers interesting new perspectives for the creative and sweet-toothed cook!

Stylish fruity desserts
Some hot, some cold

RICE RING
WITH CHERRY COMPOTE

Serves 4
1 cup arborio rice, 2¾ cups water
3–3½ cups milk, 1 piece cinnamon stick
1 strip each orange and lemon zest
5 tablespoons sugar, 1 tablespoon + 1 teaspoon gelatine
1 cup heavy cream, 2 egg whites, 3 tablespoons kirsch,
For the cherry compote:
10 oz cherries, ¾ cup raspberries, 5 tablespoons sugar
4½ tablespoons orange juice, 2 tablespoons lemon juice
good pinch each ground cloves and cinnamon
2 tablespoons Port wine, 1 cup robust red wine
4 teaspoons kirsch, 4 teaspoons crème de cassis
2 teaspoons cornstarch
You will also need:
4 x 5-inch savarin molds, oil for greasing
½ cup heavy cream, 1 teaspoon sugar
good pinch ground cinnamon

Cook the rice for 3–4 minutes in fast-boiling, salted water, refresh, and drain. Bring the milk to a boil with the cinnamon stick, orange and lemon zest, and sugar. Mix in the rice and simmer for 30 minutes, stirring occasionally. The milk should be almost completely reduced. Remove the cinnamon and citrus zest, and chill the rice. Whip the cream and

Arrange the cherries to the side of the well-chilled rice ring and serve drizzled with a little cinnamon-flavored cream that has been whipped to soft peaks.

the egg whites separately until stiff. Dissolve the gelatine according to the package instructions, transfer to a large bowl, and stir in a little of the kirsch. Stir in the rice, then one by one fold in the cream, remaining kirsch, and egg whites. Lightly oil the molds, spoon in the rice, level the tops, and chill for about 5 hours.

To make the compote, wash the cherries and remove the stalks and pits. Purée the raspberries, strain, and set aside. Heat the sugar in a saucepan, stirring, until it caramelizes. Deglaze with the orange and lemon juices, bring to a boil, and stir in the spices. Mix in the raspberry purée, Port wine, red wine, and cherries, bring to a boil, and flavor with the kirsch and crème de cassis. Dissolve the cornstarch in a little water, add to the compote, bring to a boil again, and leave to cool. Whip the cream to soft peaks with the sugar and cinnamon. Run a pointed knife along the inside edge of the molds, dip the molds briefly in hot water, and turn the rice out onto chilled plates. Serve with the cherry compote and whipped cream.

WARM MANGO-RICE PUDDING
WITH SAKE SABAYON

Serves 8
⅜ cup short-grain rice, 1 cup milk, 2 tablespoons butter
a pinch of salt, 1 split vanilla bean
grated zest of ½ orange and ½ lemon
¼ teaspoon finely chopped preserved ginger in syrup
3 egg yolks, ¼ cup sugar, 2 egg whites
½ cup (light-colored) sponge cake crumbs
1¾ cups fresh mango cubes
¾ cup freshly grated coconut
For the mango compote:
¼ cup sugar, 2 tablespoons mango purée
1½ cups fresh diced mango
For the sake sabayon:
3 egg yolks, 5 tablespoons sugar, ½ cup sake
You will also need:
8 x ¾-cup round molds, melted butter
sugar, cinnamon, and confectioner's sugar
very thin shaved coconut ribbons

To make the compote, caramelize the sugar in a saucepan, stir in the mango purée, and bring to a boil. Stir in the diced mango and leave to cool.

Wash, blanch, and strain the rice. Cook with the milk, butter, salt, vanilla, orange and lemon zest, and ginger over a low heat for 20–25 minutes, until slightly al dente. Fish out the vanilla bean,

scrape its contents back into the rice, and allow the mixture to cool a little. Preheat the oven to 375–400°F. Brush the molds with melted butter and dust with sugar, tapping out any excess. Beat the egg yolks with half the sugar until slightly foamy, then fold into the rice. Whip the egg whites to stiff peaks with the remaining sugar. Fold the egg whites and the cake crumbs into the rice. Gently fold in the mango cubes and the coconut. Spoon into the molds, place in a 175°F water bath and bake for 30 minutes. Remove from the oven, leave to rest for 2 minutes, then loosen around the edges with a knife and turn the puddings out onto a heatproof, buttered cake base. Sprinkle with sugar and caramelize briefly under the broiler.

To make the sabayon, whisk the egg yolks and sugar together in a bowl until creamy, place over a water bath at just under boiling point, add the sake, and beat until foamy. The mixture should double in volume. Arrange the puddings on plates with the mango compote and the sake sabayon, sprinkling the latter with cinnamon. Serve warm with a dusting of confectioner's sugar, garnished with coconut ribbons.

CHOCOLATE-RICE PARFAIT WITH GLAZED PEARS

Serves 12
4 squares (4 oz) semisweet chocolate, 2 cups puffed rice
4 egg yolks, 1 egg, ¼ cup sugar
3 oz hazelnut nougat, 1½ cups whipped cream
⅓ cup chopped raisins soaked in 4 teaspoons rum
For the crème anglaise (vanilla-custard sauce):
6 egg yolks, ½ cup sugar, 2¼ cups milk, ½ vanilla bean
For the pears:
6 ripe pears (4 oz each), sugar

You will also need:
12 x ¼-cup oval molds, butter for greasing
cocoa powder, puffed rice, confectioner's sugar

Melt half the chocolate in a bowl over a water bath and stir in the puffed rice. Pour onto parchment paper, spread smooth, leave to cool, and then chop into little pieces. Whip the egg yolks, whole egg, and sugar until foamy. Melt the nougat and remaining chocolate in a bowl over the water bath and fold into the eggs. Fold in the cream, and stir in the rum raisins and chocolate puffed rice. Spoon into small oval molds and freeze overnight. To make the crème anglaise, beat the egg yolks with the sugar until creamy but not foamy. Bring the milk to a boil with the scraped contents of the vanilla bean. While still hot, stir a little at a time into the eggs and sugar. Transfer to a pot and cook over a low heat, stirring constantly, until the sauce coats the back of a wooden spoon. Strain and leave to cool.

Preheat the broiler. Peel, halve, and core the pears. Slice lengthwise at close intervals toward the stalk, stopping short of the end so that the slices are still held together. Place in a buttered ovenproof dish, fan out slightly, sprinkle with sugar, and glaze briefly under the broiler. Transfer each pear half immediately to a serving plate and allow the flavors to blend for a while. Dip the parfait molds briefly in hot water, run a knife around the inside edge, and turn out the parfaits. Sift some cocoa powder over the top of each and place a parfait on each plate next to the pear fan. Briefly whisk the cooled crème anglaise with a hand blender, pour it around the pears and the parfait, and sprinkle some puffed rice on the sauce. Sift a little confectioner's sugar over the dessert and serve at once.

The chocolate-rice parfait — the individual components of which may be prepared in advance — makes a good dessert for a family celebration.

Autumnal
Ripe quinces, with their incomparable aroma, add plenty of flavor to the rice

RICE DUMPLINGS WITH QUINCES

Serves 4
14 oz quinces, 1 cup white wine
juice and grated zest of ½ lemon
1 cup milk, 1 cup cream
scraped contents of ½ vanilla bean
2-inch cinnamon stick, ½ cup sugar, a pinch of salt
1 cup short-grain rice, 2 egg yolks, 1 egg white
For the elderberry sauce:
5 oz apples, 10 oz elderberries
⅔ cup red wine, ⅓ cup freshly squeezed orange juice
½ cup sugar, 3 cloves
You will also need:
3¼ cups milk, ½ vanilla bean
½ cup heavy cream, 4 teaspoons sugar, croquant

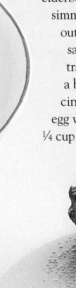

Peel, halve, and core the quinces, and dice finely. Heat the wine with the lemon juice, add the quinces, and simmer for 5–8 minutes. Strain, reserving the cooking liquid. Bring the milk to a boil in an ovenproof pot with the lemon zest, cream, scraped contents of the vanilla bean, cinnamon stick, half the sugar, and salt. Trickle in the rice, stirring, and simmer over a low heat for 25 minutes. Preheat the oven to 300°F. Stir the quince cooking liquid into the rice,

transfer the pot to the oven, and bake for about 20 minutes, until done. Remove from the oven, mix in the diced quince and the egg yolks, and leave to cool.

To make the elderberry sauce, peel, quarter, and core the apples, and cut into segments. Strip the elderberries from their stalks, wash carefully, and drain well. Bring the red wine to a boil in a saucepan with the orange juice, sugar, and cloves. Add the elderberries and apples, and simmer for 4–5 minutes. Fish out the cloves and leave the sauce to cool. Meanwhile, transfer the cooked rice to a bowl and remove the cinnamon stick. Beat the egg white with the remaining ¼ cup sugar to stiff peaks and

The fritters taste best warm and still soft on the inside, dusted with confectioner's sugar.

carefully fold into the rice. Bring the milk to a boil with the ½ vanilla bean and reduce the heat. Wet your hands and form the rice mixture into 8 oval dumplings, then simmer these in the hot milk for about 12 minutes, until done. Whip the cream with the sugar until soft peaks form. Spoon the elderberry sauce onto plates, garnish with a dollop of cream, top with the rice dumplings and serve sprinkled with croquant.

RICE FRITTERS
Serves 4

3 tablespoons chopped candied lemon zest

3 tablespoons chopped candied orange zest

2 tablespoons chopped raisins, ¼ cup chopped walnuts

1½ tablespoons pine nuts, chopped

4 teaspoons vin santo

2¼ cups milk, ¼ teaspoon salt, 3 tablespoons sugar

1 cup arborio rice, ¼ cup butter, 2 egg whites

grated zest of ½ lemon, grated zest of 1 orange

2 egg yolks, 1 cake fresh yeast, ½ cup flour

You will also need:

oil for deep-frying, confectioner's sugar for dusting

Mix the candied zests, raisins, walnuts, and pine nuts with the vin santo and steep for 1 hour. Bring the milk to a boil in a saucepan, stir in the salt and 2 teaspoons of the sugar, add the rice, and cook for 4–5 minutes, stirring. Fold in the butter and simmer for about 20 minutes, until the liquid is completely absorbed. Leave to cool until lukewarm. Meanwhile, whip the egg whites with the remaining sugar until stiff. Stir the grated zests, egg yolks, and crumbled yeast into the cooled rice. Fold in the sifted flour and the soaked fruit and nuts. Fold the whipped egg whites into the rice with a wooden spatula. Using two tablespoons dipped in water, form the rice mixture into dumplings. Heat the oil to 300°F in a deep-fat fryer, and fry the fritters for 4–5 minutes, until brown and crisp. Drain on paper towels and serve warm, dusted with confectioner's sugar.

Sweet croquant makes an interesting foil for the tart quinces and elderberries. To make it, lightly caramelize ¾ cup sugar, quickly stir in ½ cup coarsely chopped, roasted almonds, and roll out on a work surface with an oiled rolling pin into a ½-inch-thick slab. When cool, break into small pieces.

Light and quick with fruit

Use cinnamon and cardamom, hazelnuts, or orange juice to add flavor to the rice: the result is always delicious

These recipes are as digestible as they are easy to prepare. The fruit can easily be cooked in advance, and the rice itself then takes only 10–25 minutes.

ORANGE RICE PUDDING

Serves 4
1½ cups short-grain rice
1 strip orange zest, ⅔ cup orange juice
2½–3¼ cups milk, a pinch of salt
2 tablespoons butter, ¾ cup sugar
4 teaspoons Cointreau, 1 orange

Bring the rice to a boil in a pot with the orange zest, ¼ cup of the orange juice, milk, and salt. Reduce the heat and simmer for 20–25 minutes, stirring several times. Melt the butter in a saucepan, stir in the sugar, the remaining orange juice, and the Cointreau, and reduce the liquid by half. Cut a "lid" off both ends of

the orange and remove the peel thickly in segments. Cut into the orange just inside the separating membranes, release the "fillets," and reserve. Squeeze the juice from the pith and pulp you are left with, and stir it into the rice. Two to three minutes before the end of cooking time, fold the orange fillets into the rice and gently mix in the orange sauce.

HAZELNUT RICE

In this recipe a lot depends on the quality of the apricots and the hazelnuts. Buy only aromatic fruit and, because shelled nuts packed in cellophane can be affected by the light, we recommend buying hazelnuts in their shells and cracking them yourself.

Serves 4
⅔ cup shelled hazelnut, 2 tablespoons butter
heaping ½ cup sugar
1½ cups long-grain rice, 2¼ cups water
For the apricot compote:
10 oz fresh apricots, ¾ cup sugar, ½ cup water
1 tablespoon lemon juice, 2 teaspoons almond liqueur
You will also need:
lemon-balm leaves for garnishing

Preheat the oven to 400°F. Scatter the hazelnuts loosely on a baking sheet and roast in the oven until their brown skins burst. Cool slightly, until the skins

The oranges for this dessert should be fully ripe, aromatic, and juicy, since the result depends to a great extent on their flavor. Orange rice pudding served ice cold, popular all around the Mediterranean, is very refreshing on a hot day.

come off easily. Shake the nuts onto a dish towel and rub off the skins. Finely chop the nuts. Melt the butter in a pot, add the sugar, and caramelize. Sprinkle in the nuts and the rice, and stir to combine. Add the water, bring to a boil, reduce the heat, and simmer the rice for about 20 minutes, stirring occasionally.

To make the compote, blanch the apricots in boiling water, then skin, halve, and pit them. Bring the sugar to a boil in a saucepan with the water and lemon juice, and simmer for 2–3 minutes, skimming if necessary. Add the apricots and cook for 8–10 minutes until soft, keeping the heat just under boiling point. Stir in the almond liqueur and allow the compote to cool. Serve the hazelnut rice with the apricot compote, garnished with the lemon-balm leaves.

SPICED RICE WITH CINNAMON

Cardamom and cinnamon are the key flavors of this delectable rice dessert, which owes its color to saffron. The cooked rice is shaped by being packed in oval molds, then turned out. A fruity sour-cherry compote is the perfect accompaniment.

Serves 4

1¾ cups jasmine rice or Thai fragrant rice
4 cardamom pods, 1½-inch cinnamon stick
a pinch of salt, ¼ cup butter,
1 teaspoon ground saffron, ¾ cup sugar
For the sour cherries:
½ cup red wine, ½ cup sugar, 1 tablespoon lemon juice
9 oz sour cherries, washed and pitted
4 teaspoons rum, ½ teaspoon cornstarch
You will also need:
4 oval molds, oil for greasing
peppermint leaves for garnishing

Bring the rice to a boil in a pot with 2¼ cups water, the cardamom pods, cinnamon stick, and salt. Reduce the heat and simmer, covered, for 10 minutes. Pour into a strainer, refresh under cold water, and drain.

To make the sour-cherry compote, bring the wine to a boil with the sugar and lemon juice. Add the cherries and simmer for 3–4 minutes, then stir in the rum. Dissolve the cornstarch in a little water and use to bind the cherry compote. Allow to boil up and leave to cool slightly. Melt the butter in a saucepan and stir in the saffron and sugar. Mix in the well-drained rice and a little less than ½ cup water, and cook the rice for 5–8 minutes until done, stirring frequently. Remove the cinnamon stick and cardamom pods. Spoon the rice mixture into well-oiled molds, press down firmly, and turn out onto serving plates. Serve with the sour-cherry compote and garnish with fresh mint.

Sweet saffron rice
A Turkish specialty for festive occasions, served with pomegranate seeds or sour-cherry compote

Serves 4

For the saffron rice:

2 cups sugar, ¾ cup short-grain rice

1 teaspoon ground saffron

1 tablespoon rice flour, juice of ½ lemon

2 teaspoons rose water

You will also need:

1½ tablespoons pine nuts, 1 pomegranate

peppermint leaves for garnishing

For the sour-cherry compote:

10 oz sour cherries, pitted

1 cup cherry juice, 2 cloves

2 inches cinnamon stick

¾ cup sugar, ¼ teaspoon cornstarch

To make the saffron rice, bring 4¾ cups water to a boil in a saucepan with the sugar. Reduce the heat slightly, tip in the rice, and cook by the absorption method over a low heat for 20 minutes. Sprinkle in the ground saffron and stir into the rice to combine thoroughly. Dissolve the rice flour in a little water, mix it into the rice, and simmer the rice for a little while longer, stirring occasionally, until it thickens slightly. Stir in the lemon juice and rose water, remove from the heat, and leave to cool. Dry roast the pine nuts in a heavy-based pan until light brown. Break open the pomegranate, scoop out the seeds, and remove the bitter dividing ribs. Spoon the saffron rice into bowls, sprinkle with pine nuts and pomegranate seeds, and garnish with peppermint.

If you prefer to make the sour-cherry compote, bring the cherry juice, cloves, cinnamon stick, and sugar to a boil in a saucepan, stir in the cherries, and simmer for 2–3 minutes. Dissolve the cornstarch in a little water and use to bind the cherry compote. Allow to boil up, remove from the heat, and let cool. Serve the sour-cherry compote with the saffron rice in shallow bowls, garnished with peppermint leaves.

The creamy pineapple rice is served very
decoratively in the hollowed out shell of the fruit
with its green leaf crown still in place. The flavors
of the dish are rounded out by candied ginger and
roasted cashew nuts.

Aromatic and fruity
Mango and pineapple are
important ingredients in many
Thai rice desserts

PINEAPPLE RICE

Serves 4
1 pineapple (about 3 lb)
¼ cup sugar, a pinch of salt
½ cup short-grain rice, zest and juice of 1 lemon
2 teaspoons crystallized ginger, chopped
3 tablespoons cashew nuts, chopped and roasted

Halve the pineapple lengthwise, leaving the leaf
crown attached to one half. Peel the other half, cut
out the "eyes", and cut the flesh into ½-inch cubes.
Hollow out the half with the leaves, leaving a margin
of about ½ inch, and purée the flesh in a blender with
the sugar and salt. Push the purée through a fine
strainer into a measuring jug, add water to make 1¾

In Thailand, a special rice spoon like the one shown here, made
of artistically carved wood, is brought out only on special
occasions. This rice dessert combining the flavors of coconut and
fresh mango tastes exquisite.

cups, transfer to a pot, and bring to a boil. Wash the rice, drain well, and sprinkle into the thinned purée, stirring constantly. Mix in the lemon zest, lemon juice, and 1 teaspoon ginger, and bring to a boil. Reduce the heat and cook the rice by the absorption method for about 20 minutes, stirring occasionally. Mix the pineapple cubes into the rice, spoon the mixture into the hollowed-out pineapple half, and sprinkle with the remaining crystallized ginger and the cashew nuts.

COCONUT RICE WITH MANGO

Serves 4
For the coconut milk:
1 coconut, 2¼ cups milk or water
For the coconut rice:
1¼ cups glutinous rice, ½ cup coconut milk
heaping ½ cup sugar, ¼ teaspoon salt
For the coconut sauce:
½ cup coconut milk, heaping ½ cup sugar
You will also need:
2 mangoes (about 10 oz each)
⅓ cup freshly grated coconut

To make the coconut milk, open two of the "eyes" in the coconut with a hammer and nail, and pour the coconut water in a bowl. Crack open the coconut, prise the flesh from the shell, and remove the brown skin with a potato peeler. Proceed as shown below.

Soak the rice in cold water for about 2 hours, then drain. Fill a wok one-third full of water and bring to a boil. Scatter the rice over the base of a bamboo steamer, place over the boiling water, and steam for 15 minutes. Combine the coconut milk with the sugar and salt in a bowl, add the hot rice, and mix well. Cut the mangoes lengthwise into 3 pieces, with the stone in the middle section. Peel the middle section and, pressing the stone down on a cutting board, use a knife to strip off the flesh. Mix the flesh and juice into the rice. Loosen the flesh from the other two sections with a spoon and cut into ½-inch dice. Dry-roast the freshly grated coconut in a heavy-based pan. To make the sauce, stir the sugar into the coconut milk, blending thoroughly. Spoon the mango rice into dessert bowls, top with the mango cubes, drizzle with a little coconut sauce, and sprinkle with roasted grated coconut.

Either finely grate the coconut into the bowl with the coconut water, or dice the coconut flesh, purée in the blender, and then add to the water.

Pour the boiling milk or water over the coconut mixture. Transfer to a saucepan, bring to a boil, remove from the heat, and steep for 2–3 hours.

Line a bowl with cheesecloth and ladle in the coconut mixture. Gather the cloth at the top to make a bag.

Holding the bag in one hand, twist firmly with the other hand, squeezing out as much of the liquid as possible. This should yield about 2¼ cups coconut milk.

The red passion fruit, or purple granadilla, is known to plant lovers above all for its extraordinarily beautiful blossoms. It is distinguished from the yellow passion fruit by its sweet-tart flavor with delicate apricot overtones.

Stuffed papayas
Rice pudding and two varieties of tropical fruit under a meringue topping

Throughout Southeast Asia the combination of rice and fruit is predominant in desserts — hardly surprising when you consider the overwhelming selection of fruit available. The sweet delicacy here owes its full flavor to a syrup made from passion fruit and fresh ripe papayas. It is, however, prepared according to the rules of Western culinary art, a successful example of culinary "East meets West."

Of the many different varieties of papaya cultivated worldwide, the smaller ones are particularly well suited to stuffing, for example, the ones marketed under the name "Solo" or "Hawaii," which weigh about 14 ounces and are just right for two portions.

Serves 4
2 papayas (10–14 oz each)
For the rice-pudding filling:
2 cups milk, a pinch of salt
¼ cup sugar, ½ cup short-grain rice
For the fruit syrup:
6 red passion fruit (about ½ cup fruit pulp in total)
juice of 2 limes
scant 1 cup sugar
For the meringue topping:
4 egg whites, ¾ cup sugar
You will also need:
cocoa powder for dusting

To make the rice-pudding filling, bring the milk to a boil in a saucepan with the salt and sugar, sprinkle in the rice, stirring, and cook by the absorption method over a low heat for 30–35 minutes. Remove the rice from the heat and leave to cool.

To make the syrup, halve the passion fruits and scoop out the pulp with a spoon. Cook the pulp, lime juice, and sugar together in a pot, stirring frequently, until the mixture reaches a syrupy consistency.

Halve the papayas lengthwise, remove the black seeds, and hollow out the fruits with a spoon, leaving a ¼-inch edge. Cut the scooped-out fruit into small cubes. To make the meringue, whip the egg whites to stiff peaks while slowly trickling in the sugar. Stew the papaya cubes in half of the passion-fruit syrup for 1–2 minutes, remove from the heat, and mix in the cooked rice. The filling must be light and fluffy; if it has become too solid, fold in a little whipped egg white. Divide the filling evenly among the 4 hollowed-out papaya halves. Spoon the remaining whipped egg white into a piping bag with a round tip and pipe a meringue topping in the form of overlapping drops onto the stuffed papayas. Place the fruit under the broiler until the meringue begins to brown slightly.

Dust some cocoa powder over the papaya halves and transfer to 4 serving plates. Reheat the remaining passion-fruit syrup briefly and serve as an accompanying sauce.

Cakes with rice
Rice pudding with fruit is also impressive made into a cake

RICE FLAN WITH CHERRIES

Serves 6–8
For the pastry:
2 cups all-purpose flour, ½ cup butter
¼ cup sugar, 1 egg yolk, a pinch of salt
For the filling:
6½ cups milk, heaping ½ cup sugar, a pinch of salt
1 vanilla bean, split lengthwise

Spread half of the cooled rice mixture over the baked shortcrust pastry base in the flan ring.

Evenly distribute the drained cherries over the rice, stopping just short of the flan ring.

Spread the remaining rice pudding over the cherries to cover the fruit, and smooth the top flat.

Brush the second round of pastry with egg yolk, place glazed side up on top of the filling, and press down carefully.

1½ cups short-grain rice, 14 oz sweet cherries
You will also need:
1 egg yolk, 1 teaspoon light cream
1 x 9½-inch flan ring, parchment paper

To make the dough, sift the flour onto a work surface and make a well in the center. Cut the butter into pieces and rub into the flour until it resembles breadcrumbs. Add, the sugar, egg yolk, and salt. Knead quickly into a dough, form into a ball, wrap in plastic wrap, and refrigerate for 1 hour.

To make the filling, bring the milk to a boil in a pot with the sugar, salt, and vanilla bean. Sprinkle in the rice, reduce the heat, and simmer for about 30 minutes, until almost all the liquid has been absorbed. Fish out the vanilla bean, scrape its contents back into the pot, and stir into the rice. Allow to cool.

Preheat the oven to 325°F. Pit the cherries. Divide the pastry in half, rolling each half into a round about 10 inches in diameter. Use the flan ring to cut out a circle 9½ inches in diameter from each round. Chill the pastry disks for 30 minutes. Place the flan ring on a baking sheet lined with parchment paper, fold the overhanging edges in tight around the ring, and press lightly. Place a pastry disk on the base and bake for 10 minutes, until light brown. Whisk the egg yolk with

the cream, brush the second pastry disk with this mixture, and use a fork to create a fine lattice-work decoration. Bake for about 10 minutes. Remove and reduce the oven temperature to 300°F. Proceed as shown in the photo sequence on page 230. Bake the filled flan for 30–40 minutes until done, covering with foil if necessary to stop it from browning too quickly. Cool in the flan ring for 1 hour. Run a pointed knife around the inside edge to loosen the flan, remove the ring and the parchment paper, and cut into 12 pieces.

TORTA DI RISO

Serves 6–8
For the rice pudding:
4½ cups milk, a pinch of salt, zest of ½ orange
¼ cup sugar, 1¼ cups arborio rice
1 teaspoon orange-flower water
For the nut-fruit mixture:
4 eggs, separated; ½ cup sugar
scraped contents of ½ vanilla bean
¼ cup chopped pistachios, ½ cup chopped walnuts
½ cup finely diced candied orange zest
½ cup finely diced candied lemon zest
¼ cup finely diced candied cherries
½ cup pine nuts

You will also need:
1 x 10-inch springform pan
butter and fresh white breadcrumbs for the pan
sturdy cardboard and confectioner's sugar

Bring the milk to a boil in a large pot with the salt and orange zest. Stir in the sugar and rice, reduce the heat, cover, and simmer for 40 minutes, stirring several times. Remove the orange zest, allow the rice to cool, and stir in the orange-flower water. Beat the egg yolks with one-third of the sugar and the scraped contents of the vanilla bean until foamy. Stir in the rice pudding, nuts, candied citrus zests, candied cherries, and pine nuts, mixing thoroughly. Whip the egg whites until stiff, trickling in the remaining sugar gradually. Gently fold into the rice pudding. Preheat the oven to 350°F. Grease the springform pan and dust with the breadcrumbs. Spoon in the batter and smooth the top. Bake on the center rack for 1 hour, covering with foil if necessary to stop the top from browning too quickly. Cool a little in the pan. Run a knife around the edge to loosen, turn out the cake, and leave to cool. To decorate, cut the letters "r," "i," "s," and "o" out of the cardboard and place on top of the cake. Sift over some confectioner's sugar and carefully remove the templates.

Galangal Fiery-hot tasting rhizome of a shrub cultivated chiefly in China. Fresh ginger root may be substituted.

Soy sauce, shoyu Seasoning sauce made from soybeans, which may be fairly mild to salty, light to dark brown, and thin or syrupy, depending on variety.

Ginger Perennial shrub with horizontally branching rhizomes. Fiery hot, slightly-sweetish and at the same time bitter in taste. A popular spice, particularly in Asian cooking.

Curry leaves Small, spicy-aromatic leaves used like bay leaves, especially in Indian and Malay cooking (Hindi *kri patta*, Malay *daun kari pla*). Sold fresh and dried, they are usually added to a dish toward the end of preparation.

Kaffir lime Juicy variety of lime with a knobbly peel. Its juice, peel, and, above all, leaves, are favorite seasoning ingredients in Asian cooking.

Tamarind Legume whose seed pods yield a brown, sticky, sour-sweet fruit pulp, which is used as a spice, tenderizer, and acidulating agent.

Screw pine leaves Also known as pandanus leaves, these narrow, shiny, sword-shaped, rich-green leaves of the screw pine are used for their sweetish, aromatic flavor in Asian cooking in rice dishes and curries, but especially in sweet dishes.

Special ingredients
Some familiar, some new

Asparagus beans *See* yard-long beans.

Bombay duck Not duck at all, but sun-dried fish, sometimes salted, used chiefly as a seasoning, but also served fried as an accompaniment.

Candlenut The seed kernels of the candlenut tree, native to the Moluccas. Candlenuts must be cooked before they are eaten, in order to eliminate the slightly toxic effect of the oil they contain. Similar in flavor to macadamia nuts, they are used in Indonesian cooking, roasted and pounded, for thickening soups and curries.

Cassia bark Also known as Chinese or Saigon cinnamon and cassia. The dried, curved bark of the cinnamon tree or bush. The surface of the bark is brownish in color, the inner side darker. Good-quality cassia is light in color.

Chile poblano Mild, thick-walled, tapering chile, about 4 inches long and 2 inches wide. Used for stuffing, as well as cut into slices and served as a vegetable accompaniment.

Choy sum Tropical leaf cabbage with oval green leaves and edible small yellow flowers. Prepared similarly to broccoli.

Cilantro A kitchen herb also known as Chinese parsley or fresh coriander. Used fresh only. Since it is very sensitive to heat, it is always added to cooked dishes only at the end of the cooking process.

Marjoram Herb with silvery-green leaves whose flavor is milder and mellower than that of oregano.

Cumin seed The greenish-gray dried fruits of an umbellifer that flourishes in warm regions. Distinctive aroma, hot, bitter, and pungent in taste. Used whole or ground.

Enoki mushrooms: Also called golden or snow-puff mushrooms, these edible fungi have small, cream-colored caps on long, slender stems. Available fresh and canned. Cut the fresh mushrooms away from the mass at the base of the stems before using.

Fenugreek seeds A highly bitter-tasting spice when raw, fenugreek seeds are quite palatable when cooked. The ripe light-brown to grayish-red seeds are dried and used whole or ground, especially in Southeast Asian cooking, in curries and chutneys.

Fish sauce Thin, salty seasoning sauce with an intensely fishy flavor. Used like soy sauce. Available in supermarkets and Asian groceries.

Garam masala This Indian spice mixture for curries and spicy side dishes can consist of up to twenty different spices. The basic ingredients are always cardamom, coriander seed, cumin, cinnamon, cloves, and pepper.

Garlic chives A perennial herb cultivated in California and Southeast Asia, the thick, flat leaves have a discreet garlic taste and smell.

Ghee Clarified butter, available in Asian groceries in cans. It can be replaced by rendered butter. To make it yourself, melt some sweet (unsalted) butter in a pot and simmer for 45 minutes, during which time the solid constituents will take on color and settle at the bottom. Strain through a cloth and store refrigerated in tightly sealed jars.

Ginkgo nuts The seed kernels of the ginkgo tree, native to China and Japan. Raw, they taste like rancid butter, but after roasting or boiling they have a flavor reminiscent of mild Swiss cheese. Popular ingredient in both sweet and savory dishes in Chinese and Japanese cooking.

Jerusalem artichoke Also called sunchoke. A tuberous vegetable, available on the market from October to May. The white-to-cream-colored flesh is pleasantly sweet in taste.

Ketjap asin, Kechap asin Thick, salty seasoning sauce made from dark soy sauce, spices, salt, and a little sugar.

Ketjap manis, Kechap manis Thick, sweetish seasoning sauce made from dark soy sauce, lots of sugar, and spices.

Lotus root Perennial aquatic plant distributed chiefly throughout Southeast Asia. The characteristic tubes supplying oxygen to the plant are visible in cross-section. Available fresh and canned in supermarkets and Asian groceries. Peeled lotus root cut into slices is an ideal ingredient for exotic rice dishes and curries.

Mo-er mushroom Tender-fleshed Asian cultivated mushroom, also called cloud ear, wood ear, or black fungus. Very popular in Chinese cooking.

Nori Species of seaweed. Dried, pressed, and cut into squares, it is used as a wrapper, or, cut into thin strips, for seasoning and garnishing. Store in a dry place.

Palm sugar Also called jaggery. Sap collected by tapping the trunks or the tips of date, coconut, toddy, and palmyra palms, which is boiled down to a light-brown, clear syrup and then crystallized. Malty in taste. Can be replaced by raw brown sugar.

Pio-pini mushroom Popular Italian cultivated mushroom with a small cap and long stem.

Rau ram Vietnamese cilantro. This herb has reddish-purple-ribbed leaves that taper to a point. Hot-tasting, with a peppery, mint-like aroma and flavor.

Peppermint may be substituted.

Salsiccia Dry sausage from Italy and Switzerland.

Scotch-bonnet pepper Infernally hot, thin-walled variety of chile pepper from the Caribbean with a highly wrinkled, lantern-like shape. Used like other fresh chiles.

Shiitake mushroom An edible mushroom, originally from Japan (*take* is Japanese for "mushroom"), but also widely distributed in China. It has a large brownish-gray to reddish-brown cap and firm, juicy but not watery flesh. Available fresh and dried. Can be stored in the vegetable compart-ment of a refrigerator for up to one week.

Straw mushrooms Edible mushroom cultivated on rice straw, distributed throughout Southeast Asia. Best fresh, but also available canned.

Taro root Undemanding swamp plant cultivated in the tropics and subtropics. The starchy tubers with their white-to-light-gray flesh are prepared in a similar way to potatoes, but take longer to cook.

Wasabi Strongly aromatic pale-green powder or paste made from a Japanese species of horseradish. Hot mustard may be substituted.

White cabbage sprouts Marketing term for white cabbage cultivated in the tropics. Owing to climatic conditions, the cabbage ripens very quickly and does not "head" nor achieve the weight usual in the West.

Winged beans Also called Goa beans. These owe their name to the wavy wings running the length of the 2- to 16-inch-long pods. A good source of protein, they have been cultivated for centuries throughout Asia, East and West Africa, and the Caribbean. Both seeds and pods are cooked and eaten as a vegetable.

Yard-long beans Also know as asparagus beans and snake beans because of their length (up to 3 feet). The pods contain 10–30 seeds. Native to Southeast Asia, this bean has a sweeter, meatier taste than the string bean, and is prepared in the same way.

Long red and bird green Chiles lend their background heat to countless Far Eastern dishes, sauces, and spice mixtures. The unripe green peppers are even hotter than the fully ripened red ones.

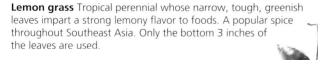

Lemon grass Tropical perennial whose narrow, tough, greenish leaves impart a strong lemony flavor to foods. A popular spice throughout Southeast Asia. Only the bottom 3 inches of the leaves are used.

Oyster sauce A condiment that is very popular in Chinese cooking, made from fresh, puréed oysters and various seasonings.

Bibliography

Brücher, H.: *Tropische Nutzpflanzen*, Springer-Verlag Berlin/Heidelberg, 1997.

Chandler, R.F. Jr.: *Rice in the Tropics*, Westview Press, Colorado, 1979.

Elmadfa, I., Leitzmann, C.: *Ernährung des Menschen*, 2nd rev. edn, Verlag Eugen Ulmer, Stuttgart, 1990.

Franke, W., *Nutzpflanzenkunde*, 4th rev. edn, Georg Thieme Verlag, Stuttgart, 1989.

Geo Journal 35, 1995, Vol. 3: *Feeding 4 Billion People*.

IRRI: *Filling the World's Rice Bowl*, 1994

IRRI: *Planning for the 1990's*, 1990.

Luh, B. S. (ed.): *Rice*, 2nd edn, Van Nostrand Reinhold, New York, 1991.

Otsuka, S.: *Japanese Food Past and Present*, About Japan Series, Vol. 21, Foreign Press Center, Tokyo, 1996.

Ramseyer, U.: *Reis*, Edition diá, St. Gallen/Cologne/São Paulo, 1988.

Rehm, S., Espig, G.: *Die Kulturpflanzen der Tropen und Subtropen*, 3rd rev. edn, Verlag Eugen Ulmer, 1996.

Täufel, A. *et al.*: *Lebensmittel-Lexikon*, 3rd rev. edn, Behr's Verlag, 1993.

Trauffer, R. (ed.): *Manger en Chine — Essen in China*, Ausstellungskatalog Alimentarium Vevey, 1997.

United Nations: *Industrial Statistics Yearbook*, 1991.

Villa, E. (ed.): *Rice and Restaurants*, Ente nazionale risi, o. J.

Vollmer, G., *et al.*: *Lebensmittelführer*, Georg Thieme Verlag Stuttgart/Deutscher Taschenbuch Verlag, Munich, 1990.

Yoshioka, Y.: *Food and Agriculture in Japan*, About Japan Series, Vol. 18, 3rd edn, Foreign Press Center, Tokyo, 1996.

Zürcher, K. in Heiss, Rudolf (ed.): *Lebensmitteltechnologie*, 4th edn, Springer-Verlag Berlin/Heidelberg, 1991.

Acknowledgements

The authors and publishers wish to thank all those who have contributed to this book with their advice, help and expertise, in particular:
AIRI, Associazione Industrie Risiere Italiane, Mr Carriere, Pavia, Italy; Antica Riseria Artigiana FERRON, Isola della Scala, Italy; Agentur Headware, Ms Kraus, Königswinter, Germany; Bar Food, Düsseldorf, Germany; Central Union of Agricultural Cooperatives, Mr Yasuko Abe, Tokyo, Japan; California Dept. of Food and Agriculture, Sacramento, California; Ms Huali Chen, Wendlingen; Consejo Regulador de la Denominación de Origen C.R.D.O. Arroz Delta del Ebro, Mr Benet Arce, Amposta, Tarragona, Spain; Culinary Studios, Mr Yim Chee Peng, Singapore; Delta Research & Extension Center, Mr Joe E. Street, Stoneville, USA; Department of Agricultural Extension, Mr Sooksanti Malithong, Bangkok, Thailand; Ente Nazionale Risi, Dr Anna Callegarin, Milan, Italy; EURYZA GmbH, M/S/C/ Lebensmittel GmbH, Ms Blunck, Hamburg, Germany; Mr Ferrarini, Bologna, Italy; Freeze-Dry Foods, Ms Lübbeling, Greven, Germany; Georg Fles GmbH, Ms Lappase, Hamburg, Germany; Getreidenährmittelverband e.V., Mr Hees, Bonn, Germany; Gourmet House, Mr Joseph Schneider, Clearbrook, Minnesota; Huber-Mühle KG, Dr Landerer, Mannheim, Germany; IRRI Japan, Mr Kazuko Morooka, Ibaraki, Japan; IRRI, Los Baños, Manila, Philippines; Mr Saeed Khoie, Teheran, Iran; Kikkoman Trading GmbH, Ms Loos, Düsseldorf, Germany; Küche - Redaktionsbüro, Mr Schaber, Darmstadt, Germany; Lundberg Family Farms, Richvale, USA; Ms Fabienne Maillen, Brussels, Belgium; The Mansion, Kempinski Bangkok, Mr Rafael Neitzsch, Bangkok, Thailand; MAS DE NANS, Mr Griotto, Arles, France; Mietens & Co. Realitäten-Service, Ms Helga Mietens, Hamburg, Germany; Müller's Mühle, Ms Götz, Gelsenkirchen, Germany; Museum für Ostasiatische Kunst, Ms Girmond, Cologne, Germany; Nestlé Côte d'Ivoire, Mr Alexander Klein, Abidjan, Côte d'Ivoire; Mr Oberacher, Munich, Germany; Philippine Dept. of Tourism, Ms Beltran, Frankfurt, Germany; Mr Roger Poletti, Bourg St. Maurice, France; Rice Research Institute, Chatuchak, Mr Chanyanuwat, Mr Veerasak, Bangkok, Thailand; Rickmers Reismühle GmbH, Dr Barbara Hess, Mr Ralf Lange, Bremen, Germany; Riso Gallo, F&P s.p.a. Mr Paolo Pignataro, Robbio, Italy; Ritz-Carlton, Peter Schoch, Mr Yap Wing Sang, Singapore; Mr Roland Sager, Manila; Seminar für Sinologie und Koreanistik, University of Tübingen, Mr Seifert, Ms Stein, Tübingen, Germany; Spanish Consulate-General, Ms Pérez, Mr Sanz, Düsseldorf, Germany; Stadtbibliothek Kempten, Mr Brock; Syndicat de la Rizerie française, Paris, France; Ute Middelmann PR GmbH, Ms Steffens, Hamburg, Germany; University of Hohenheim, Institut für Pflanzenproduktion in den Tropen und Subtropen, Dr Thomas Hilger, Stuttgart, Germany; University of Munich, Institut für Ostasienkunde, Prof. Jungmann, Munich, Germany; USA Rice Federation, Ms Beatrix Rückert, Hamburg, Germany; WARDA/ADRAO, Association pour le développement de la riziculture en Afrique de l'Ouest, Mr Monty P. Jones, Bouaké, Côte d'Ivoire.

Index

Picture credits

The authors and publishers wish to thank the following for kind permission to reproduce photographs:
pp. 6, 7: Bildarchiv Preussischer Kulturbesitz, Berlin; pp. 8, 11, 25, 33: Ente Nazionale Risi, Milan, Italy; pp. 9, 11, 14: Seminar für Sinologie und Koreanistik, Tübigen; p. 13: WARDA/ADRAO, Bouaké, Côte d'Ivoire; pp. 14, 16, 17, 18: Dr Lampe; pp. 16, 18, 19: IRRI, Los Baños, Philippines; pp. 22, 24, 26, 28, 30, 32, 34, 36, 38, 40: Bayerische Staatsbibliothek, Munich, Germany; pp. 27, 39: USA Rice Federation, Hamburg, Germany; pp. 31, 35: Bon Color Photo Agency, Tokyo, Japan; pp. 42, 43, 50: Euryza, Hamburg, Germany; pp. 60, 61, 62: Du Bois Wild Rice Ltd., Canada (Georg Fles GmbH, Hamburg, Germany).